NEVER CALL ME A HERO

NEVER CALL ME A HERO

|||||||||||||||||||||||||||||||||||||||||||||||||||||||||||||||||||||||||||||||

A LEGENDARY AMERICAN

DIVE-BOMBER PILOT REMEMBERS

THE BATTLE OF MIDWAY

N. JACK "DUSTY" KLEISS

WITH

TIMOTHY AND LAURA ORR

WM

WILLIAM MORROW

An Imprint of HarperCollins*Publishers*

HarperCollins books may be purchased for educational, business, or sales promotional use. For information, please email the Special Markets Department at SPsales@harpercollins.com.

FIRST EDITION

Library of Congress Cataloging-in-Publication Data has been applied for.

ISBN 978-0-06-269205-4

17 18 19 20 21   DIX/LSC   10 9 8 7 6 5 4 3 2 1

For Jean, my love.

—NJK

This book is also dedicated to the memory of our friend Gregory A. Coco, who taught us to listen to veterans when they speak.

—TJO and LLO

CONTENTS

||||||||||||||||||||||||||||||||||||||||||||||||||||||||||||||||||||||||||||||||||||||||||||||||||||||||||

||||||||||||||||||||||||||||||||||||||||||||||||||||||||||||||||||||||||||||||||||||||||||||||||||||||||||||||

FOREWORD

After he retired from the Navy, Dad (aka Captain "Dusty" Kleiss) became a schoolteacher in my high school. I don't remember anyone asking me what Dad did in the war. If they had, I'm not sure I would've known to tell them that he bombed three Japanese ships in the Battle of Midway. I guess the students knew something about his accomplishments because they nicknamed him "Commodore."

I learned more about Dad at dinnertime, when, slowly, he started to speak about the war. Bruno Peter Gaido was the first squadron mate Dad talked about with us. Dad told me, "Peter jumped into a Dauntless parked on the flight deck and he manned a .30 caliber machine gun. He fired at a Japanese bomber intent on making it a bad day for our crew on USS *Enterprise*." Dad chuckled. "It was a good day for Gaido, a not-so-good day for that Japanese bomber crew." Dad later learned that Peter had been captured by the Japanese. It is speculated that he and his pilot endured torturous interrogation before being thrown overboard. There must have been rumors that Gaido revealed secrets because Dad often said, "I knew Peter. I know he never talked."

Bill West also "visited" us. Dad often recounted how Bill's plane made a water landing, and what should have been an easy rescue ended in a freak accident. Dad watched from the railing of his ship as his friend Bill unhitched his harness only to have his boot get caught in an antenna wire. Unable to free himself, Bill held on as his SBD Dauntless dive bomber plunged downward, nose first, taking him as a passenger. Leaning against the ship's rail only feet away, all Dad could do was watch as his friend died.

Dad had a penchant for practical jokes, puns, and a never-ending store of belly laughs. He'd laugh at his own jokes, others' jokes, and laugh just because he could. He would humbly say, "I'm a very lucky man. I don't know why I lived and God didn't take me."

Slowly, I learned about my dad through the historical documents he kept. I became a keeper of the logbooks; in the process, I learned about the meticulous notes Dad had made during the war. I became keeper of the love letters he wrote my mom, which helped me combine sound with sight, hearing his words to her, hers to him, captured in the kiss the day he was awarded the Navy Cross. I became keeper of a small thin wire twisted into the shape of a ship. It was no larger than an inch square. "This was the pin from the bomb that I fired on the *Kaga*," he said.

Now he's gone, and I have the Virgin Mary medal he always wore, his war medals, and a few bullet casings fired during his military funeral. The flag that adorned his coffin is also mine. And I have all those wonderful stories. I extend my warmest gratitude to Laura and Tim Orr, who captured for all time my dad's stories through interviews and countless conversations. He told anyone who would listen, "They [the Orrs] are writing a book about me!" With sheer determination Dad made it to his one hundredth birthday, but he fell short of his goal to see the book in print. From his current spiritual plane (pun intended, Dad), I can see him smile. I'm certain Dad is proud that his heroics are captured, but he's even more grateful to honor those with whom he served, allowing readers to appreciate the actions of what has been called the "greatest generation."

—*Jill Kleiss*

INTRODUCTION

My name is Norman Jack Kleiss. I'm ninety-nine years old. Long ago, I fought in the war against Japan. I served with Scouting Squadron Six, a U.S. Navy dive bomber squadron assigned to USS *Enterprise,* a *Yorktown*-class aircraft carrier. During the first six months of 1942, I participated in several battles in the central Pacific. On June 4–7, I fought in the epic Battle of Midway, our navy's first decisive victory over the Empire of Japan. In a single day, our fleet's dive bomber squadrons destroyed four enemy aircraft carriers, a stunning feat that has never been repeated so long as I've been alive. Many historians have called Midway the "turning point" of the Pacific War. What's indisputable is that the Battle of Midway now stands as one of the most famous naval engagements in world history. Somehow, I was lucky enough to survive it.

Nowadays, when I look back on the events from the Battle of Midway, I remember them as if they happened yesterday. But it wasn't always like that. When I returned to the States immediately after the battle, I had plenty of other things to think about. I wanted to marry the love of my life, for starters. I also had a new career path in mind as part of the U.S. Navy, and I wanted to embark upon it. Further, I did not want to dwell on the awful images I had seen. I had lost many good friends on June 4 and it hurt to think about the strange quirks of fate that caused them to die and me to live. Unwilling to confront it, my memory of the battle quickly faded. When I finally retired from the Navy in 1962, it formed only a small footnote in my very long career.

In 1979, some of my old friends from Scouting Six planned to attend a Battle of Midway symposium at the Wyoming State Museum. I wished to see them and catch up on old times. This was my first big Battle of Midway commemoration. I learned something during my visit. I was shocked to see an enthusiastic public, thirsty for knowledge about the battle. Even thirty-seven years after those important days in June 1942, Americans still wanted to hear war stories from the people who lived it. This surprised me. I didn't think my tale was terribly interesting. True, I had helped sink two Japanese carriers, but that did not strike me as something irregular. I only did what the Navy had trained me to do, nothing more.

As the years passed, more and more attention came my way. Historians wanted to interview me. Television studios asked to include me in their historical documentaries. As the twenty-first century dawned, the Battle of Midway wouldn't leave me alone. To answer the flurry of questions accurately, I had to relive the battle over and over again. I had to come face-to-face with memories I'd long since buried. I had to recall the smell of the salt air, the roar of the wind as it rushed past my cockpit, the sight of red flames coming up from the exploding ships, and other such vivid sensations for which words will never do justice. I had to summon the faces of friends I'd lost and the sadness that tortured me as I whiled away the aftermath of the battle in my bunk. Today, that day—Thursday, June 4, 1942—hovers over my shoulder like an annoying friend, constantly chirping in my ear, "I am the most important day of your life." It will not leave me alone.

In recent years, my memory of the Battle of Midway has only

become more intrusive. In August 2010, after the death of Vernon Micheel, I became the last living pilot from my squadron. Then, in January 2011, after the death of Clayton Fisher, I became the last living American dive bomber pilot who fought in the battle. I may very well be the last living American pilot who fought in the battle, period. Without anyone else to interview, historians seeking new information now come to me. Lately, I've been asking myself, *why? Why has God seen fit to make me the last one? Why must I be forced to remember Midway for every remaining day of my life?* After considerable meditation and prayer, I've determined that I have one last calling. I must tell my story.

I want to do it for history's sake and to honor my friends who gave their lives so that our nation could live on. I hope that long after my earthly remains have turned to dust, historians can still use my narrative to their advantage. They can praise this book, they can ridicule it, or they can say whatever they like about it—I don't really care—but I don't want it to be said that I lived so long and never contributed to the battle's memory. The only way I can make peace with myself is to describe what I saw and narrate it as honestly and faithfully as I know how. The passage of time has dimmed my recollection of certain events, but I faithfully checked my logbook, my personal diary, my letters I wrote to my girlfriend (who later became my wife), my squadron's after-action reports, and as many primary sources as I could find to reconstruct what happened during those tumultuous opening months of the Pacific War.

However, this memoir is more than just a narrative of battle. It is also a love story. Shortly before the world erupted in the bloodiest war in human history, I met a charming young lady named Jean. I was smitten. Thankfully she didn't find me too obnoxious, so we started dating. While I was fighting in the Pacific, I thought of little else than getting back to the States to marry her. Nevertheless, I have to admit the tale of our love isn't a simple "boy-meets-girl" story. Several complicating factors came into play that nearly ruined our romance. In short, after "boy-meets-girl," a bunch of other things happened: boy stupidly lost girl, boy regretted losing girl, boy apologized for being a fool, boy won back girl, boy sailed away to fight in a couple of battles, and, finally, boy spent the bulk of his Navy days worrying that he had made the biggest mistake of his life by initially losing girl in the first place. My narrative is an embarrassing litany of personal mistakes I made in matters of romance; this much I know. Somehow, I turned things around and ended up with the best partner a man could ask for. My affection for Jean got me through my dark days of the Pacific War, and, if anything, this memoir is a testament to her kindness and compassion. Jean, if you can read this in heaven, I'll always love you, more than life itself.

My memoir is also a history of naval aviation and its coming of age. Prior to the outbreak of the Second World War, I wanted to be a pilot. I fell in love with aircraft during a time when U.S. naval aviation was new and largely untested by the rigors of combat. We pilots had to surmount all kinds of obstacles: prejudice from surface warfare officers, faulty equipment, and the perils of our preferred method of attack, which we called dive bombing. We had to learn to navigate the blank canvas of the Pacific Ocean to find our targets with no discernible landmarks to help us. We had to learn to dodge enemy fighters that swooped behind us in battle. We had to learn to release our bombs in the midst of a 240-knot dive. We had to learn to push our planes to the limit, to endure the dangerous g-forces that threatened to black us out. We had to learn to conserve fuel to return to our carriers. We had to learn to locate and then land on a tiny, pitching carrier deck in the middle of the night or on a stormy sea. We had to learn to grieve quietly when our friends were shot down or went missing, when no earthly remains could be recovered. We had to do all this when U.S. naval aviation was still young, when the dangers of dive bombing were still being discovered by trial and error.

Finally, this is a memoir about a specific battle and its legacy. Although I commence my narrative from my humble beginnings in southeast Kansas, I focus on my time as a pilot assigned to Scouting Six and even more on my role in the Battle of Midway, where in just five minutes' time the pride of the Japanese carrier fleet was wrecked by forty-eight American Douglas SBD Dauntless dive bomber aircraft. I served alongside many brave men, pilots and gunners in whom I placed unshakable trust. Many of them did not come back. My comrades in Scouting Six ran out of fuel and died slow deaths out on the lonely ocean. My best friend—a member of Torpedo Six—died an equally horrible death, shot down by Japanese fighters. Two of my friends were captured by the Japanese, interrogated, and executed. They all died doing their duty, trying to give our navy a victory when the cloud of defeat appeared darkest.

After years of keeping quiet, I've accepted that it is time I gave back, that I complete something permanent, a testament to my comrades' bravery. Without them, I don't believe I would have had sufficient skill or confidence to have survived that awful battle. I've done my best to follow their example, to be brave like them. It requires a certain amount of bravery, I think, to share one's life story with the public—including some of my embarrassing moments, miscues, and regrets.

Dear reader, please be generous to me, but never call me a hero. During the Pacific War, I did my job and that's it. I know I performed a dangerous task—dropping out of the sky with a bomb— and that I lived in an exceptional time, when the world was torn apart by war. But in the end, I'm just a lucky fool, blessed with a long life and lasting love. Fortune favors me, but I have yet to comprehend why.

—*Norman Jack Kleiss*

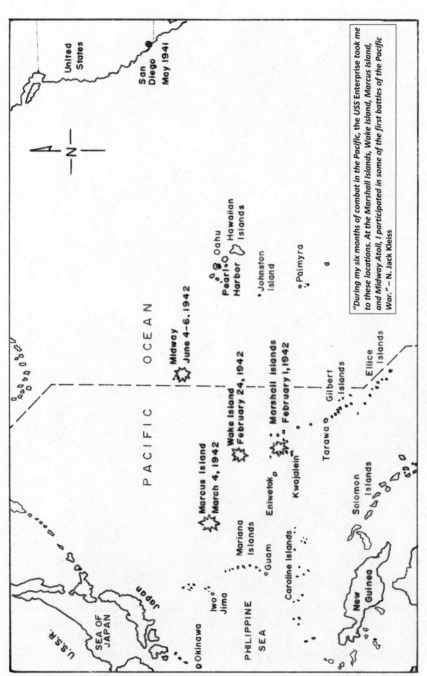

"During my six months of combat in the Pacific, the USS Enterprise took me to these locations. At the Marshall Islands, Wake Island, Marcus Island, and Midway Atoll, I participated in some of the first battles of the Pacific War." — N. Jack Kleiss

Map of Lt. Kleiss's war, 1942. *(John Heiser)*

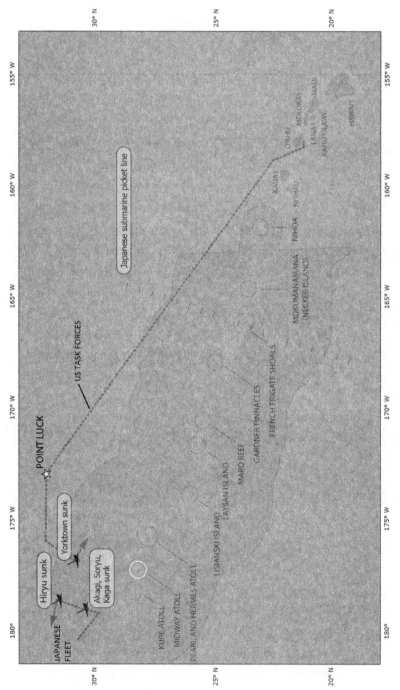

The Battle of Midway: regional map (NOAA)

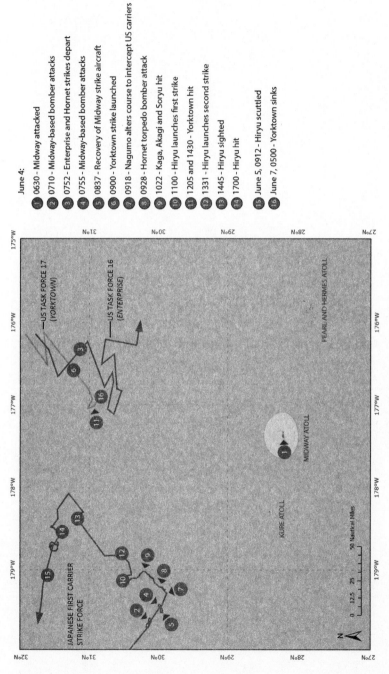

June 4:

1 0630 - Midway attacked
2 0710 - Midway-based bomber attacks
3 0752 - Enterprise and Hornet strikes depart
4 0755 - Midway-based bomber attacks
5 0837 - Recovery of Midway strike aircraft
6 0900 - Yorktown strike launched
7 0918 - Nagumo alters course to intercept US carriers
8 0928 - Hornet torpedo bomber attack
9 1022 - Kaga, Akagi and Soryu hit
10 1100 - Hiryu launches first strike
11 1205 and 1430 - Yorktown hit
12 1331 - Hiryu launches second strike
13 1445 - Hiryu sighted
14 1700 - Hiryu hit

15 June 5, 0912 - Hiryu scuttled
16 June 7, 0500 - Yorktown sinks

The Battle of Midway: local map (*NOAA*)

NEVER CALL ME A HERO

CHAPTER 1

||||||||||||||||||||||||||||||||||||||||||||||||||||||||||||||||||||||||||||||||||||||||||||||||||||||

KANSAS CHILDHOOD
1916–1932

I was born on March 7, 1916, in Coffeyville, Kansas. My parents
were John Louis Kleiss and Lulu Dunham Kleiss. In 1859, the
Kleiss family left its home in Germany and settled in Wisconsin.
My grandfather, John B. Kleiss, was born during the year of the
immigration, the first of my line to be born in the United States.
My father—who was called "J. L." by his friends—was born on August 21, 1888. He lived in Wisconsin for much of his life, working as a master woodworker for a railroad company, but he later
found employment as an insurance salesman for Mutual Life Insurance Company of New York. That job brought him to Kansas.
My mother, Lulu Isabel Dunham, was born on March 17, 1882, in
Logan County, Illinois. Her family traced its lineage to Peter Banta,
a New Jersey scout for the Continental Army during the Revolutionary War. My mother was an expert typist, possessed exquisite
handwriting, and worked for the local Dorcas Society, a sewing
club that donated homemade clothing to the poor. She was a perfect mother, always kind and caring, looking out for my needs. In
looking back through my "archive" of personal documents I can
see that my first written word was *mother*.

My hometown, Coffeyville, was one of twelve townships in Montgomery County, a flat, grassy patch of southeast Kansas. The southern edge of town stopped only a few miles short of the Oklahoma border. On the east side of town, a winding 270-mile river called the Verdigris, one of the principal tributaries of the Arkansas River, flowed lazily to the south. My hometown is famous for one event. It's the place where the Dalton gang met its ignominious end. In 1892, Coffeyville possessed two banks, making it a tempting target for ambitious robbers. On October 5, five members of the infamous Oklahoma-based gang arrived in town, attempting to hold up the two banks simultaneously. It was a bold plan, but foolish; the unnecessary dispersal of the robbers' numbers allowed a mob of Coffeyville residents to gather at a local hardware store, borrow its firearms, and dispatch the thieves. After a twelve-minute shootout, four gang members lay dead, as did four Coffeyville citizens. We children grew up hearing the thrilling stories of the townsfolk who resolutely defended their prairie boomtown from these villainous interlopers. I remember listening to a bewhiskered veteran of the gunfight, a garrulous man who regaled children about how he had been "wounded" (pronounced in such a way that it rhymed with "pounded") in the legendary battle.

My parents' house stood in the midst of an expanding urban oasis. The home usually smelled of flowers and asparagus, thanks to a large patch of each in the backyard. The noise of frolicking children echoed up and down the short road. Our neighbors, Russell and Effie Tongiers, boasted a large house with nine children. The Tongierses' house came courtesy of Effie's brother, Walter Johnson, the star pitcher for the Washington Senators and one of the first five players inducted into the Baseball Hall of Fame.

As a child I had dark—nearly black—eyes, exactly like Mom. My hair was straight and light-colored, although it gradually darkened as I aged, and I had large, protruding ears. I was shorter than most boys my age, and as the youngest of three siblings, I tended to draw plenty of attention from my mother. I don't remember much about my personality, but Mom kept an annotated photograph album that described my misadventures. She noted how I had an uncontrollable fondness for exploring. One photograph depicts me wearing a knit bonnet standing in the center of a dusty trail, surrounded by overgrown weeds. Mom captioned the image, "There's a long, long trail." I wanted to be the first to see the end of it. I loved the water, too. When I was six years old, I preferred to don a sailor's outfit. I wore it as often as possible, an easy accomplishment because Mom also admired it. Once, she wrote, "When you first wore this suit you looked in the mirror and remarked (hands deep in pockets), 'Now I'm a real boy, ain't I mother!'" In 1924, my parents took me on a visit to California and I saw the Pacific Ocean for the first time. It didn't take long for me to love those waves. I splashed around in the surf for hours and had to be dragged away from them. My thirst for adventure came from my admiration of my siblings, both of whom took well to the rigors of the Kansas prairie. Louis (my older brother by six years) and Katherine (my older sister by three years) both possessed an unrequited sense of wanderlust. They were quick, clever, loving siblings. It wasn't hard to be the youngest of the brood; with a smart, attentive older brother and sister, all I had to do was sit back and learn.

However, I liked to do things my own way. First of all, I named myself. I was baptized "Norman Jack Kleiss." For the first four years of my life, everyone called me Norman. I hated it. I insisted on going by my middle name, Jack. When condescending adults asked me, "How is little Norman?" I set them straight. I huffed, "My name Jack!" (I left out the verb.) By age five, my parents accepted the name change. I was Jack. It became *my* name, now and forever. Also, I loved to act like a daredevil, and sometimes that backfired on me. One day, when I was three, while visiting my aunt's farm, I insisted on riding my cousin's mule. Although Mom and Dad protested, I climbed into the saddle with help from my cousin. Suddenly, as if to prove my stupidity, the mule reared its legs, flinging me violently into the air. As Mom later described it, "We were horrified and fully expected you to be killed." With a sickening thud, I landed hard on the ground. The mule tromped off, glad to be rid of me, and my parents rushed to my rescue. They feared they would find a broken boy, but amazingly, I stood up and dusted myself off with only a single bruise on my left arm. I had survived my first brush with death. As Mom told it, for the next few days I reprimanded the mule comically, with my minor speech impediment, saying many times, "Bad ol' 'ule."

My symptoms of independence often got me into trouble. One of my first memories involved me being tied to a tree at the edge of our property. I must have been four or five years old. One day, my father took me on a short walk from the house to his office. The trip traversed about eight blocks and the busiest thoroughfare in town. This was my first walk with Dad to see what he did for a living, and I loved it. I enjoyed the sights of Coffeyville, the streetcars and buses, the locations of the Dalton gang robbery, and my father's office. The next day, after Dad left for work, I decided to follow him. I had memorized the route sufficiently, and I said to myself, "Hmm, I'll just go downtown and see where everyone else goes. They keep busy and I'm left out of all the fun stuff." Although I had made the trip only once, I crossed the tracks successfully, passed through the intersection, ascended a flight of stairs, and arrived at my father's office as if I were a regular client. Dad flew into a fury. He dragged me back home, and to teach me a lesson—that I should never travel without an adult—he tied me to a tree. At first, I didn't seem to get it. Why did Dad immobilize me? I tugged at the ropes, shouting defiantly: "I wish I could pull this *tee* down!" (At the time, I never pronounced the letter *r*.) Nobody would help me. I was stuck there for two or three hours until Dad finally released me.

I guess my father's lesson stuck. I never followed him to work again. However, I'm not sure if he was successful in getting me to stop exploring. As a youngster, I wanted to see more of the world, and no one—not even Mom and Dad—could stop me. None of this is to say I was incorrigible. In fact, I learned the lessons of right and wrong fairly early. One day, my father hired a man to clean the pump attached to our cistern. For some childish reason, I decided I wanted to hear the splash of an object dropped down that hole. When no one was looking, I grabbed the family's finest silverware and released them, one by one, into the gaping chasm. I giggled when I heard the splash, but my thrill was short-lived. My parents fired our part-time maid, accusing her of stealing the silverware. I felt horribly guilty about it. Six months later, the man returned to clean the cistern's gutters and recovered the missing silverware. My parents discovered my misdeed and summarily punished me. I learned my lesson. My misbehavior had resulted in a terrible consequence for our maid, who was innocent of the crime for which she was accused. This incident has lingered in my mind for years, a reminder of the definition of "consequences." Since then, I've done my best never to let others suffer for my transgressions.

Religion played an important role in my childhood. Every Sunday, Mom and Dad donned their finest to attend morning services at Coffeyville's First Methodist Episcopal Church, a stately brick edifice at the northwest corner of Tenth and Elm. After listening to my teachers at Sunday school, I came to believe God routinely intervened in the affairs of humankind. All of the inexplicable occurrences—good or bad—were part of His plan. I imagine this message influenced my outlook on life. I believed that life was a mission. Only after mortals completed their earthly duty could their souls be called to the Kingdom of Heaven. I preferred to be-lieve that God had a special plan for me. I just had to figure out what it was.

At age six, I commenced my public education, heading off to Garfield Elementary School, a small public facility in the center of town. I loved to learn. My first report card contained a healthy mix of M's, B's, and E's, meaning I performed at average or above average in all of my subjects.* During my first term, I was never tardy and I missed only four days due to illness. I also loved to play pranks. In January 1922, on a wintry day, as I waited to enter class, a schoolmate and I hid behind the corner of our building, watching an English teacher approach the door. Without warning, we tossed two well-aimed snowballs at her. The snowballs struck her squarely in the chest, causing her to lose her balance and fall ungracefully, her legs thrashing comically in the air. We had planned to run, but the ludicrous sight of our upended teacher caused us to laugh so hard that we forgot to make a break for it. Eventually, the humili-ated proctor righted herself, caught us by the arm, and declared us suspended from first grade for a full week.

The snowball assault was symptomatic of my love of taking risks. As a child, I exhibited no trouble embracing daredevilry. Whenever my friends needed me for some dangerous task, I com-plied. When playing ball, items sometimes got caught on the roof. As the smallest of my playmates, I was the easiest to hoist atop a neighbor's house. I volunteered for these missions, rescuing lost toys for friends, performing feats that would have appalled my par-ents if they had been there to see. Even games of tag came with a

---

* At Garfield, teachers graded students with U for unsatisfactory, M for aver-age, and E for exceptional. Every academic subject followed that rating. Only "scholarship" and "industry" followed a rating system of A through F. I received straight B's.

violent edge. My brother and I frequently went across the street to play with the Rosebush boys, Kenneth and Robert. Of course, the Coffeyville version of tag differed greatly from the original. At the beginning of the game, we determined who would be "it." That person stood in the center of the Rosebushes' backyard while the others ran in a circle around him. Then the "it"-person lit a flash-cracker and dropped it into an old World War I shell casing. Next, he dropped in a tennis ball, so the casing became a cannon. The "it"-person could not move, but he could rotate, waiting for the flash-cracker's fuse to burn down. When it exploded, the tennis ball shot out like a rocket. If you got hit, it knocked you down. Those were the kinds of games we played.

By today's standards, cannon-fired tennis balls might seem unusual, but this was par for the course. People didn't worry much about kids in those days. You either lived, or you didn't. We grew up hard and fast and learned to look after ourselves. In the summers, my father didn't mind dropping us off for daylong boat rides in the Verdigris River. My friends and I took lumber from wrecked houses and we built ourselves a scow called the *Punkin' Creek Special,* named for one of the tributaries of the Verdigris. Later on, I even built my own boat. Using surplus flooring pilfered from construction sites, I cobbled together a small dinghy. Each morning, Dad hooked the tiny rowboat to the back of his car and drove it up the Verdigris River and dropped me off. All day long, I floated downstream. At about 2:30 in the afternoon, Dad drove along the road, looking for the boat, picking me up wherever I happened to land.

Because we floated for hours without any adult, we learned to look after each other. The crew of the *Punkin' Creek Special* consisted of six boys, one girl, and one dog: me, my brother, my sister, the two Rosebush boys, Bill Mitchell, and Jack Isham; the Rosebushes' dog, an Airedale named Dan, whom I loved dearly, sat near the rudder. It was fun enough, but we learned to share responsibility. Someone always manned the rudder. One of us always kept a lookout for danger. Although we enjoyed fishing and chatting, the experience taught plenty of valuable life lessons: always be alert, always be responsible for your job.

I learned responsibility in others ways, too. My first pennies came from household chores. Dad awarded me an allowance for refueling the kitchen furnace. I hauled coal from the garage about three times per day, receiving one cent per bucket. As I grew older, Dad gave me more demanding work: a nickel for mowing the lawn, a dime for climbing up on the roof and removing unwanted tree limbs, or a quarter for putting more sand underneath the brick walkway. I began my first paid job at age eight. Taking designs I had seen on discarded Singer Sewing Machine kits, I painted pictures of birds on cigar box lids and sold them to neighbors for about fifteen cents apiece. Two years later, I earned ten cents per day by hauling buckets of paint atop towering scaffoldings for building painters. It was dangerous labor, as it required that I remain focused and keep my balance. Working with painters allowed me to learn plenty of curses, words that Dad would never teach me. The painters made the air blue with obscenities whenever one of them goofed up, which was often. As I grew older, work did not get any easier. In junior high, I was a carhop at a local drugstore, earning fifteen cents each evening. My hours were 9 P.M. to midnight. By high school, I worked for the local newspaper, the *Coffeyville Journal*, delivering newspapers for two dollars per week. I had to get all of my papers to my customers within an hour of printing. If not, I received a "kick," a nickel reduction in pay for each customer who complained. Typically, I suffered one kick per week, usually caused by the last house on the route. In short, money came hard, and regular pay was never guaranteed.

A Kansas childhood meant growing up with guns. Coffeyville residents took their reputation for frontier justice seriously, and they imparted children with the skill to shoot. My aunt (on my father's side), Helen Ruthrauff, was the women's shotgun champion of Kansas, and she gave me some valuable pointers. However, I learned most of my marksmanship lessons from my neighbor Earl Alfonso Rosebush, the father of my two playmates. Although Mr. Rosebush was not a competitive marksman, I considered him one of the best shots I had ever seen. Rosebush always carried a revolver. One day, I accompanied him for a ride in his Chandler automobile. As the car whizzed along a sandy road, churning up grit, Rosebush sighted a jackrabbit as it bolted from the brush. Without pause, he drew his pistol, rested his wrist on the side of the door, and fired. In one blast, he shot the rabbit dead. He brought the car to a halt and told me to go fetch it. (He intended to bring it home for dinner.) This was an incredible thing: Rosebush had hit a moving target from a speeding vehicle. He saw the astonished look on my face. He asked, "Do you wanna learn to shoot like that?" I nodded. He took me under his wing and let me practice with his pistol. I prefer to believe that his instructions contributed to my excellent aim as a dive bomber pilot. After all, leading a jackrabbit is not too different than leading a ship. For both, the shooter must aim for where the target is going to be, not where it is.

In general, I lived a pleasant childhood, as agreeable as the Kansas prairie could be for a young boy. However, childhood brought sad times as well. Nothing prepared me for my family's greatest tragedy, the untimely loss of my mother on February 14, 1929. Mom died from the effects of stomach cancer. It had been a long, troublesome illness. The cancer had left her bedridden for more than a year, and it put such a strain on Dad that he had to separate the family temporarily. He took Mom to Johns Hopkins Teaching

Hospital in Baltimore to find some form of relief, and accordingly, he sent me to live with my uncle, William Coleman, in Lincoln, Illinois.

My stay in Lincoln had the potential to change my life aspirations. Uncle William was a larger-than-life character. After marrying Mom's sister, Nellie Dunham, Uncle William served as a surgeon in the First World War. He had one son, Walter Dan Coleman, and he hoped that Cousin Walter might follow in his footsteps and become a physician, too. Instead, in 1929, Walter chose to accept an appointment to the U.S. Naval Academy. With his son shying away from medicine, Uncle William attempted to impart his passion for medical knowledge upon me. I liked the idea and I spent many months following my uncle to surgeries and house calls. I loved watching him work in his white suit, taking care of various maladies. Mostly I enjoyed his care for babies, as he tried to deduce their ailments even though they could not speak. My interest in medicine impressed Uncle William to the point that he promised financial support if I ever declared my intent to go to medical school. For a time, I was certain I wanted to be a doctor.

In the winter of 1929, I returned to Coffeyville for my mother's funeral, a terribly sad affair. Saying goodbye to Mom was one of the hardest ordeals in my very long life. Although my family surrounded me, I felt cold and alone, detached from emotion in a way I had never felt before. The only solace was religion. According to the scriptures, Mom was in heaven—no longer in pain—and sitting at the side of her maker. That thought gave me some sense of closure. However, I must have been visibly upset. To ease my melancholy, the Tongierses bought me a small dog named Ginger. I appreciated the gesture, but she wasn't the greatest dog. After a few months, Ginger ran away. It seemed as if I was destined to bear my sadness alone during that gloomy winter.

I returned to my last year of junior high school more pessimistic and increasingly aware of important world events. I think my pessimism bubbled up in my written work. As the Great Depression carried Kansas into deeper economic troubles, I had become convinced that war—another conflict greater than the one seen by Uncle William—was on the way. I won't go so far as to say that I predicted the Second World War, but I will say I developed a cynic's eye toward lasting peace. In 1933, during my senior year at Field Kindley Memorial High School, I chose to write a report on the Kellogg-Briand Pact of 1928, the international settlement that was intended to outlaw war. I questioned the idea that savvy diplomacy and moral progressivism could make war obsolete. Nations would always go to war, I concluded. There would always be a need to fight. I don't know if the despair caused by my mother's death influenced my writing with such a dark philosophy, but in any event, my report was accidentally prophetic. I expected another war to come along and shake the United States out of its naïve assumptions.

Little did I realize, the bloodiest war in human history was on its way—and I would be swept up in it.

||||||||||||||||||||||||||||||||||||||||||||||||||||||||||||||||||||||||||||||||||||||||||||||

CHAPTER 2

THE LURE OF FLIGHT
1932–1934

On January 18, 1932, at age fifteen, I enlisted in the Kansas National Guard to serve on weekends after school. I lied about my age, but my recruiting officer didn't seem to care. I wanted to serve in the armed forces. I can't really explain why. As a teenager, I was seeking a place in society. The anguish of my mother's death had stirred in me a desire to prove myself. With that, I decided to try my luck at being a soldier. I joined Troop B, 114th Cavalry. My post was not especially accommodating. Fort Riley possessed only one ambulance and it lacked a starter. The soldiers had to start up the engine by pushing the dilapidated vehicle downhill. Working with similarly obsolete pieces of equipment quelled my desire to remain. Only my love of horses kept me in the ranks. I had an opportunity to ride atop many four-legged friends. In fact, I have a better memory of the equine soldiers at Fort Riley than any of the humans in my company. Every horse had its own personality. No two were alike.

I loved one horse above all the others. His name was Jeff, and he could jump, swim, prance, and gallop in all conditions and through all types of terrain. He loved it when I offered him challenges. If I wanted him to leap a hedge or ford a stream, Jeff never shied away. After surmounting the obstacle, Jeff preened and postured with pride, jubilant that he could display athletic grace the other horses lacked. It was as if he had something to prove, just like me. Maybe it is strange to say this, but Jeff was my first experience with military courage. He taught me its value and what it means to meet a challenge. When I rode him to an obstacle, I'm sure he never knew if he could surmount it, but he always felt it was worth the try. That is a form of courage, I think. We test our fears by seeing what we can do against the unknown. Jeff possessed only one odd personality quirk. He hated it if a rider refused to look him in the eye. If you turned your back on him, he'd bite you on the butt. I learned this the hard way several times. I guess I absorbed another military lesson from him: respect your superiors. Clearly, he believed he outranked me.

Although I loved my horses, I learned that cavalry no longer commanded the battlefield. As the months went by, I grew certain that airplanes represented the future of combat. One day, we held a massive mock battle outside Fort Riley. We divided our forces into Red and Blue Teams. Operating with the Blue Team, I mounted up and went off to test my mettle in simulated combat. When the Red Team's biplanes appeared, one of my teammates called out, telling me to take cover. Curious to see the planes operate, I moved my horse to the edge of the woods and peered through the trees to get a better look at one incoming aircraft. Suddenly, a referee stopped me. He pointed at me and said, "You're dead!" Mock battles sometimes followed arbitrary rules, but I could not doubt the veracity of the referee's decision. If that swooping plane had been armed, I would have been slaughtered. I thought of Charles Lindbergh, my childhood hero. It took bravery to be a pilot, I thought. Perhaps I could combine the two. I could be an aviator and a soldier. A new dream hatched. I wanted to become a cavalryman mounted on wings, a knight of the airborne battlefield.

Piloting, though, was not my only dream. As my teenage years sped by, I pondered my career path. I weighed several options, but none truly delighted me. I might follow in the footsteps of my brother and go to college. A few years earlier, Louis had packed his bags and gone to Kansas State Agricultural College, in Manhattan. His gregarious nature allowed him to thrive and he even helped to establish a fraternity. In 1932, to get a sense of campus life, I went for a visit. What I saw disappointed me. Louis's fraternity was little more than a boardinghouse. The wealthier students paid a little extra in dues to live inside the edifice, but most of the students encamped on the porch or on the street. I visited during the winter, which required me to endure the cruel weather alongside Louis. I had a hard time considering the possibility of living outdoors. Further, Louis's pitiful income made the prospect of college appear even less appealing. In the summers, my brother worked as a pick-and-shovel-man for a streetcar company, earning two dollars per day. He came home covered in grime and sweat, with little money to show for his effort. Was this the value of a college education? There must be a better way to earn money. It seemed silly to spend so much time at college and have another job on the side.

I considered another possibility, applying for the Solon E. Summerfield Scholarship. Solon Summerfield had earned wealth in New York City as the owner of a ribbon factory. His father had been a law professor at Kansas University. To honor him, in 1929, Summerfield established a foundation that allowed "deserving boys" an opportunity to attend Kansas University for four years on full scholarship. At Kansas University I might continue the dream I had concocted in Illinois. Maybe I would become a physician. The scholarship exacted high standards. To qualify, I had to possess the best grades at my high school. Specifically, I had to stand among the top four boys. I worked hard to be in that quartet, spending all my time in the study halls, reading numerous books while others were out goofing around.

When the application deadline arrived, I found myself in that elite group of four male students. However, to gain the scholarship, I had to pass three competitive tests. We four contenders from my high school went to a civil service center and took our first examination, which offered an assortment of questions from the social sciences and humanities. When I exited, I thought I had performed poorly, particularly because the test had quizzed us heavily on our knowledge of Latin, about which I knew little. I talked over matters with the other three applicants. I admitted I had performed badly, but the other three boasted they had done well. The next day, the test scores revealed the reverse. Only I had passed the test and the other three had failed. I had performed well on the history questions and that got me to the next round. Another test followed, narrowing down the state-wide finalists to ten, all of whom had to take a third and final test at Kansas University. In preparation for this final test, I studied in a cleared-out room in Dad's office building. One day, Dad introduced me to a friend, an attorney whose brother was employed at Kansas University as a professor. Dad asked, "I know we can't ask you too much about it, but is there anything my son should be working on?" The attorney looked at us and answered in one word, "Evolution." He said no more.

I understood the attorney's cryptic hint. The Scopes Monkey Trial had happened nine years earlier. In Kansas, controversy surrounded the teaching of evolution. I took the warning seriously and spent time pondering my answer to this potential question. I felt no desire to compromise my belief in the biblical account of Creation, but at the same time, I respected the natural sciences, subjects I enjoyed. Clearly, the question was intended to vex Kansas boys who had religious upbringings. If asked, we would simply dismiss evolution as hokum and then get booted from the program. I vowed not to let that happen. When I arrived at Kansas University, several professors screened me, and exactly as the attorney predicted, one of them asked me if I believed in evolution. I hemmed and hawed, talking about the advantages of a biblical understanding of Creation versus the scientific foundations of the origins of the universe. Then, when it came time to deliver a definite answer, I explained, "I really can't come to any conclusion on the matter, but what I'm hoping is that I'll go to Kansas University and after spending four years there, I'll be able to come to the right conclusion." This answer must have placated the professors. I won the scholarship.

At that moment, it looked as if I had chosen my path. I expected to go to Kansas University; however, I also weighed another option: the U.S. Naval Academy, at Annapolis, Maryland. I still wanted to become a pilot, and I figured the best way to achieve that goal was to become a midshipman. Although Army aircraft at Fort Riley had inspired my love of aviation, I selected the Navy because its aviation program was expanding rapidly. While in high school, I had read newspapers that described the launching of two new aircraft carriers, USS *Lexington* (CV-2*) and USS *Saratoga* (CV-3). At the time, the Navy was in the process of completing another carrier, USS *Ranger* (CV-4), and then in August 1933, it awarded a contract to Newport News Shipbuilding to build a larger type of aircraft carrier, the *Yorktown* class. With naval aviation growing annually, I figured now was the best time to become a pilot for the fleet. The decision to go to the academy was not to be taken lightly. The curriculum prepared midshipmen to be leaders, not pilots. Even if I

----

* A glossary of military acronyms appears on page 297.

spent four years at the academy, I had to wait another two years to begin flight training. After graduation, all ensigns had to spend two years in the surface fleet, and if we didn't give up on aviation by then, we set out for the aviation cadet training program headquartered at the air station in Pensacola, Florida. In short, becoming a pilot through the Naval Academy required six years to reach completion.

I required congressional recommendation for a posting, and I possessed that through my connection to Congressman Harold Clement McGugin, a graduate of Coffeyville High School and the representative of Kansas's Third District. To be more specific, I knew McGugin's wife, Nell Bird McGugin, who was several times smarter than her husband. She took an instant liking to me and appreciated my thirst for adventure. After putting considerable pressure on her husband, she convinced him to give me a position as "fourth alternate" to the Naval Academy. The Secretary of the Navy could appoint two midshipmen per congressional district. If a vacancy opened up, I was fourth in line to receive the appointment. To get admitted, I had to hope the other nominees ahead of me would fail to meet the admissions requirements or otherwise leave the academy.

All of my anxieties collided on graduation day at my high school in May 1933. After receiving my diploma, my principal stopped me. "Wait a minute!" he said. "We have just received word of your four-year scholarship to Kansas University. Congratulations!" The principal escorted me to a room to meet with some Kansas University professors who had shown up. "Wait a minute, again," the principal began. "We have also received word that you are fourth alternate to the Naval Academy and you passed all your tests." I basked in the accolades. However, the KU professors took note of what had just happened. The next day, I received a phone call from Kansas University, telling me that I could not possess both the scholarship and the Naval Academy position. The representative of the scholarship program said, "Although you are fourth alternate, you can't have both. Either you go to KU next year and immediately cancel your appointment to the U.S. Naval Academy, or your scholarship is over." I did not expect to be put on the spot. I thought about it for four or five minutes, and decided to accept the Naval Academy position.

As an alternate, I had to wait a full year to enter the academy. In June 1933, one month after graduation, I sought employment to keep myself occupied. I found a position at Oil Country Specialties, a company that made drilling equipment for oil wells. I got the job because my sister, Katherine, was dating one of the managers, Ben Beal. Initially, I worked as a sweeper, earning thirty-five cents an hour, but I soon became an apprentice toolmaker, earning fifty cents an hour regular pay and one dollar an hour for overtime. It was dangerous work. I usually found myself hardening tools with cyanide, a poison; however, I considered it the best job I ever had while living in Coffeyville.

In an indirect way, Oil Country Specialties offered me my first opportunity to fly. Douglas Brown, one of the company's managers, happened to be an associate of Roger "Rolley" Inman, the oldest of three brothers who had formed a flying circus a few years earlier. The Inman Brothers were famous because their act included a two-year-old male lion who would ride in the stunt planes. Rolley Inman owned the lion and often drove with it in the rumble seat of his automobile, eliciting stares from shocked Coffeyville residents. One day, Douglas Brown introduced Rolley Inman to my father and me. The Inman brothers had just purchased a new Model-17 Beechcraft Staggerwing, a twenty-six-foot biplane with the lower wing thrust slightly forward of the enclosed cockpit. Showing off the aircraft, Rolley asked, "Would you like to see what it looks like in the cockpit?"

I answered, "Yes!" Rolley Inman offered Dad a cup of coffee and escorted both of us into the plane. I sat in the copilot's chair, and Dad took a seat in the back. Without much of a wait, Inman engaged the throttle and we soared into the air. Later on, without warning, while Dad stood between the pilot's and copilot's chairs, Inman put the Staggerwing into a perfect loop. Somehow, not a single drop of coffee spilled. When the plane landed, I looked over at my father. He wasn't exactly shaking, but he was very perplexed.

Dad stuck out his hand. He said, "Thanks again for those flights."

"Flights?" Rolley Inman laughed. "I gave you only one flight!"

Dad rejoined, "No, you gave me two flights, the first and the last!"

Dad may have hated flying, but I loved it. I wanted to do another loop, to feel that weird sensation of defying gravity. I was seized by the idea of becoming an aviator, now more than anything. Any doubts about turning down the scholarship to Kansas University evaporated in that loop.

To survive the Naval Academy, I took time to prepare. In August 1933, I enrolled at Coffeyville Junior College, taking classes in calculus and French. I learned from an excellent teacher, a woman named Edith Steininger, who made calculus come easily. In fact, I learned more mathematics from her than from all of my instructors at the Naval Academy combined. I split my time, attending classes in the morning and then working at Oil Country Specialties in the afternoon, sometimes clocking out around midnight. On the weekends, I cleaned and repaired firearms, unwanted weapons once used by the famous big-game hunters Martin and Osa Johnson. The Johnsons routinely returned to Coffeyville to visit relatives, bringing back old or broken rifles. I cleaned and repaired them, and for every four or five rifles I fixed, I usually got to keep one for myself. It was a tough year of work, but as it turned out, it was for the best.

Every day, sweat poured from my brow and my eyes strained from all of the studying, but I finally reached the day when I left Coffeyville for good. Annapolis beckoned.

|||||||||||||||||||||||||||||||||||||||||||||||||||||||||||||||||||||||||||||||||||||||||||||||||||||||||||||||||||||||||

CHAPTER 3

MIDSHIPMAN

1934–1938

In May 1934, I arrived at Annapolis, Maryland, and entered the U.S. Naval Academy. I found no sprawling prairie there; the campus consisted of a compact 224 acres and 125 buildings. I arrived at a realm steeped in tradition and indoctrination. At the time, the U.S. Naval Academy was eighty-nine years old, and its faculty knew how to mold naval officers through a time-tested, inflexible manner.

By that point, more than eleven thousand midshipmen had graduated. My class—the future Class of 1938—contained 575 people. I was just one of many hopefuls. When we arrived, we received a pocket-sized, two-hundred-page tome called *Reef Points*. The staff considered it a "bible" for plebes—the slang term given to first-years—and the book warned us to read every word in it. It said, "Read it; 'bone' it; live by it! Your cruise here at the Academy will be more pleasant if you do; just as a mariner's cruises are more enjoyable when he knows that his actions are those his 'sailing directions' recommend." *Reef Points* told us that we plebes would soon discover we knew next to nothing about the service we had just entered. We might wonder why we were denied certain privileges accorded to older students. We might complain about performing certain repetitive, apparently useless tasks. The Plebe Bible instructed us not to raise questions. It said, "You will find yourself, for the time being, on the wrong end of nearly all the rates, but it must be so, and as time goes on you will see the 'why' of them and be glad they exist. . . . The seemingly pointless tasks will teach you resourcefulness and cheerful obedience. We all learn it; never for a moment think you are being subjected to anything which has not been included in the training of every naval officer." *Reef Points* listed eighteen random examples of disciplinary changes we had to monitor—maintain correct posture, keep off certain benches, don't wear fancy belts, always use "sir," try out for a sport—among others. I remember the first imperative more than the rest. If a plebe received an order from a senior midshipman, we were instructed to say, "Aye, aye, sir!" and then carry it out to the best of our ability. It said, "*Never* argue."

As I discovered, most of the Naval Academy's colorful traditions came not from the faculty, but from the minds of sadistic upperclassmen. The social code as devised by the First Class of midshipmen (the seniors) came crashing down upon the Fourth Classmen (the incoming class) as soon as we got there. The upperclassmen taught us the value of rank by inflicting all manner of illegal hazing on us. (Officially, hazing was not allowed at the academy, and it was punishable by court-martial, but few upperclassmen paid this rule any mind.) No matter our social standing, we plebes now held the most inferior position at the academy. The First Classmen imposed a severe form of discipline, meting out "swattings," physical punishment inflicted upon those who failed to act the part of a gentleman, the centerpiece of our code of conduct. Quite often, First Classmen awarded swattings for petty trivialities. For instance, I received one for failing to remember the number of bricks in a certain campus building. I took this beating without complaint, but this punishment was terribly unfair. The upperclassman who ordered it had simply wanted to apply his authority and watch someone get swatted. I endured this humiliation as gracefully as I could. I took the advice from *Reef Points* and held my tongue.

I shouldn't speak too ill of the swattings. Sometimes they had a positive effect. The First Classmen "awarded" them for serious infractions. If they discovered alcohol squirreled away in the dormitories, or if they conducted a random sobriety test and a Fourth Classman failed it, a series of abuses followed. They made us plebes "sit for infinity," that is, sit on an imaginary chair for hours. Other offenders had to row a bathtub across the floor until their arms tired. It all served as a way of correcting any aberrant plebe's pattern of misbehavior. Intelligent plebes corrected their errors; intractable ones became so overwhelmed by the abuse that they washed out. By the end of the year, I grew tired of dodging the cruel First Classmen. Finally, I happened upon a solution. I joined the wrestling team and excelled at the sport. The sports teams tended to stick together. Even if I got into trouble, no First Classman would dare challenge me, for fear of facing reprisals from his classmates on the team, all of them thickly muscled. Consequently, my swattings decreased and I never had to endure public humiliations, such as "sitting for infinity" in the mess hall.

No plebe ever wanted to incur the wrath of the upperclassmen, but the junior midshipmen loved to pull pranks and act disobediently, anything that ran in defiance of the institution's strict codes of conduct. We newly arrived plebes had already heard the strange tales of the mythical Zigon, a midshipman who possessed masterful skills as an electrician. I don't know if this fellow Zigon really existed, or if any of the tales attributed to him are true, but they took on a life of their own during my time at the academy. Midshipmen gossiped about Zigon as if he were a folk hero. I knew these stories because my cousin Walter Coleman claimed to know him personally. These wild tales told of a midshipman who had full run of campus. As the legends told, he built an electric chair that shocked people when they sat in it. He stole a pay phone from downtown, hooked it up to his room, and arranged it so the bill went to the administration building. Once, Zigon even crank-called the super-intendent, shouting obscenities into the phone. When the superin-tendent tried to catch the mysterious culprit, entering an elevator on an Ahab-like manhunt, Zigon managed to stop the elevator be-tween floors, trapping the hapless admiral. Zigon even penetrated a steam tunnel that went underneath the promenade, using it as an access point to enter the academic buildings. He stole tests and fashioned a black-market trade, selling answers to needy midship-men for fifty cents per test. These tales went on and on. Eventually, Zigon's pranks got him dismissed, a truth that few of us doubted.

Tales of the merry prankster Zigon set a standard of horseplay that we tried to meet and surpass. I had been a bit of a prankster as a child, but as a midshipman, I participated in few illicit activities. When I arrived at the Naval Academy, I thought of nothing but my goal of becoming a pilot. Walking through campus—or "the Yard," as we called it—reminded me of the seriousness of my enterprise. Monuments to great admirals and naval commanders filled me with confidence that, with the right education and a profound sense of responsibility, I could reproduce similar acts of valor. The chapel contained a beautiful painting of the 1812 battle between USS *Constitution* and HMS *Java*. The main entrance to Macdonough Hall contained two British cannon captured at the Battle of Plattsburgh Bay. I loved to march past the memorial to Tecumseh, the Shawnee warrior who had defied the United States during the War of 1812. Located in front of Bancroft Hall, the Tecumseh Monument was a life-size bronze re-creation of the figurehead that once adorned the bow of USS *Delaware*. Before every football game, the regiment delivered a left-handed "penny salute" to the bust, tossing pennies in the direction of the monument for good luck.

If Tecumseh ever favored our fortunes, it certainly came during the Army-Navy game of 1934, the first event I can remember when the campus unified intensely and completely. On a cold, drizzly day, December 1, we filed into Franklin Field, Philadelphia, to participate in the football rivalry that had existed between the two service academies since 1890. Our team was under pressure; the Navy had not won a game since 1921. Dressed in our overcoats, the Army cadets and Navy midshipmen paraded along the edge of the field, which quickly turned into a sopping mud pit. A number of midshipmen even lost their shoes, sucked off by the thick mire. When the game got underway, the two teams flailed wildly at each other, the players sliding comically in the grime. I cheered excitedly because the team's punter, Bill Clark, was my mentor. (Each plebe had an upperclassman assigned to look after him.) After hours and hours, neither team had scored a touchdown. At one point, a mud-spattered referee attempted to find the ball but accidentally handed the quarterback a dirt clod that fell apart in his hands. Finally, our team made it to the eleven-yard line and called up Midshipman Slade D. Cutter to kick a field goal. Cutter placed the field goal perfectly, and when the game ended with a score of 3–0, we jubilant midshipmen stormed onto the field and pulled the goalposts out of the ground.

The football games were fun, but I always made sure to keep graduation in sight. To that end, I surrounded myself with equally studious friends. One of my closest chums was Elton Lewis Knapp, an exceptionally bright student who eventually graduated forty-third, within the top 10 percent of our class. Having him alongside made it easy for me to hit the books. I admired him because he put in the time and effort to become a naval officer. As a bonus, Elton also improved my chances with the ladies. In those days, I wasn't terribly suited to courting. If I found any recreational time at all, I spent it building guns. I often went to the campus machine shop, and using scrap metal, I welded together a .22-caliber submachine gun. By the end of my term, I had constructed four guns and practiced with them. My fondness for firearms gained me a reputation as something of an eccentric. Indeed, the Naval Academy's yearbook said this about me: "No biography would be complete without telling of Jack's passion for guns. During his years here he built everything from a pocket pistol to a machine gun. When he really gets out working for Uncle Sam, he will probably make the Germans and their Big Berthas look like pikers." All the gun toting might have put a damper on my social life, except that Elton usually took me along whenever he went searching for romance. Elton possessed good looks and charm, which attracted local girls to him. No gal would ever ask me on a date without Elton's help, for whenever a pretty girl invited Elton out, he always insisted on a double date. He made sure his lady friend—whoever she was— could find an equally pretty partner for me.

Of course, more than chasing girls or building guns, I took time to sharpen my leadership skills. I learned that yelling and screaming did not attract respect. I remember one midshipman on the parade ground who preferred to act the part of the martinet. Whenever any of the junior midshipmen anticipated his commands, he admonished us, ordering us to continue as instructed until he uttered his next command, apparently eager to hear the crescendo of his own voice. One day, the formation made its way along the drill field—called Farragut Field—with the martinet in the lead. He was walking backward so as to observe the formation. Suddenly, he disappeared. He fell into an enormous hole dug by a maintenance crew, an unmarked excavation intended to root out a troublesome pipe. The formation adhered to the midshipman's words, marching over the seawall and into the Severn River. When the water reached our knees, we halted. Our unfortunate commander hoisted himself out of the hole, spied his dutiful, waterlogged troops in the river, and said, "Permission to laugh."

Each June, July, and August, we midshipmen conducted "summer cruises" before our September leave, the brief furlough before the new academic year began. The summer cruises gave the First, Second, and Third Classmen practical knowledge in navigation, seamanship, electrical engineering, gunnery, and radio operations. I joined them twice, once in 1935 and again in 1937. The academy's midshipmen served on one of three battleships. Each time I went out, I received assignment to USS *Arkansas* (BB-33), a 26,000-ton *Wyoming*-class battleship laid down in 1910. The massive vessel was well past its prime. USS *Arkansas* had no means of modern communication. Instead of telephones, the ship used voice tubes and annunciators. When all eight boilers were working it could steam very slowly at only fifteen knots and the tightest circle it could make was almost a mile in diameter.

The 1935 cruise offered plenty of instruction. I served in one of *Arkansas*'s six turrets. Each turret housed two twelve-inch guns. All summer long, I worked as part of the turret crew, loading and firing the guns. It was not terribly rewarding work, but from the inside, I learned how a battleship operated. The second cruise, however, offered greater rewards. *Arkansas* departed on June 4, 1937, bound for Europe, and made its first stops at Sweden and Norway, exciting places for a young sailor. Blond-haired, blue-eyed ladies met us at all the ports, welcoming us to Sweden with delicate pastries. I adored the food and the giggling girls. Also, *Arkansas* received important dignitaries. Crown Prince Olav V of Norway was our most remarkable visitor. The finely dressed monarch sauntered along the deck with his characteristic slicked-back hair and an arrangement of jangling medals on his chest. He defied expectations when he intermixed with us sailors, shaking our hands. An officer asked Prince Olav if he wanted to see anything on the ship. All he wanted was an apple.

During this second cruise I focused on becoming an expert in naval gunnery. Having already won "expert" at pistol and rifle marksmanship, I felt the urge to have that award for naval gunnery. I served in turret No. 5, one of the stern turrets, a raised battlement that abutted the superstructure. A more senior midshipman operated as the pointer, raising the guns to their proper elevation. Because of my academic standing, I served as the trainer, rotating the turret. To fire the turret guns safely, we ran through a checklist of thirty-one different items, carefully marking down important details, including the temperature of the powder, the temperature outside of the turret, and the temperature inside the turret. In running the guns out, we had to make certain they did not collide with each other or with any equipment or personnel on the deck. I worked night and day, memorizing the complex loading and firing procedures. I knew them all by heart.

To test gunnery, the captain of *Arkansas* had each turret's crew fire at a target pulled by a tugboat. The best crews could zero in on a target within a few seconds. To sight, we used twelve-inch gun-sight mirrors, the only modern pieces of technology on the ship. These gargantuan binoculars were incredible. I swear, I think they could read the print on a newspaper nearly a mile away. At first, my turret crew demonstrated little desire to win the rating of expert, but I devised an ingenious incentive. One day, while cruising off the coast of Norway, I looked through the gun-sight mirrors and saw a beach full of beautiful women. All of them had stripped off their swimwear, thinking that there were no men around to see them skinny-dip. I decided to hold gunnery practice by targeting the nude Norwegian girls. Every drill, I'd choose a good-looking woman and swing the sights on her. When the crew had finished the drill, I asked one of them to look through the mirrors and confirm the target.

I'd ask, "Do you see the girl?"

"Aye, aye, sir!"

I continued, "Is she wearing a swimsuit?"

They'd giggle, "No, sir!"

Needless to say, my lonely sailors came to enjoy gunnery practice. Thanks to the girls, we made the rating of "expert" pretty quick.

Arkansas left Scandinavia in late June, making a stop at Kiel, Germany, before heading to Funchal, Madeira, off Portugal. The stopover at Germany opened my eyes to the rise of Nazism. I had visited in 1935 when accompanying the crew of *Arkansas* during my first summer cruise. Back then, the Germans spoke fondly of their new chancellor, Adolf Hitler. They told me how Hitler intended to end unemployment and bring "glory and strength" to the nation. Now, in 1937, the situation did not appear so rosy. I noticed crowds battling in the streets; many supported the government's actions against free speech, communism, and Jews. Like many Americans, I didn't quite grasp the chilling portent of things to come; however, I saw a glimpse of a nation racked by turmoil, snapshots of Germany's deteriorating political situation.

After leaving Germany, USS *Arkansas* headed to Madeira and we ran through gunnery drills in the archipelago. I believe this visit was intended to suggest to Spain that it needed to respect American neutrality. At the time, Spain was involved in a civil war between fascist and leftist forces and our ship gently reminded them that neither faction would be wise to hurt American interests.

Honestly, for us sailors, the civil war could have been a million miles away; my memories of the Madeira cruise are mostly filled with drinking and mayhem. One day, I witnessed a comical sight. *Arkansas*'s captain came running past me, trying to put his pants on as he navigated the ship's narrow passageways. A damage control team had reported an explosion in the forward magazine. Several sailors had tried to create a "Pink Lady," an alcoholic cocktail made from medicine and torpedo propulsion fluid. The sailors lit a fire to burn off the denaturant, and the rising temperature accidentally ignited some loose explosives. I remember that sound: "Boom! Boom! Boom! Boom!" The captain ran down to the forward magazine, thinking the ship was going to explode. That's the fastest I've ever seen a captain run. Eventually, marines captured the culprits.

Shore leave brought additional problems. When the midshipmen went ashore, the cheap but potent Madeira wine was too tempting to pass up. Even I drank more than I should have. One day, I was terribly drunk when I returned to the ship, because I had consumed a whole bottle at a restaurant. I don't know how, but I managed to find the ship and returned to my quarters without incurring punishment. (Incidentally, Arkansas's captain had instructed us not to drink the water. If caught, I would have argued that getting drunk was a consequence of the captain's orders.) During my lucid moments, I admired the scenery. The streets were made of a picturesque cobblestone and not a single automobile choked the thoroughfares. I remember that another sailor was so blissfully drunk on wine and reverie that he refused to leave. I had to badger him to come back to the ship. If it hadn't been for me, he would have stayed there. Upon leaving Madeira, I reported to the bridge with a head-pounding hangover. The captain ordered the crew to haul anchor and get the ship moving.

As it got underway, Arkansas drifted toward a shoal. The captain ordered, "Full speed ahead," issuing his commands through the annunciator. Slowly but surely, the behemoth continued to drift toward the shallows. The captain bellowed into the voice tube, "Give me full speed down there!" Again, the engine room did not respond. Finally, the captain turned to his warrant officers and chiefs.

My stars! His face went from red to purple. The captain realized the engine room could not hear his commands because the voice tubes were choked with wine bottles. We had used those tubes as a trash bin, dropping the empty bottles into them. The captain screamed, "Give me full speed ahead and get those bottles out of that tube or there's hell to pay!" The chiefs ran full tilt, hurrying to the engine room. Pretty soon the smoke started billowing and we went "full speed ahead," a pathetic ten knots.

For all the humor and miscues, the summer cruises brought me much-needed experience in the surface fleet. However, flying was still my dream. Ever since my days in the Kansas National Guard, when army planes buzzed my regiment and "killed" me in mock combat, I believed that planes, not surface ships, would win the Navy's future battles. And so I learned on my own. I logged a few hours flying the Naval Academy's Martin PM-1 flying boat, a giant twin-engine floatplane that boasted an open-air cockpit that sat right atop the nose. This was the only opportunity the Naval Academy could offer to a would-be aviator. Consequently, I had to find places outside the academy. Whenever I went to and from Coffeyville, I made arrangements to pass through Washington, D.C., so that a friend from the Army Air Corps could let me fly the route between Bolling Field and Annapolis. At one point, I visited a different Army Air Corps facility at Scott Field, Illinois. There I met a helpful lieutenant who noticed my interest in aircraft. After spending several evenings at the lieutenant's house—where I ingratiated myself by flirting with the officer's attractive daughter—I convinced him to let me pilot some of the aircraft at Scott Field. Thus, through these personal acquaintances, I got my first chance to be behind the stick of an airplane.

Four years of antics, studying, training, gunnery, and flying passed quickly, and within a flash, graduation day came. My class—the Class of 1938—counted 607 midshipmen on its full roster, the 575 admitted back in 1934 and thirty-two others added since. In four years, we had lost 174 students: one to death, three to dismissal, 128 to resignation, thirty-four held back, and eight removed by honorable discharge. In order of merit, I graduated 245 out of the remaining 438.* Despite all my studying, I never mastered a few classes. I still possess a booklet of my grades as a "Third Classman," my sophomore year. According to that, I performed excellently in all my engineering classes, gaining above a 3.0 in Marine Engineering, Electrical Engineering, and Mathematics. I did not perform as well in English, History, and Languages, where I hovered at a 3.0 or just below. Clearly, Edith Steininger's lessons in calculus had helped me immensely, but my prairie education in southeast Kansas didn't quite prepare me for the liberal arts taught at the academy.

President Franklin Roosevelt delivered the commencement address. Our commander in chief recommended we possess multiple talents, saying, "No matter whether your specialty be naval science, or medicine, or the law, or teaching, or the church, or civil service, or business, or public service—remember that you will never reach the top and stay at the top unless you are well-rounded in your knowledge of all the other factors in modern civilization that lie outside of your own special profession. That applies to all of world thought and world problems, but it applies, of course, with special emphasis to the thought and the problems of our own Nation." Continuing, he offered that our learning lay ahead of us, and that education, the best of it, would be attained through the pro-

---

* I should point out that my class—the Class of 1938—faced the intensity of World War II like few others. Of the 438 graduates, 421 of us served in the war. Forty-two died in battle. Twenty-four earned Navy Crosses, seventy earned Silver Stars, 146 earned Bronze Stars, and forty-four earned Distinguished Flying Crosses.

cess of making the right decisions at the right time. He explained, "You will be called on for decisions in your line of duty where such knowledge will be of at least daily desirability—daily help to you in coming to your own conclusions and carrying out your own assigned tasks. Preliminary knowledge of that kind you have; but the best of it, the most important part of it, will come to you through the passing years."

Partway into the address, Roosevelt paused to introduce the mayor of the Canadian city of St. John, New Brunswick, who presented the Naval Academy with a rare artifact, John Paul Jones's quadrant. Then the president returned to the task at hand, conferring us with our newest mission. He concluded, "And now there will be no more speaking, there will be something more important. Before you actually become Bachelors of Science, let me stress that in the days to come you do not place too much emphasis on the word 'Bachelor.' And so, I congratulate you on your graduation. Your Commander-in-Chief is proud of you. Good luck and happy voyage." I guess I should have been listening to this part more carefully. Roosevelt had told us to find the love of our lives and get married as quickly as we could. Perhaps if I had taken his sage advice I wouldn't have nearly messed up my chances at finding true love. But that is a story for later.

On that happy day, I hefted my cover into the air. More than four hundred other white caps went airborne with it. I was off to sea.

CHAPTER 4

|||||||||||||||||||||||||||||||||||||||||||||||||||||||||||||||||||||||||||||||||||||||||||||||||||||||||||||||||||||||||||||||||

FINDING LOVE

1938–1939

In the summer of 1938, I arrived in Long Beach, California, and joined the crew of USS *Vincennes* (CA-44), a 9,400-ton *Astoria*-class cruiser assigned to Cruiser Division 7. Sleeker and lower in profile than USS *Arkansas* from my midshipman cruises, *Vincennes* was a model of perfection when it launched on May 21, 1936. It went to sea with 952 officers and men and possessed top-of-the-line armament. It boasted eight-inch guns mounted in three turrets, along with five-inch deck guns and .50-caliber machine guns. In the spring of 1938, it participated in Fleet Problem XIX (a mock attack against Pearl Harbor), and then it made port at Long Beach. That's where I joined the crew.

Vincennes's commanding officer, Captain L. M. Stevens, assigned me to the position of turret officer, a decision undoubtedly influenced by the fact that I had won "expert gunnery" during my summer cruise aboard USS *Arkansas*. I joined a forty-person crew belonging to *Vincennes*'s No. 2 turret, a 250-ton rotating casemate that held three of the cruiser's Mark-12 naval guns. I worked hard to win the "expert" rating a second time and I think my devotion won the admiration of Captain Stevens. I didn't have stiff competition.

Another ensign insisted on heading that turret. He spun the turret so far that its guns slammed into the bridge, and it took a full two days to extricate them. After that, Captain Stevens instructed me to take command. I spent a few days preparing my crew for the test. An impartial test crew arrived to see if my gun crew could manage the turret. At the word *go,* I had to locate a target moving on an unknown course three miles away, hitting all projectiles on a white canvas sheet above a wooden raft pulled by a boat with three-mile towlines. My crew had to make no errors, spill no powder, and suffer no injuries in the loading process. We passed the test, getting the chance to mark a rare *E* on our turret.

Captain Stevens took a shine to me, and my friendship with him allowed me to request specific duties. I wasted no time in asking for a position as *Vincennes*'s aircraft recovery operations officer. While performing this task, I superintended recovery of the cruiser's Scout Observation Curtiss (SOC) Seagull seaplane, a two-seat scout plane. During recovery operations, the crew had to execute a series of tricky maneuvers. First, the helmsman made a sweeping turn, calming the water. Next, the pilot landed the plane, taxiing it over a cargo net dragged by a boom connected to the ship. The pilot then had to maneuver the seaplane so that a hook attached to its floats caught hold of the net, and then, once the SOC stopped, the pilot had to stand up and attach the ship's crane hook to an aircraft sling. Finally, the crane operators lifted the SOC seaplane out of the water and returned it to a sixty-foot deck-mounted catapult. I had the job of making sure all of these components functioned in harmony. Any minor mistake could cost the seaplane pilot his life or potentially damage the expensive piece of aviation equipment. It wasn't easy to accomplish all this with the ship rolling and the plane bobbing.

Although it was a fretful task, I enjoyed seaplane recovery operations. It offered me valuable experience, a chance to see naval aviation in action before my inevitable journey to flight school. However, in learning the ropes of SOC launching and recovery, and in getting to know the Seagull aviators, I learned that prejudice existed between surface warfare officers and pilots. Since the introduction of naval aviation in the form of the U.S. Naval Air Service in 1914, officers divided into two classes: "black shoe" and "brown shoe." These classifications derived from the noticeable distinction in the color of officers' footwear. For years, Navy uniform regulations insisted that its officers wear polished black. In 1922 the Navy altered the shoes assigned to aviators, requiring them to wear russet brown. Of course, the shoe color did not cause the rift, but rather the attitude that followed from it did. The "black shoe" surface officers believed that aviation represented a short-lived fad, and that battleships and cruisers would always remain the vital backbone of the U.S. Navy.

Because of my love of flying, I had cast my lot with the "brown shoe" aviators. On *Vincennes,* I witnessed a degree of resentment toward pilots because they received 50 percent additional hazard pay beyond the normal $125 per month base pay of the "black shoes." The war between "black shoes" and "brown shoes" never made life uncomfortable for me while I served on the cruiser, but I detected an air of mistrust. I knew that aviators would only earn their place through success in combat.

Despite these murmurings, I absolutely loved my billet. California represented something of a paradise. It had all the things of which I dreamed: beach, sun, ocean, and girls. At the time, I wanted to be there forever. Of these four circles of nirvana, I spent most of my energy on understanding the female component. By the end of my first month in California, friends from Coffeyville arranged a meeting. A neighboring family from Lincoln Street had a son, Lawrence Coverdale, who worked as a professor at Long Beach City College. Wanting to help me in matters of romance, the Coverdales implored Lawrence to take appropriate measures so that I might find a girl. Lawrence invited me to campus and told me to watch the women as they entered the parking lot after class. If any of them caught my eye, I should report back immediately. This method of courting probably sounds strange by today's standards—and maybe it was odd even at the time—but it worked for me. I was always shy around women, and I'm not sure I could have followed my instincts or made a good impression if I was seeking romance on my own.

As I watched the women saunter out of the college buildings, I noticed a particular blue-eyed beauty. I hurried back to Lawrence and asked who she was and if he might provide me with her address. He said, "Yes," but only on the agreement that he call her parents first, making sure this arrangement would be acceptable to them. He told me she was twenty-seven-year-old Eunice Marie Mochon, a woman who worked for Calavo, a farmer's cooperative in Los Angeles.* I'm not sure what he told her parents, but apparently he was convincing. He gave me an address and a date to pick up Eunice. Unfortunately, I don't remember what day that was, but I recall my anxiety. I was nervous as hell when I showed up at the Mochon residence. The house struck an imposing visage; a high wrought-iron fence surrounded it, and when I entered the front yard to ring the doorbell, a massive three-foot-tall Chow rose to its full height and growled menacingly. This was the family dog, named Ming. Any bulldog appeared like a puppy to him. Bravely, I passed by the purple-tongued sentry and rang the bell. Ming watched me as if I were some interloper, but not the first to try his hand at winning Eunice's heart. He looked at me as if to say, "You fool. You'll be gone in a few hours!"

---

* Eunice was born on January 5, 1911. She was five years older than me.

Eunice's parents, a French-Canadian couple, answered the door and ushered me inside. They commenced a pleasant interrogation of me, asking many personal questions about my family, my life experiences, my job, my goals, and my religion. I answered everything to their satisfaction, and much to their enjoyment, I answered a few sentences in French. In turn, the Mochons shared their own history, the story of their family and their quest to change from Canadian to U.S. citizenship. "Mama" Winifred Mochon asked most of the questions, and if I would mind speaking to their many French-Canadian visitors in their native language. Without hesitation, I answered, "Bien sûr" (Of course). I'm not sure why I agreed to do this; I guess I was just eager to end the interrogation and go on the date. When I felt sufficiently courageous, I asked if I could see Eunice. They agreed, but they insisted upon being present through our first meeting. She came down and—my stars!—she was beautiful! We spent our first evening talking as her parents monitored us. When night finally came, and I had overstayed my welcome, I asked Mrs. Mochon if I could stop by again and take her daughter on a real date. "Yes," she said out of earshot of everyone else. But she warned me to telephone first for an appointment, as her daughter had many suitors and she did not want them colliding or potentially fighting on the front steps.

I did not expect so frank a response, but I gamely persisted in my effort to court fair Eunice. So it happened, and for the next several months I visited the Mochon household regularly. Usually I played bridge with Eunice and her parents, or I listened to Eunice play her grand piano. I got along well with her father, Albert, and we spent many fond evenings drinking wine, one of his favorite pastimes. Additionally, I got to meet many of the Mochon relatives—and it always seemed that they had someone staying in the guest bedroom. The visitors usually spoke French, and I believe my knowledge of the language impressed them.

Although her parents liked me, I wasn't sure I was getting anywhere with Eunice. We never went on any dates by ourselves, and with all of my visits to her family's home, I was feeling more like some kind of freeloading cousin than a boyfriend. I had precious few opportunities to see Eunice outside of her house. Sometimes I accompanied her to school plays, but this only worsened the situation. I could see she was good at everything, but she was exceptionally known for her acting ability. She liked to perform girl-meets-boy plays where actors hugged and kissed each other and professed to love each other forever. It shocked me the first time I saw her kiss an actor passionately onstage. I was suddenly racked with self-doubt. How could she kiss him so devotedly unless she secretly loved him? And what did she really feel about me?

Our courtship became a long, difficult process. Eunice approached all her relationships cautiously. Although she had no problem acting romantically onstage, she didn't want to be hugged or kissed early in the game. At times it was difficult for me to know exactly where we stood. Complicating the picture, she had many boyfriends, true to her mother's words. If I wanted to win her affections, I had to outdo a slew of competitors. Eunice's exquisite beauty and her list of accomplishments made her a popular target. In addition to her secretarial skills, musical expertise, athleticism, and multilingualism, she was also an accomplished stenotypist, capable of typing fifty words per minute. I couldn't quite wrap my head around the idea that she'd consider me, a gun-loving Kansan, as suitable boyfriend material.

In fact, so many suitors hounded Eunice that her mother had trouble keeping a schedule whereby we avoided meeting each other. One evening, I came over to play bridge. The telephone rang in the middle of the game. Mrs. Mochon answered it, and I could tell from the conversation that it was one of Eunice's other suitors at the other end of the line. Luckily, Mrs. Mochon lied, saying that

Eunice was out and could not answer the phone. A few weeks later in the summer, a more embarrassing moment occurred when Eunice mistakenly invited two boyfriends to her house at the same time. I was one of those two, arriving second. As soon as I entered the house, I could tell something was amiss, judging by the look of horror on Mrs. Mochon's face. Unwilling to risk a confrontation, Mrs. Mochon sequestered me. She put me in the family room and the other suitor in the kitchen. She kept us separated all evening, and my rival and I never met. Luckily, Eunice spent more time with me that night. We talked all evening. She was apparently oblivious to the fact that the other beau waited impatiently in another room. My most troublesome competitor lived across the street. The lad's mother desperately wanted her son, who had entered into a lucrative automotive dealership business, to marry Eunice. The suitor's mother was an artist, and consequently she showered the Mochons with paintings, trying to win their blessing.

Of all Eunice's suitors, I always believed I possessed the greatest handicap because the Navy could call me away from Long Beach at any moment. Indeed, it did. Until that point, *Vincennes* had gone to sea only twice, and we still needed to fix a multitude of problems the crew had noticed during the shakedown cruise. After six months of training at Long Beach, *Vincennes* went up the coast to Mare Island in the San Francisco Bay for repairs. I hated leaving Long Beach, especially since I worried about losing touch with Eunice, or losing her to a rival boyfriend. Further, Mare Island Shipyard in Vallejo—*Vincennes*'s destination—appeared like a den of iniquity when compared to the picturesque Eden of Long Beach. I think it had the longest stretch of bars of any place in the world. I took a peek inside one as soon as I got there. One look was all I could stand. It was filled with drunken sailors, prostitutes, and mean-looking shipyard workers.

I visited one of Vallejo's smaller, less dingy establishments and seated myself at the bar next to two wealthy-looking "gents." One of them said to the other, "I just sold an old car for ten dollars to make room for my sailboat." I spun my head around and blurted out, "I sure wish I could have bought that car for ten bucks!" The gentleman looked at me from head to toe and said, "Well, I have another one for sale." They finished their beers and then I hopped into the stranger's car. We drove into the countryside and there, outside a spacious barn, was a Model 1927 Oakland Motor Car. The man repeated, "Ten dollars and it's yours." The car did not run, but I paid for it anyway. I returned to *Vincennes* and asked Captain Stevens if I could sign out necessary tools on a ten-day loan. He agreed. I borrowed the tools and fixed up the Oakland—which I named "Windy"—and asked for liberty in five months, when *Vincennes* would sail back to Long Beach. Stevens granted it, and I drove my new automobile back to Southern California. At last I had the means to take Eunice on an unsupervised date.

Immediately, I went to the Mochon residence and asked to take Eunice on a drive. Normally the Mochons would have said, "No, sir," but I guess by then they liked me so much they gave me every chance to win over their daughter's affections. They set a curfew, requiring me to return Eunice before sundown. I staked much of this date's potential success on my car's appearance and my superb driving skills. I made certain to point out that I had cleaned and repaired it all on my own. Sadly, bad luck intervened. I had not bought any new tires, and during the drive the left rear tire blew out on a busy street in downtown Los Angeles. Undaunted, I pulled over, unpacked my jack, and affixed the spare; however, I believed this stroke of bad luck had ended my chances. As I repaired the tire, I thought, Oh, what a way to start a first date! I really messed this thing up. She'll never have another date with me! With much of the evening wasted in getting my buggy started again, I drove Eunice home. Ming, apparently, had not moved from the porch during the few hours we'd been gone. When I returned her to the front door, the devoted Chow rose to his feet and eyeballed me suspiciously, making sure I wasn't causing any trouble. Almost mockingly, Ming sat down on the porch and smiled when I made my sheepish exit.

I thought I had struck out, but the date had not gone badly at all. In fact, Eunice did not see the flat tire episode as a failure; rather, she adored my quick thinking and my knowledge of automobile mechanics. If I had been at all flustered by the flat tire, she had not detected it. Once I purchased new tires I asked her on a second drive, and she accepted. With Windy at my command, I became a frequent visitor at the Mochon home. I picked up tools for them and helped move a screen door. Additionally, I fixed items around the house, including the door chimes and an ailing furnace. I think I won the day when I invited Eunice to visit *Vincennes*. Captain Stevens saw the two of us touring the cruiser, and he made it a point to introduce himself and "talk up" my accomplishments. This convinced her that I might be the best of her many boyfriends.

Events moved rapidly after that. One day I dared ask Mrs. Mochon about her daughter's ring size. Without hesitation she replied, "Size number eight and she'd like a wedding ring just like mine." Using my meager salary, I went out and bought an engagement ring. I had only to kneel down and propose marriage, but that moment never arrived. I balked at the opportunity, due to an argument with my father. Dad sent me several letters intended to talk me out of marrying a Catholic girl. In his typical old-fashioned way, he argued that families should not cross religious lines and that if I decided to marry into a Catholic family, I would be disrespecting the Kleiss family traditions. I knew from conversation with Eunice that she intended to stay Catholic and send any children to Catholic schools. These letters have always been a source of embarrassment for me, largely because they filled my head with doubt. I couldn't bear to start a rift with my father, so I decided not to propose marriage unless I had an assurance that she'd give up Catholicism for me. Ultimately it was a stupid decision on my part, one that I still regret to this day. I decided not to follow my heart, succumbing to the inflexibility of stodgy family pride.

I didn't have much time to talk about this wrinkle with Eunice. Right after I bought the ring, I learned that the Navy had decided to transfer Cruiser Division 7—and *Vincennes* with it—to the Atlantic Squadron. *Vincennes* and four of its sister ships had orders to head to Norfolk, Virginia, a continent away. This meant I had only one week to propose marriage or else keep forever silent. I called at the Mochons' house every day, but I never caught her. Finally, the day *Vincennes* left port, Eunice called me on the telephone. She told me that she loved me—a big step indeed—and promised to await my return. I was overjoyed with this news, but lacking a face-to-face conversation I missed my chance to discuss the troublesome question about her religion.

Vincennes was about to sail off, leaving the sunny shores of California behind. It was an awful day for me. I had found love, but I was too dim-witted to go after it.

CHAPTER 5

|||||||||||||||||||||||||||||||||||||||||||||||||||||||||||||||||||||||||||||||||||||||||||||||||||||||||||||||||

THE NAVY'S SURFACE FLEET
1939–1940

My cruiser, *Vincennes,* set sail on May 26, 1939. A gang of yard workers went to sea with us as we got underway for Panama. They were desperate to complete their contracted upkeeps within the deadline. We left the shipyard with two or three people finishing the deck and we had to slow our speed to allow a boat to pick them up and bring them back. During the first day of the cruise, I did something unusual. I changed my girlfriend's name. I never really liked the name Eunice, and neither did she, apparently. I wrote this in my letter to her: "It all came to me last night at 12:16:46, . . . that your nickname (or at least one of them) should be 'Jean.' It's a name I've always loved, tho' I'm sure you deserve even better." I guess it's strange to change a person's name, but I had changed my own when I was five, and my parents caused me no trouble. Eunice carried her name for twenty-eight years, and oddly enough, she offered no resistance, either. In fact, she wrote, "I really like my new nickname," and starting on June 12, she became "Jean," carrying that name forever after.

On June 2, *Vincennes* arrived off the coast of Panama, entering a sweltering atmosphere, with temperatures in the upper nineties.

We traveled along the coast for three more days and on June 6 entered the Panama Canal. The painfully sluggish canal transit offered opportunities for us to go ashore, our first shore leave since leaving the alcohol-soaked city of Vallejo. On the first night of the passage, I served as the officer of the deck, with a burly chief to help me preserve order. At first it seemed as if the sailors on *Vincennes* intended to keep their high jinx to a minimum. As the night proceeded, I noted only one minor disturbance. Twenty yards ahead of the ship, I spotted an inebriated sailor disrobing, apparently intent on diving into the lock. I dispatched two men to grab him, and thankfully they apprehended the nude sailor only seconds before he attempted his dangerous swan dive. The two enforcers dragged him up the gangway, where I confronted him. "What's this all about?"

The naked sailor replied, "Well, he dared me!"

"Wait, what?"

The drunken man elaborated. Apparently one of his companions had confronted him and said, "You wouldn't dare swim across the lock." Not to be taken for a coward, the sailor had prepared to dive in. Flummoxed by the sailor's unusual answer, I asked him how he expected to survive the fall. Had he actually jumped into the lock, he would surely have struck concrete and broken his neck. Further, I argued, what about the wildlife? Didn't the sailor realize that alligators patrolled the lock? He grumbled an obscenity in response, and I ordered him back to his quarters.

Hours later, Captain Stevens arrived at the gangway. He asked me if the crew had caused me any trouble. I regaled him with the story of the drunken, naked sailor and then said, "But otherwise nothing." Just as I uttered this sentence, a military police wagon backed up to *Vincennes*'s gangway. The police opened the back door and an angry sailor burst out, running up the gangway onto the ship, apparently eager to flee their custody. The burly chief held out his hand. "Whoa, slow down there, little fella." Undaunted, the sailor plowed into the chief and knocked him out. Embarrassed that my earlier report now appeared woefully inaccurate, I took a step to intervene on the chief's behalf. Suddenly, Captain Stevens admonished, "No, don't you get involved! An officer is not allowed under any circumstances to hit an enlisted man!" The violent sailor made his way belowdecks, leaving the unconscious chief in his wake. Acting calmly, knowing that Captain Stevens was watching me, I rounded up eight sailors, tracked the man to his bunk, and then ordered the sailors to tie him down, which they did, even though the man thrashed about violently. I couldn't imagine that anyone so small would be able to do this, but we needed all eight men to subdue him. Next I asked the Military Police what the angry sailor had done to merit his arrest. The MPs explained that the sailor had been drinking at a club and became unruly, causing some damage. I asked, "Well, how much was the damage?"

With unflappable seriousness, one of the MPs replied, "Oh, the damage is pretty great. We had to pay them two dollars to get a broken window fixed."

My jaw dropped. The MPs had arrested a sailor over a matter of two dollars! Captain Stevens reached into his pocket, saying, "Here's your two dollars."

On June 13, *Vincennes* finally reached its destination, Norfolk, Virginia, the home of forty-eight Navy warships. After we had a few days' rest, Captain Stevens informed the crew of the ship's upcoming schedule. He expected *Vincennes* to make a series of short cruises to various ports to pick up supplies and receive additional repairs. (Our eighteen-day cruise had revealed that some of the Vallejo repairs were insufficient.) The next three months amounted to a series of cruises along the Atlantic coast, none of them long enough to settle anywhere. Nevertheless, I did my best to visit the different cities and have fun. After voyaging between various shipyards all summer, *Vincennes* finally returned to its home at Pier 7, Norfolk, during the last week of July. We had just one more month to train until worldwide events altered life for every sailor. On September 1, 1939, the German army invaded Poland, touching off the first military action of the Second World War. Additionally, Adolf Hitler unleashed Germany's submarines against Allied shipping lanes in the Atlantic. On September 5, fearing that Hitler's submarine force might threaten America's neutrality, President Roosevelt issued a proclamation declaring his intent to protect American territorial waters from all belligerent vessels. Accordingly, Chief of Naval Operations Harold Stark ordered the Atlantic Fleet to mobilize for "neutrality patrol," long-range operations designed to report the movement of enemy ships. Stark expected our ships to patrol more than three thousand miles of coastline between Canada and South America and do so at the height of hurricane season.

The results of Roosevelt's Neutrality Patrol proclamation had an immediate effect on me. At midnight, September 6, 1939, an officer telephoned my quarters. He told me that one of my Naval Academy classmates, ENS Jamie Adair, had fallen off a gangway and broken his ankle. Someone needed to take his place, and the officer said it had to be me. In the dark of night, I packed my gear and made haste for a new ship, USS *Goff* (DD-247), which was to sail in two days. Annoyed that the Navy had changed my assignment without warning, I angrily gathered my equipment from *Vincennes*, which, coincidentally, also would depart in two days. As I wrote at the time, "No sleep in two days, but by propping both eyelids open I still find a good set of officers."

I had mixed feelings about heading to *Goff.* On one hand, it was a smaller ship, and not well suited for patrolling the Atlantic's rough autumn seas. *Goff* was a 1,200-ton *Clemson*-class destroyer, launched in 1920, and now assigned to Destroyer Division 21. At only 314 feet long, it was almost half the size of *Vincennes*. A noticeably smaller crew operated it, only 106 enlisted sailors, about 10 percent of the crew of *Vincennes*. On the other hand, *Goff* boasted a tight-knit officer corps. Six officers and eight chiefs completed *Goff*'s complement of men. When I arrived, I became the destroyer's commissary officer. The ship's commander, LCDR Noble Wayne Abrahams, liked me instantly, and he assigned me a host of collateral duties, including assistant navigator, battery control operator, spotting officer (gunnery), assistant engineering officer (boilers and turbines), coding board officer, athletic officer, and torpedo officer.

I also reunited with an old friend from the Naval Academy, ENS Elton Knapp, who served as *Goff*'s communications officer. Unlike *Vincennes*, the officers of *Goff* seemed more like a family. In writing to Jean, I explained, "How do I like the ship? Well, except for the fact that I can't figure out why she's stayed afloat these 19 years (she had a birthday party and birthday cake last week), I think she's swell. The skipper, Lt. Comdr. Abrahams, is full of vim and vigor and lots of nice sea stories, and the Exec., and the Doc and Eli and Pack and Knappsie rate with the best." Compared to life on a heavy cruiser, *Goff* represented a carefree environment, one where the rigorous requirements of the Navy tended to relax. For example, as commissary officer, I discovered I had plenty of opportunity to decide the ship's bill and fare. My duty was to determine the ship's menu, and naturally, I thought we ate like kings. Further, I arranged it so the officers' mess bill stood at only $10 per month. The government allowed $18.75 per month for expenses, so the officers pocketed the difference, a vast improvement over the bill on *Vincennes*, where we routinely overrode our mess expenses by $7 to $12 each month.

Another unusual difference pertained to civilian visitors. On *Vincennes*, Captain Stevens had allowed female visitors to come on board only between the hours of 4:00 P.M. and 10:00 P.M., and lifted an eyebrow if one brass button was out of place. On *Goff*, LCDR Abrahams allowed female visitors late into the evening. During the first night of a two-day stay in Newport, Rhode Island, Abrahams invited the officers and their lady friends for a late-night cocktail. On the second night, *Goff*'s wardroom "was once more covered with women"—that's how I described it at the time—who stayed until 3:00 A.M., drinking the ship's entire stock of Coca-Cola. I think some from that bevy of New England beauties wanted romance. They had no luck because all of the officers had wives. Only I lacked a wedding band, and all evening I dodged clusters of amorous women, now supercharged with caffeinated soft drinks. Five minutes after clearing the vessel of the visitors, *Goff* set sail at fifteen knots, dodging tugs and ferries with the officers standing watch in their usual apparel, white shirts and leather aviation jackets, not uniforms.

Goff sailed out of Norfolk in mid-September, traveling first to the Naval Torpedo Station at Newport, Rhode Island, and then to the New York Naval Shipyard in Brooklyn. *Goff* remained laid up until mid-November as workers overhauled the old ship, preparing it for its Neutrality Patrol to Puerto Rico. As we waited for the workers to prepare it for service, I considered the significance of our Neutrality Patrol assignment. As of October, Congress was poised to pass another Neutrality Act, one that would allow the United States to trade weapons to Allied nations on a "cash and carry" basis. Nowadays, it's hard to remember how I felt about it, but my letters to Jean offer a clue. On October 8, I wrote: "Hope this so-called 'neutrality' legislation doesn't pass. Not only do I think it's bad business, but it will keep more ships on this coast. And there's no telling how many good looking 'native sons' of California (if such there be) you'll run across between now and then (our date—remember?)." I preferred to be on the west coast, where I could be close to Jean; however, if I had to remain in the Atlantic, I felt confident because *Goff* intended to go south rather than north. I wrote, "While all the older ships are 'barking in the sunshine of southern climes,' the newer ships, like the VINCENNES will be pounding the North Pole run, stubbing their toes on icicles."

As it turned out, *Goff* never embarked on its patrol to Puerto Rico. Unaccountable delays held my ship in port. At one point, the local labor union refused to release the destroyer's anchor chains until the contracted work had been completed. Eventually, LCDR Abrahams sent a squad of marines to retrieve the chains by force. The marines accomplished this, but sadly, not knowing anything about them, they forgot to retrieve the shackles, the pieces that held the links together. Later, when the crew turned up the propeller in preparation to leave, by a stroke of bad luck it struck a wooden camel—a float ordinarily placed between a dock and a ship— ruining two boilers. After patching up the damage by working for twenty-four hours, we put *Goff* to sea on schedule, November 13, but as we steamed away from New York, strange noises issued from the turbine, so Abrahams insisted on putting the ship back to port. *Goff* limped dejectedly back to the navy yard "at about the speed Ming walks when you call him to take a bath," as I wrote to Jean, in order to put the awkward moment in some perspective for her. Then, as *Goff* made it back, we passed a civilian tanker that suddenly exploded. We dutifully sent over fire and rescue workers, helping the tanker crew abandon ship, but the fire melted off some of *Goff*'s fresh paint. When our aging destroyer finally made it back to the yard, as I put it in a letter, "New York welcomed us like a case of diphtheria." Rather than repair the damaged turbine, the yard workers insisted on replacing it. After hours of arguing, Abrahams decided to set sail again to find a different yard.

Eventually, *Goff* limped into Norfolk with a failing, overworked turbine. After an inspection at the nearby navy yard, Abrahams determined that we could not set sail for Puerto Rico any sooner than December 15. Frustrated, I wrote, "Nope, instead of basking in the sunny climes, here we sit, parked in another Navy Yard, with a turbine literally torn to bits." Naïvely, I added: "Honest to gosh, Jean, we've suffered every casualty known to sailor men."

Goff eventually went on its Neutrality Patrol, but not until June 1940, seven months behind schedule; however, I did not accompany it. After spending a quiet Christmas in Norfolk, I learned that I had been transferred yet again. I received a telephone call and an officer instructed me to transfer my gear in twenty-four hours. On January 3, 1940, I joined the crew of USS *Yarnall* (DD-143), a 1,150-ton *Wickes*-class destroyer.

Compared to *Goff* or *Vincennes*, *Yarnall* represented a significant downgrade. This ship had been launched back in June 1918 in the midst of the First World War. It did not see any combat, and after four years of peacetime service, the Navy ordered it decommissioned. *Yarnall* came out of retirement from 1930 to 1936, until the Navy again decommissioned it due to its advanced age. Then, in September 1939, shortly after Germany's invasion of Poland, the Navy recommissioned *Yarnall* for a second time, adding it to the Atlantic Fleet's Destroyer Division 61. I would have rather stayed aboard *Goff.* This new assignment already had a bad feel. I had seen some of *Yarnall*'s poor luck firsthand. When the crew took it out of mothball status, a boat captain died. From the deck of *Goff,* which anchored alongside, I watched as *Yarnall*'s crew lowered a lifeboat. Suddenly a rusty davit broke, and the crew spilled into the water. The boat slammed atop the boat captain, breaking his neck. Atlantic Squadron's sailors considered *Yarnall* an ancient relic, utterly incapable of deepwater transit. At the time, I wrote this about my transfer: "This old sea-going bucket is really a lulu. . . . [I] Certainly miss the good ship GOFF. She's one of the finest of the finest."

Even before I came on board, *Yarnall* lost its anchor, an embarrassing incident that should never have happened. This occurred on November 25, only six hours after the ship set sail for the first time in three years. Somehow *Yarnall* ran aground at Lynnhaven Roads. I did not serve on *Yarnall* at the time, so I do not know what happened from firsthand experience, but I heard many whispers. Gossipers blamed *Yarnall*'s commander, LCDR John Greeley Winn. For whatever reason, he ordered the anchor dragged to slow the ship in a heavy breeze. Then, forgetting that his anchor had latched, he ordered, "Full speed ahead." *Yarnall* snapped its anchor chain and plowed into the sand. No damage occurred, but Winn sent out an SOS distress call. Afterward, residents of the area derisively called the beach "*Yarnall* Shoals." I got a good look at the stricken vessel after it grounded.[*]

Naturally, the morale of *Yarnall*'s crew dipped low after the grounding incident. When I arrived with orders to become the ship's gunnery officer, I noticed how the crew harbored an intense hatred of their skipper. Writing to Jean, I declared, "Most of the men are offering 50 bucks for a transfer to any other ship." I tried my best to learn Winn's peculiarities and accept him for what he was, but within hours of my transfer, I formed the same negative opinion. This passage appeared in my letter of January 8: "The old captain isn't exactly mean: he just 'forgets' to start liberty, pipe down to meals on schedule, and so forth. Like today. He had the

---

[*] USS *Yarnall*'s logbooks confirm the story I heard. The grounding occurred around 3:30 A.M., November 25. The previous evening, *Yarnall* had been anchored in five fathoms of water. After getting underway, the watch officer suspected one of the anchors of dragging. At 3:20, he informed the executive officer of his suspicion, and when word reached the skipper, LCDR Winn ordered, "Let go starboard anchor." By 3:40, *Yarnall* had run aground, and the port side engine could no longer turn the screw, it being so badly jammed into the sand. On November 26, CAPT Robert Griffin reported on board, convening a court of inquiry. The inquiry lasted until December 1. Ultimately, the inquiry resulted in Winn having to face a court-martial.

gunner's mates work in freezing spray to get all the guns ready for firing, got all the men at the guns, got up ammunition, threw overboard the target, made the approach, and decided to shoot to-morrow." Winn's incompetence might have been excusable if he had attempted humility when he erred in judgment, but each mis-take only increased his arrogance. For instance, Winn loved cream with his coffee. One day, he desired it particularly, so he altered *Yarnall's* heading, directing the helmsman to enter a narrow river. After steaming past some shocked Virginia residents, he ordered his sailors to put a boat ashore, sending them with money to pur-chase the cream. The whole message of this drama, I supposed, was to prove to everyone that he was the skipper, and that when he wanted something, so went the ship.

I guess I wouldn't have minded his behavior so much, except that we all got punished for infractions of an ill-disciplined few. Sometime during my thirteen days under Winn's command, *Yar-nall* failed to offer a proper salute to a passing admiral's barge, the result of an inattentive lookout. As a rule, every time an admiral's barge went by, all vessels, no matter how large or small, had to pay proper honors by blowing their bugle, assembling their crew, and offering up a salute. When the admiral noticed how *Yarnall* had snubbed him, he sent a message to Winn. Under the admi-ral's orders, we had to assemble our crew and make a mail call at another port, thus depriving the crew of their preassigned shore leave. After this, I looked forward even more to leaving the surface fleet. I believed incidents like this wouldn't trouble me as often. As a pilot, I'd be my own boss in the cockpit, beholden to no one else's mistakes.

By the end of the first week of January, Winn received word that he had to face a court-martial regarding the grounding incident of November 25. Consequently, he had to relinquish command.

When this news spread, *Yarnall*'s crew began to cheer openly. In fact, the officer of the deck had to hold the helmsman by his arms in order to prevent him from blowing *Yarnall*'s whistle and siren to celebrate the occasion. Upon learning he had to give up command, Winn worried the court-martial proceedings might reveal that he had never fired *Yarnall*'s four-inch guns during the ship's month of operation. Before returning to port, he ordered me, as gunnery officer, to fire the forward gun. When the gunner's mates loaded it, they discovered they could not ram a shell. The gun tube was so filled with hardened Cosmoline—a smelly, waxy anti-rust agent— that the end of the shell protruded from the barrel. The gun could not be fired until we cleared the bore. The gunner's mates told me this might take all day. This was a terrible lesson in procrastination; nothing had been done to check the status of the guns during the three months since *Yarnall*'s recommissioning.

Undeterred by this news, Winn wanted to fire the gun anyway. He turned to the gunner's mates and said, "This time, really throw the shell in there. Stop messing around!" As ordered, the crew rammed the shell hard, but it still stuck out of the breech by a couple of inches. Undaunted, he ordered, "Slam the breech on it!" I couldn't believe what I was hearing. I thought he was going to kill us all! I interrupted him. I asked, "Permission to go to the fantail, sir?" Without waiting for a reply, I walked away. I've always been a combative individual, but rarely have I flouted orders. That day was an exception. I didn't wish to die in a gunnery accident all because my commander wanted to save his reputation. I might well have been punished for my disobedience except that the rest of the gun crew followed me. Apparently getting the message, Winn shouted, "Belay that!" canceling the order to fire. He ordered the gun cleaned and repaired, but the crew never did get a chance to fire it under his command. Eventually, on January 16, *Yarnall* made it back to Norfolk. Winn stood his court-martial, but I never learned the results. Scuttlebutt said he received a reduction in rank, and he became a chief engineer on a gunboat. In any event, I never saw him again.

CDR Thomas Edward Fraser, a graduate of the Naval Academy Class of 1924, replaced Winn and put *Yarnall* back to sea. When Fraser came aboard, things changed immediately. He insisted the crew work night and day to bring *Yarnall* out of mothball status. He began removing incompetent members of the crew, even if it took creativity to get them transferred. For instance, he despised the head boy and called him into his stateroom to assess his performance. When asked why he routinely failed to meet expectations, the lad complained, "My feet hurt." Sensing an opportunity to remove him, Fraser ordered the medical officer to put the boy's feet into massive casts, such that he could no longer serve on the destroyer, or any ship. Fraser removed *Yarnall*'s executive officer, or XO, the same way. He offered the XO shore leave for one month, and while the officer dawdled, looking for something to do, Fraser surreptitiously signed in a replacement. Fraser also took pains to enforce discipline. He noticed how *Yarnall*'s sailors tended to get drunk easily, and the ship always had to refill its alcohol stores more frequently than the other destroyers in the division. Fraser soon discovered the problem. The enlisted sailors had drilled a hole into the bottom of the alcohol stores, and every so often they drained it, painting over the drill hole to cover their crime. Upon realizing this, he ordered all of the alcohol drained from the stores. He told me to put the alcohol in one-gallon cans and then store those cans under my bunk. Essentially I became the destroyer's alcohol warden.

More than anything, Fraser demonstrated boldness, and one particular episode impressed me. We had just finished repairs at the Brooklyn Navy Yard. Brooklyn boaters had a habit of intentionally ramming Navy vessels that exited the yard. Maneuvering in smaller craft, they knew that if they jerked the rudder at the last minute they could make it appear as if an inept naval helmsman had caused the accident; thus, after months of litigation, they might win damages in civil court. Destroyer skippers had to watch carefully when they exited the yard. Because of the depth of the draft of their ships, they had to proceed along a straight path through the shipping channel, sailing past Governors Island. Consequently, if one of the accident-seeking mariners wished to ram a Navy ship, the destroyer had no room to maneuver. On the day *Yarnall* left Brooklyn, I stood watch. Sure enough, a commercial boat came careening along, cutting across our path. Immediately, I alerted Fraser. I pointed to the boat and warned him of its intention.

I asked, "What shall we do?"

Fraser smiled. He answered, "I'll take charge."

He grabbed the intercom and called to engineering: "Emergency speed! Full speed ahead; I mean emergency!" Within seconds, *Yarnall*'s engines burned at full, and we picked up speed, barreling along at forty knots. In fact, we kicked up a thirty-foot flare, a massive spray of water from the fantail. Obviously, Fraser meant to play a game of chicken with the commercial boater. If the boater wished to ram us, he had to risk death. At flank speed, a *Wickes*-class destroyer could have sliced the boat in half. When he saw us coming, the boater wisely slowed down to avoid collision. After we passed the boat, Fraser calmly grabbed the intercom. With a little smirk he ordered, "Normal speed."

I must say, Fraser's ingenuity produced immediate dividends. We had a better ship and a finer crew. I admired CDR Fraser greatly. Writing to Jean, I described him as "a rough old sea dog, good as they make them." The only thing I disliked was his Siamese cat, which became the problem child of the ship. He spoiled his pet, the sole member of the crew allowed to get away with violations of naval decorum. Writing to Jean, I complained, "The old black and yellow monster howls like a mountain lion, hates to be shut up in any room, and sulks for hours when he burns his feet on the hot steel decks. I wouldn't trade even the laziest hound dog for all the best cats."

By mid-January 1940, *Yarnall* was ready for sea. We set sail, reaching the coast of Venezuela. Once there, we turned north, docking at Guantanamo Bay, Cuba. We returned to Norfolk on March 1. I noted to Jean that we had been "mucho busy." I told her that I averaged only four and one-half hours of sleep each night. I wrote, "[I] have just about got the affairs of my predecessor straightened out, have fired all the guns many rounds, and have inspected another ship from stem to stern, and been inspected." When *Yarnall* returned to port, I knew I had less than two months to go before completing my obligatory time in the surface fleet. I needed to contemplate my future. My two years on *Vincennes*, *Goff*, and *Yarnall* had left me with conflicting opinions. I learned that poor destroyer crews did not always get top-of-the-line equipment and got sent on dangerous assignments. But I also admired the surface fleet. Although the destroyer divisions contained a few incompetent officers, it also possessed many capable ones, with Abrahams and Fraser standing tall among that contingent. Perhaps most important, there was reason to believe staying with the surface fleet might lead me back to Jean. I wanted to return to the west coast, and if I joined the crew of a cruiser, I might find my way back to Long Beach.

However, I still wanted to fly. In an airplane I could be my own commander, make my own decisions. Indecision paralyzed me. Only days before *Yarnall* returned to port, I wrote Jean: "Have to take the much-delayed physical exam for Pensacola pretty soon. Can't make up my mind whether to pass it or not. I like to fly and there's an extra 50% pay (about $187 a month instead of $125). But there's a lot of other branches of the Navy I like too. It's one of the toughest decisions I've ever had to make."

At this moment of hesitancy, I received a push from Fraser. He caught me staring at a picture of Jean, something I did often in my bunk. Fraser told me to hurry up and marry her before she got away. Or, this is how I later narrated his words when I recalled them in 1943: "I remember most vividly Capt. Frazer's [sic] advice one night[.] . . . He saw me looking at [Jean's] picture and roared, 'For @!~~*'s sake, why don't you marry the girl'?!!" Actually, to drive me toward the prospect of marriage, Fraser promised to give me a pair of antique sabers as a wedding present. Somehow, an admiral who counted Fraser as a friend had acquired these two historic weapons, which had once been the property of officers who had served aboard USS *Philadelphia,* the forty-four-gun frigate that had been seized by Tripolitan corsairs back in 1803.[*]

Thus prompted, I decided to telephone Jean on my birthday, March 7. I had one mission: to propose to her. In three months I would pass the two-year mark that prevented me from marrying, and if I chose to pursue becoming an aviator, I expected three weeks' furlough before heading to flight training at Pensacola Naval Air Station in Florida. Sadly, this phone call did not go well. I proposed, but she did not say, "Yes," at least not unconditionally. She said she would accept my proposal only if I accepted a few proposals of hers. Jean objected to my proposal for two reasons: first, she was older than I, and second, she wanted to raise the family Catholic. She wrote to me on March 7, apparently hours after our

---

* Fraser kept his word. He presented the swords to me after I married Jean in 1942. Later on, I presented these sabers to my eldest son, Jack Jr., as his wedding present, and they remain with him to this day.

telephone conversation, reiterating her main points: "[I]f we do become partners your happiness would be foremost in my endeavors, so I want you to remember that there's a few years between us, even though it would make no difference now, do you think there is any possibility of your being sorry later on? Also, honey, I'm Catholic, and that means I'd want to be married by a Catholic priest and if we were to have a family (and no home is complete without 'kids') I'd want them to be the same faith as I have. I've enjoyed my own home so very much that I'd like to build my new home on the same foundation."

Honestly, I didn't care about the age difference. To me, this was a little bump in our relationship, "just a tiny piece of gravel which will be ground smaller by the sands of time," or so I wrote. Age mattered not. I explained, "I know you'll always be young and healthy—the way you are now." However, the other bump loomed larger. My father's warning echoed in my ears. I couldn't consent to marrying into a Catholic family. I expected her to convert to Methodism. I took responsibility for this mistake. Religion meant a great deal to her and I had failed to recognize it. I wrote, "This whole business has been my fault for not being more careful in finding out the 'dope.' There's no way I could repay the anxieties and troubles I've given you."

Stubbornly, I held my ground. I cannot remember what I said during the telephone conversation, but my letters to Jean approximately described my reservations in converting to Catholicism. I wrote, "One of my deepest beliefs—and I've been trying to question it unsuccessfully these last two days—is that all the family (that is, mama and papa and the kids) should have the same religion; otherwise the Highway will be a steep one with numerous 'detour' and 'road closed for repair' signs. . . . I'd have to know more about being a Catholic . . . to see if I could accept the doctrines and abide by all the rules. But even then we'd have great difficulties because my

Father and Grandmother are strong Methodists (in fact everyone in the entire Kleiss family) and I doubt if they'd either forgive me or you if I'd change religions."

My dispute with Jean lasted into August, and it grew worse with each passing week. At first it appeared that I had just misinterpreted her. She did not want me to convert, but I had to accept a Catholic wedding and Catholic children. "After all," she later wrote, "every man has a right to his own opinion. The only thing I wanted to make clear was that you have no objections to being married in a Catholic Church. How do you stand on that score?" This did not settle matters. I believed that if we married, one or the other had to convert, and I could not accept Catholicism. I explained: "According to my very meager knowledge of the Catholic religion, it exacts too many promises for people like me, and I doubt if I could believe in Confessions or miracles by Saints. . . . The thing I can't promise to do, Jean, is to promise to make someone else believe them. I guess we'd better try to forget the whole affair unless you can come over to my side. That looks cold, cruel, and demanding the impossible." To this day, I don't know why I was so stubborn. I guess my father's words had gotten to me and I worried about the scandal that would ensue in Coffeyville if he learned that I married a Catholic. Oh, the stupid decisions we make to appease our parents! I said and wrote many ugly things that demeaned Catholicism, and today, decades removed from those awful days, I regret what I said.

Jean tried to convince me to stop being so stubborn. She replied, "Have you forgotten that there are two sides to every fence? It would be just as difficult for me to change my beliefs as it would be for you to come over to my way of thinking. So [if] . . . we both carry on in our same old way, I'm afraid we've got a hurdle to[o] big for either one of us to get over." Eventually, the dispute deadlocked any chance of marriage. In May, in utter anguish, I wrote flatly, "I can't—and I know you can't—go on like this much longer.

I've tried to be fair, but I just can't become Catholic or be married in a Catholic Church." We nearly broke up. This was one of my greatest mistakes. If two people who love each other cannot overcome religion, what hope is there? Sometimes I hate to look back at my twenty-four-year-old self. What a fool I was, sacrificing love on behalf of pride.

The dispute accomplished one thing: it pushed me toward aviation. Because some doubt now existed in the possibility of marriage, I had no desire to sacrifice my dream to become an aviator. In April, I went for my physical, a daunting process that involved intense psychological and physiological testing. I described it in a letter to Jean: "First, they place you in a bunk and ask you all sorts of foolish questions about family history and worries and what you think about so-and-so." Next, the flight surgeons sneaked up behind me and took my pulse and blood pressure, followed by a quick instruction, standing me up and taking more readings. Then the physicians ordered me to jump up and down a dozen times and pass the "Snyder Test," a numeric system that quantified blood pressure readings to determine flight readiness. Finally, the surgeons whisked me off to the "revolving chair," literally, an elevated chair that spun around at high speeds to simulate g-forces, which mimicked gravity during a high-speed turn. After spinning me around several times, the surgeons asked me to stand up and then noted the direction in which I fell over. Then they told me to focus on a chart six feet away and read a number pasted on it, recording the seconds it took me to focus. After that, the flight surgeons made me try the same experiment again, but this time with colors, and then again after adding eye drops. "In conclusion," I narrated in one of my letters, "they ask you why you're darn fool enough to want to be an aviator and scratch 'temperamentally fitted' at the bottom of [the] check off list." By the beginning of April, I had passed all my tests. In July, I would be heading to Pensacola.

I wanted to know what Jean thought of my plans. I wrote, "This flying business is something where you'll have to help me because I haven't got much ability to judge danger. I can only go by what other people (most especially you) would call 'dangerous.' I helped Louis, my big brother, build nitro glycerin and gas pipe cannons years and years ago. Now I walk through the magazines every day and handle tanks of powder the same as you would a basket of groceries." Jean had mixed feelings about my decision to become an aviator. On one hand, she loved the allure of dating a daredevil. "I've always had a secret desire to take it up myself," she wrote. "I've always loved planes, & streamlined trains." However, she worried about the danger connected with it. When she made her final assessment, she preferred I take the safer course, which meant staying in the surface fleet. She wrote, "I hate to discourage you in aviation, 'cause it's no fun working unless we enjoy what we're doing, & if that's what you like, that's what you should do, but if that means taking any chances, then I'd wish you'd try and see if you couldn't get out of it."

I disregarded her advice. *Yarnall*'s last trio of voyages carried me to this decision. The destroyer put to sea three more times in late April and early May, heading out on various patrols, either to escort American submarines or to conduct weapons tests. During the third excursion, *Yarnall* hauled a towline and target for patrol planes to practice their bombing techniques. Even though the towline was a half-mile long, the other crewmen ducked their heads when they saw the 1,000-pound bombs drop. By contrast, I was mesmerized by the sight. Once again I was on the receiving end of a mock air attack. I wanted to be flying the planes, not incurring their wrath. The excitement of the event only further reinforced my decision to become an aviator.

I canceled my plans to visit Jean in California. In early August, shortly before traveling to Pensacola, I penned a letter that tried to end our romance. I wrote, "This is good-bye. . . . Things are so tangled up that my coming to California wouldn't help matters any. . . . We haven't been in agreement on anything even for so long as a week. . . . Long ago I dreamed that you and I would be the star actors in a movie made real; but somehow these last few weeks didn't develop the way we planned. So now it is the hour to say, with love, and all the best wishes at my command, to the nicest girl I've ever known, Adieu, Jack." Jean wrote a tearful reply, a final plea to keep our relationship alive:

> When I read your last letter, I felt like weeping, but tears don't solve problems, so I bit my upper lip & kept on going. I did so want you to come to Calif. for a few days. Even if nothing had come of it, we still would have had the pleasure of being together again for a short while. I've always been & always will be very much of a fatalist. If things are to be they will be. Religion seems such a trivial thing to keep us apart, 'cause after all we both believe in the same God & what He taught. . . . I feel privileged in being a Catholic, so consequently I want to stay one, & I do think the day will come when you will be able to understand it a little more clearly. I don't want you to be a Catholic 'cause I know you couldn't be happy as one, but I wish you could be a little more tolerant of its principles. . . . You're everything that's fine, Jack, and I'll always love you whether we're together or apart. I'm wishing you the best of everything—lots of luck, health & happiness. Love, Jean.

Nothing came of it. I could not be deterred. I sallied forth to Florida, intent on earning my wings. At long last, or so I put it at the time, I had my chance to whisk on "golden skies and ruby-red suns, or maybe diamond shaped clouds against a silver background."

The open sky beckoned.

|||||||||||||||||||||||||||||||||||||||||||||||||||||||||||||||||||||||||||||||||||||||||||||||||||||||||||

CHAPTER 6

FLIGHT TRAINING

1940–1941

In late August 1940, I reported to Ground School at Pensacola Naval Air Station to begin flight training. I joined a class of ninety-two, which included a few of my former Naval Academy classmates. Naval reservists constituted the bulk of the trainees. The instructors imposed harsh rules about when the reservists could leave the base. As an academy graduate I received preferential treatment, and I had plenty of opportunity for fun—when not studying—and I enjoyed days at the beach, horseback riding, and duck hunting. Training moved at a brisk, uninterrupted pace. Half the time, we spent our days in the classroom; during the other half we were in the air. At least once a week, we flew at night. I embraced the challenge and used my previous flight experience to my advantage. I had already flown aircraft from Scott Field and Bolling Field as a midshipman, and I had flown with Rolley Inman back in Kansas. At the time, I wrote, "I like aviation fine, and apparently it likes me because I've gotten along pretty well so far and have had more than my share of luck in missing other planes and keeping from 'ground looping.' Just now I'm performing stunts like this. [Here, I inserted a drawing of a plane doing a loop and roll.] It's fun!"

Several instructors trained me, but LT Jewell Earl Lanier served as my primary mentor. During my instructional flights, Lanier and I flew the NAF (Naval Aircraft Factory) N3N-1, a two-seat trainer biplane, popularly known as the "Yellow Peril" because of its bright canary-yellow paint job and the fact that it was mostly flown by untrained student pilots. Lanier taught trainees to think fast, often fabricating emergencies to test our instincts. On almost every flight, he unexpectedly cut the throttle to simulate a failed engine. With the plane gliding under no power, he gave me only a few seconds to act, to pick out the best place to land, dead stick, and line up the N3N-1 for approach. At the last minute, Lanier engaged the throttle and pulled up. When we landed he graded me on my choice of an emergency landing zone.

My first instructional flight with Lanier occurred on September 10, and exactly one month later, October 10, I performed my first solo flight. I climbed aboard an N3N-1 with sandbags weighing down the rear seat. A photographer snapped a picture, and I gave a cheery "thumbs-up." With no fear, off I went. In January 1941, I switched to more complex aircraft. I began flying the Vought (SU-2, SU-3, O2U, and O3U-1 models) Corsair, a scout-observation biplane, and the North American (NJ-1 and SNJ-1 models) Texan, a two-seat monoplane. By February 21, I had logged 149 hours in the air, during which time I had not suffered a single crash or problematic incident. The only unusual moment came back on October 11, after my third solo flight. While I was returning to the landing strip, a solid layer of clouds moved in. As I neared the area, I saw a dozen other Yellow Perils circling the cloud bank, waiting for it to dissipate. Suddenly a small hole appeared. I looked down, recognizing a familiar drugstore on the street below. I put my plane into a dive and flew just above the main road, flying low enough to count the traffic lights to make the right-hand turn. By following the road network, I reached the airstrip, landing almost where the runway started. I taxied off at the first exit, and as I raised my goggles to applaud myself on a job well done, suddenly—Whoosh! Whoosh!—the other student-pilots zoomed past my plane, using the remaining stretch of runway to land. Apparently one of them had seen me break below the clouds, and in a panic, they all followed me to the airstrip.

My time at Pensacola awarded me with some special friendships. I was closest with John Thomas Eversole—or simply Tom, as I called him—a Naval Academy classmate from 1938. We bonded during a long car ride over the Christmas holiday. We left Pensacola on December 18, taking turns driving my new 1940 Ford Coupe to Kansas City, Missouri. From there, Tom caught a train to his hometown of Pocatello, Idaho, while I drove on to Coffeyville. I had fun visiting with family and friends, but unfortunately I caught a bad illness, which spelled potential disaster. If I failed to return for the additional weeks of instructional training, I might be held back. Generously, Dad drove my Ford to Kansas City so that I could pick up Tom. I slept for most of the trip, trying to recuperate, but I gradually awoke when I felt the car traveling at a dangerously high speed. To my surprise, Dad was cruising along a vacant stretch of highway with the pedal to the floor.

Dad smiled and said, "This Ford has got more power to it than my Mercury!"

The scenery whizzed by in a blur. Groggily, I asked, "Well, how fast are you going?"

My father replied, "I dunno. Seventy miles per hour, maybe?"*

With Dad at the wheel, we reached the train station, where Tom took over—albeit driving less recklessly—and we made it

---

* If I remember correctly, the speedometer on that car went up to 100 miles per hour, but versions of that car rarely went above 80.

back to Pensacola for our seven additional weeks of training. Although I remember this trip because of Dad's high-speed driving, the Christmas break excursion solidified my friendship with Tom. Unarguably, he was my best friend in the Navy. We did everything together afterward. Two closer chums could not be found.

I didn't complete my flight instruction at Pensacola. Since I intended to serve aboard an aircraft carrier, I required six weeks of "combat instruction" at the new Navy fighter school at Opa-Locka, Florida. I arrived there on February 26. At Opa-Locka, the instructors offered more specialized training, focusing on naval landing and takeoff procedures as well as dogfighting techniques. Opa-Locka was a brand-new base—so new, in fact, that it did not even possess a fully built control tower. To observe the trainees, the instructors watched from improvised platforms boosted on wooden sawhorses.

At Opa-Locka, we trained with the Boeing F4B-4, a small, single-seat biplane. I liked the new aircraft. It was fun to fly and versatile in its acrobatics. Unfortunately, the F4B-4 possessed a few problems. Notably, the engine quit whenever a pilot rolled it upside down. If a pilot possessed the wherewithal to roll over immediately, the engine started again, but more than a few biplanes crashed during the training period. Crashes occurred so frequently that the flight instructors limited the training airspace to the swampy region to the north of the base. The Navy had no desire to bear the blame if one of its trainees went down inside one of Miami's populated suburbs. Consequently, if a trainee crashed, he had to wait hours for the Navy to find him in the swamp. The Opa-Locka base possessed a swamp buggy, a vehicle capable of cruising over the water and brush. Unfortunately, it drove no faster than five miles per hour. The instructors issued pilots a solemn rule. If we landed in the swamp, we had to unravel our parachute so it could be seen from the air. That way, another plane could spot us and radio our position to the rescue team in the buggy.

This system did not always work well. One pilot crashed and could not be found for hours. None of the search planes could see his unfolded parachute from the air. Eventually, a swamp buggy scoured the scene of the crash, finding the shaken pilot standing in chest-high water, surrounded by curious alligators. One of the instructors berated him, asking him why he failed to unfold his parachute. Angrily, the trainee replied, "Sir, the water was up to my chin. I had to stand on my parachute just to get my head and shoulders above the water." Luckily, I never experienced a crash. Always careful, I did my utmost to avoid disaster.

I observed one horrible accident firsthand. I sat on a plank between two sawhorses alongside an instructor, helping him record the results of the students' acrobatic stunts. As per the exercise, one new pilot put his plane into a spin and then tried to recover. Three times the pilot tried to end the spin, but three times he failed. Realizing he could not recover the plane, the pilot jumped out and pulled his parachute ripcord. The parachute emerged, but it failed to open. It stayed above the falling pilot in a vertical column. With paralyzing fear, the instructor and I watched the poor man plummet to the ground. He hit horizontally and bounced twenty feet into the air. The noise he made when he hit was simply awful. The instructor and I raced to the scene. The poor pilot had broken every bone in his body. Amazingly, he was still alive, at least for the moment. I expected him to curse the man who failed to pack the parachute correctly, or say loud spells for pain, but no, he only looked at me and the instructor saying, "Pray for me and tell my family to pray for me." Those were his last words. He closed his eyes and died.

After acrobatic training, we learned to dogfight. Now we flew the

Grumman F2F-1, a single-engine biplane. The instructors rated us on our ability to dodge incoming attacks. Similar to the F4B-4, the F2F-1 was a troublesome plane. It boasted two enormous wheels attached to its landing gear that had to be cranked into place. I also flew the Grumman F3F-1, another single-seat biplane, and the Curtis SBC-4, a two-seat scout-bombing biplane. By the time I had finished at Opa-Locka, on April 17, I had logged another ninety hours of official flying time.

More important, I reopened communication with Jean. I began writing letters to her again sometime in November 1940. Our relationship had been on a three-month hiatus. Jean pronounced herself pleased with the fact that I wanted to continue communication, but I wrote to her cautiously. I tried to tell her that I did not consider myself in love. "Me in love," I wrote in February 1941. "I guess not, because they all still look pretty good to me." My lukewarm feelings toward her grew in intensity as spring came, primarily because I could not refrain from thinking about the young pilot who had died when his parachute failed to open.

This period allowed me to think about the wisdom of that young man and how he knew that we humans have only a short abode on earth. No religious thinker could surpass the fallen pilot's utterance. Nowadays, I look back at my youthful shortcomings with disgust. Did it take that pilot to die to make me come to my senses? For some unexplained reason, God decided to bless me with physical skills and endurance, but insufficient clairvoyance to see true love when it was right in front of me. How stupid I was to think that Jean was just an actress, a deceiver capable of feigning her affections. Thankfully Jean was a patient angel who helped me become sensible. Finally, I believed her intentions toward me were sincere. I trusted her. I realized that my own shortcomings were all that stood in the way of my happiness. I never wanted to be a Catholic, because of its oath-taking. When I was twelve years old I made an oath to the Methodist Church that I'd never use tobacco or use alcohol. Since I couldn't keep that oath, I resolved never again to make an oath that I couldn't keep. But in the spring of 1940, that belief seemed trivial to me. It was only that horrible experience of the dying young pilot that cleared my brain.

Then fate offered me a second chance at love. In late April, right after I received my wings, I learned that I would be heading to San Diego for assignment.* "Have I got wings!" I wrote Jean jubilantly. "Am I good!" At last, I had my opportunity to reconnect with Jean. My new assignment was Scouting Squadron Six, or simply VS-6. It was a scout-bombing squadron, an eighteen-plane unit that could perform both long-range scouting missions and massed dive bombing missions. The name, VS-6, indicated the squadron's particular assignment. "V" stood for "heavier-than-air aircraft," "S" stood for "Scout-Bombing," and "6" indicated that it was the sixth scout-bombing squadron put in service by the U.S. Navy and consequently part of Carrier Air Group Six, the unit assigned to mighty USS *Enterprise* (CV-6). Honestly, I don't know why the Navy assigned me to this particular squadron, or why I became a dive bomber pilot as opposed to a fighter pilot or a torpedo bomber pilot. I've spoken to other dive bomber veterans and they all say the same thing. The Navy appeared to have assigned us randomly, or based on something as simple as alphabetical order. I really wonder how this decision was made because, in the end, it caused Tom Eversole and me to be split up. We both graduated from the Naval Academy at the same time and we both graduated from flight training together. However, he joined a torpedo bomber squadron—Torpedo Six—and I joined a scout-bomber squadron.

I delighted in my new assignment. Writing to Jean, I joked

---

* I earned my wings on April 27, 1941.

about the challenges now confronting me as a carrier pilot. "[I'm going] to the ENTERPRISE and see if I can land on her, or whether they'll have to fish me out of the brink. 's a good thing they furnish us with life jackets!" I was filled with hope and energy. I left Opa-Locka in my Ford Coupe, first visiting with my family in Coffeyville. After a few days in Kansas, I made haste for Long Beach, arriving there on May 2. It proved to be a momentous reunion. Jean and I saw each other and our love rekindled. In fact, we patched our differences and forgot all about our arguments over age and religion. I promised never to be so pigheaded ever again.

Once I settled into my new billet at San Diego, I promised to marry her. Writing to her a few days after that visit, I declared, "Jean, darling, you're the biggest problem I've ever had. A year ago I couldn't think of anything but you, and this year I thought I had you pushed clear of my mind. And then I had to go and kiss you again, and now you've got me all confused. Why do you have to be so nice and so full of tiny little magnets?" Jean felt the same way about me, that our love should overcome all other matters. She wrote a few days after this meeting, "You know, darling, I'm definitely a dreamer, I guess, & all my dreams include you. Somehow, regardless of the fact I botched things up very beautifully to begin with, I just know everything's going to right itself & maybe we'll be able to start out again where we left off."

For a few days, at least, I felt as though I was on top of the world. Two years had passed since I graduated from the Naval Academy. I had finally rid myself of my obligatory time in the surface fleet. I had acquired my wings. I had reunited with my lady love and I no longer had to worry about the Navy's marriage restriction on recent academy graduates. Everything seemed grand.

Unfortunately, in two days' time, the U.S. Navy changed my life forever.

CHAPTER 7

||||||||||||||||||||||||||||||||||||||||||||||||||||||||||||||||||||||||||||||||||||||||||||||||||||||||||||||||||

SCOUTING SQUADRON SIX, PART 1
May–June 1941

W hen I arrived in San Diego on May 6, 1941, I expected to
spend the next six months onshore, taking time to accli-
mate myself to my new unit. Instead, when I reached Naval Base
San Diego, I received a rude surprise. Within forty-eight hours, the
Navy whisked me off to Pearl Harbor, Hawaii, in the belly of an
aircraft carrier.

My first few blissful hours in San Diego seemed like a fresh
start. I anticipated a long summer, during which time I could
make friends and learn the nuances of my squadron and my plane.
Upon arrival, I said to myself, "I'm going to do this right!" I went to
work immediately, procuring an ideal apartment at the Bachelors
Officers Quarters (BOQ). They were splendid quarters, with two
large rooms and nice furniture, and within slingshot distance of a
tile outdoor swimming pool. I unpacked, sent my uniform to the
dry cleaners, put my personal items into laundry, and signed up for
the officers' club. With only a few hours remaining in the day, I decided to visit the residence of LCDR Ralph D. "Smitty" Smith, my
new commanding officer. All I wanted to do was introduce myself.

When I got there, Smith looked me over, and then brusquely

informed me that our aircraft carrier, USS *Enterprise,* had orders
to leave San Diego on May 8. *Enterprise's* sailors had just finished
stripping down the combustible material: wooden furniture, canvas, excess rope, and inflammable paint. This work, which had
begun weeks earlier, had proceeded faster than expected, and
Enterprise planned to put to sea in two days. I already knew this.
Accordingly, I expected to train with VS-3 (or Scouting Three) temporarily, until Scouting Six returned to port. I explained to Smith
that the Navy's personnel officers had already made arrangements
with Scouting Three. I just stopped by to say that I looked forward
to joining Scouting Six when it returned in six months. Better informed about the conditions of *Enterprise's* deployment, Smith did
not expect Scouting Six to return at all. If hostilities escalated with
Japan, *Enterprise* might remain in Hawaii indefinitely.

At the time, diplomatic relations between the United States
and the Empire of Japan were nearing the breaking point. Over
the course of several years, Americans had come to see Japan as
an aggressor nation. It had lost favor in the United States because
of atrocities committed by its soldiers in China. In December 1937,
Japanese bombers sank one of our gunboats, USS *Panay,* in the
Yangtze River, killing three sailors and wounding more than forty
others. Although Japan made a formal apology, claiming the attack
had been unintentional, relations continued to sour. In July 1939,
the United States ended its commercial treaty with Japan, and later
on it imposed a gasoline embargo. In the face of these overtures,
Japan only escalated its commitment to conquest, invading French
Indochina in September 1940 and joining the Axis nations by signing the Tripartite Pact. When I arrived in San Diego in May 1941,
no one could be sure of Japan's next move. Would they attack the
Philippines? Or Hawaii? War's shadow seemed closer than ever.

LCDR Smith did not indulge in any small talk. He grilled me
with a series of questions, asking me about my experience with

surface ships and aviation, and after a while, he instructed me to have a seat, excusing himself to make a telephone call. A few minutes later, he returned. "Your orders have been changed," he told me. "The day after tomorrow you are to go to the *Enterprise* at eight o'clock with all of your gear for an indefinite time." This news came as a shock. For some reason—known only to him—Smith had decided to retain me. I could not argue. Because of that telephone call, I had to be on *Enterprise* when it left the docks in two days. I raced back to my quarters and called Jean. I had no time to put my belongings into storage. I asked her to drive down from Long Beach and take them. On May 7, I repacked my possessions, arrived for a physical examination, and received a series of shots to prepare me for the tropical climate. I wrote a letter sometime later that month. It accurately depicted my state of mind. I penned, "Eleven o'clock ~ bedlam, confusion, ???!!! Transfer back to [Scouting] Six. Report on board. Sailing Immediately. Packing up. Paying Bills. Endorsements to orders. Retrieving laundry. Storing car. Headache. All thumbs. Two hours later ~ One O'clock ~ all ready to sail." At 8:00 A.M., May 8, after bidding Jean farewell, I ascended *Enterprise's* gangway, all of my gear slung over my shoulder. I said goodbye to San Diego, having been in it only two days.

The sudden departure of *Enterprise* meant that I had to learn the intricacies of my new ship out on the open ocean. *Enterprise* was a *Yorktown*-class aircraft carrier, 827 feet long, 114 feet wide, displacing 25,500 tons fully loaded. It was one of the Navy's largest ships—a huge city of sailors who lived in an unnavigable labyrinth of hatches and dimly lit passageways. Describing one of my first days on the ship, I wrote this in a letter: "The ship's so darned big that even I—the old-man-of-the-sea—am not above getting lost now and then, and several times I've had to inspect a perfectly good steam valve to keep the seamen from lifting an eye brow after I've followed a dead end passage to the bitter end."

Although it was confusing at first, I appreciated the fine accommodations of *Enterprise,* a world apart from the rough, cramped life I had encountered in the destroyer fleet. I entered the best of all worlds. The ship had all the latest features and equipment available at the time, yet it had made a shakedown cruise to correct the problems always encountered with a new ship and its new crew. *Enterprise's* mammoth wardroom (its officers' mess cabin), six times the size of the wardroom on *Vincennes,* always appeared full, and despite its impressive size, *Enterprise's* officer corps overflowed the room if all of the officers sat together. The captain instructed the officers to eat in shifts to prevent overcrowding. It was a lively place, full of spirit, freshness, and a sense of humor. Ten minutes before dinner, music usually rolled out of the speaker system, playing a swing-time version of "The Campbells Are Coming," "Pop Goes the Weasel," or some other lighthearted ballad.

Enterprise's various decks offered plenty of distractions. Every night, the officers played movies on the hangar deck, the cavernous bay where the crew stored the planes. I tended to stay away from these amusements if I could, because the officers in charge of the films played too much Shirley Temple. But some nights, I had to attend the movies whether I liked it or not. During our voyage, the squadron's flight surgeon, Dr. J. M. Jordan, insisted on testing our night vision. He required the pilots to drink carrot juice and then told us to find an empty seat as quickly as possible. He wanted us to walk out of the bright sunlight and into the movies and spot an empty seat—if there was one—and climb into it in a couple of minutes without stumbling over too many people. If we couldn't do this, he supercharged us with carrot juice and made us try again.

In addition to learning the ins and outs of *Enterprise* and its crew, I learned the peculiarities of the officers assigned to Scouting Six. In May 1941, the squadron consisted of twenty officers: a squadron commander, two senior lieutenants, two junior-grade lieutenants, and fifteen ensigns. At the top of our hierarchy was LCDR Ralph Dempsey Smith, a Naval Academy graduate, Class of 1923. He was one of our best and most careful fliers and a real prince of a man. Thirty-nine-year-old LT Halstead Lubeck Hopping, or "Hal," Class of 1924, served as Scouting Six's XO. A New York City native, six foot one, and powerfully built, Hopping possessed an active, outspoken mind. He had one negative trait: he exhibited exceptionally poor piloting skills. I don't like to criticize a man's flying talents, but his deficiencies were noticeable. Another squadron mate said it best: "Men don't fly with equal skill any more than they play tennis with equal skill. We were always a little leery flying on him." The squadron's third-in-command, or flight officer (FO), was thirty-four-year-old LT Wilmer Earl Gallaher of Wilmington, Delaware. He too graduated from the Naval Academy, and he had earned fame as a gymnast, nearly winning a spot on the U.S. Olympic Team in 1928. After the academy, Gallaher served aboard USS *Arizona* (BB-39), the battleship destined for slaughter at Pearl Harbor. By the time I joined Scouting Six, Gallaher had been flying dive bombers for a year. I liked him instantly. He possessed a friendly demeanor and had excellent skill. Undoubtedly, Gallaher had the best aim of any of the dive bomber pilots in the Navy at the time. He was easily the true genius of our squadron.

I spent most of my time getting to know the other junior officers, my peers. On my first day aboard, I met my roommate, ENS Perry Teaff, a twenty-five-year-old Oklahoman who had already served on *Enterprise* for twenty months. As a token of friendship, I showed off my Remington, my favorite sidearm. Perry didn't ridicule me for my fondness for guns, a fortunate fact because I had brought along six rifles and pistols. I was probably the best-armed man on *Enterprise*. (Of course, I had to keep my guns in a trunk belowdecks near the forward elevator. Only my Remington stayed with me in my quarters.) Perry was garrulous and acted as the social epicenter of the squadron. He possessed a goofy sense of humor. For instance, Perry and his wife, Maggie, owned a pet alligator, which they kept in their bathtub. Naturally, guests who used the restroom at Teaff's house in California received a shocking surprise. They'd hear a weird swishing in the bathtub, pull back the shower curtain, and let out a shriek, which caused Perry and Maggie to laugh at their expense. Perry always told me he loved owning the alligator. How shall I put this? It helped his guests "drop their load."

Perry and I talked a lot and really enjoyed each other's company. He introduced me to the other pilots, and I joined a circle of friends down in the bowels of *Enterprise*. My inner circle presented a dynamic cast of characters, and nearly all of them answered to nicknames. The gang consisted of ENS John R. McCarthy, known as "Mac," a chatty Minnesota aviator from the Navy Reserve. I also befriended ENS Cleo John Dobson, a tall, burly man from Oklahoma. Back in 1935 Dobson had earned fame as the captain of the Oklahoma A&M basketball team. Dobson's unusual first name came from the fact that his mother had always desired a girl, wanting to call her "Cleopatra." She gave birth to a boy instead, but insisted on keeping the name and shortening it to "Cleo." We gave Dobson grief about this, but when he responded with needless bravado, we simply took to calling him "Dobby." I also became friends with ENS William Price West, a Navy Reserve pilot who had been on *Enterprise* for about five months. We called him "Little Westie" to distinguish him from another member of our group, Norm West, who for height reasons was known as "Big Westie."

Bill West earned a reputation for possessing the best luck in the squadron, largely because he avoided bizarre accidents. I witnessed one such moment. On a beautiful day near Hawaii as we strolled along *Enterprise*'s flight deck, the centerline elevator—which also doubled as part of the flight deck—suddenly sank down to the hangar deck. For some reason, the warning Klaxon did not sound off, and we reached the gaping hole just as the elevator began to drop. I stopped short, avoiding a life-threatening spill, but Bill did not. He tumbled over the edge, gone from view. I looked down, expecting to see him smashed to bits by the thirty-foot fall. I ran down the ladder to the hangar deck, sure I would find a man with multiple broken bones. Instead I saw Bill dusting himself off. I asked him what happened. Bill explained how his fall had been perfectly timed with the elevator's descent. They had fallen at roughly the same pace, so it felt like landing on a feather bed. Bill grinned goofily, unfazed by the whole ludicrous experience. I stared spellbound, happy my friend was okay.

Scouting Six consisted of two other elements, the maintenance crew and the enlisted gunners. The maintenance crew reported to one of two chiefs, Myers and Dodge. Chief Dodge handled all matters related to the aircraft engines and Chief Myers handled everything else. They were the finest in the whole Navy, intelligent, dedicated, and physically strong. I guessed the Navy appointed the best chiefs to our squadron, because, as a scout-bombing squadron, we required only 165 feet of takeoff space on the flight deck, and thus, our planes needed to be tip-top. Those who worked for Myers and Dodge received blessings and curses. Their blessing was a fast track to higher rank and pay. Their curse was working day and night with no relaxation. Chief Curtis Myers had a one-track mind, or so it seemed, relentlessly making sure Scouting Six's planes functioned at their best. He did not want any deaths to be accountable to his crew. I don't know when he ever slept, because he worked relentlessly. That work paid off, as we pilots trusted his judgment. When he left an airplane and said it was ready to fly, it was ready to fly.

Chief Myers and Chief Dodge offered another service to our squadron. They selected the best sailors to serve as rear-seat gunners. Any sailor who wanted "flight skins" and the accompanying aviation pay had to meet a strict set of requirements. He had to be able to start the plane on the flight deck, operate the rear machine guns, record ship signals, operate the radio, and be able to fly the plane if anything happened to the pilot. (Each Scouting Six plane possessed emergency controls in the rear seat.) About two dozen sailors served under Myers and Dodge: twelve radiomen (RM) and aviation ordnancemen (AOM) under Myers, and twelve aviation machinist's mates (AMM) under Dodge.

The *Enterprise* Air Group (EAG) consisted of four squadrons, about ninety planes altogether: Scouting Six (VS-6), Bombing Six (VB-6), Torpedo Six (VT-6), and Fighting Six (VF-6). Two squadrons, Scouting Six and Bombing Six, operated a mix of Douglas SBD-2 and SBD-3 Dauntless dive bombers. Each squadron had eighteen planes, plus two or three "spares," SBDs that could be added to an attack if any plane experienced engine trouble on the flight deck. Torpedo Six, under command of LT Eugene E. Lindsey, flew eighteen Douglas TBD-1 Devastators (plus spares). Finally, Fighting Six, led by LCDR Clarence Wade McClusky, rounded out the air group. McClusky's pilots flew Grumman F4F-3 Wildcats, single-seat fighters armed with four wing-mounted .50-caliber Browning machine guns, making them capable escort planes or Combat Air Patrol (CAP) craft.* A senior officer, the "Commander, *Enterprise* Air Group," or CEAG, directed all of the squadrons from a special SBD-3. LCDR Howard Leyland Young, from the Naval Academy Class of 1923, served that role. Normally two SBDs flown by junior pilots drawn from Scouting Six or Bombing Six accompanied Young's plane for the purpose of taking photographs of the action.

I paid particular attention to the happenings of Torpedo Six, largely because my good friend Tom Eversole served in it. Particu-

---

* The later model, the F4F-4, contained six machine guns.

larly, Tom and I worried about the capabilities of the TBDs, three-person torpedo bombers that entered the Navy's arsenal back in 1937. In combat, these planes were supposed to waft one hundred feet above the water in order to drop a 1,800-pound torpedo at an enemy ship. The lumbering, 9,200-pound plane could make only 108 knots, and while flying at low altitudes, it maneuvered poorly. Further, we worried about the capabilities of the TBD's primary weapon, the Mark-13 aerial torpedo. During the previous year's annual gunnery exercise, our torpedo planes dropped ten torpedoes. Five of those torpedoes ran erratically, veering away from their intended target, and four torpedoes simply hit the water and sank. In essence, 90 percent of the sample size failed to work. From my point of view, the pilots in Torpedo Six always worried that, unless something was done to modify the torpedoes, they would continue to fail 90 percent of the time.

On May 11, *Enterprise* arrived at Oahu. We were eager to see our new port. We crowded the gangway at Pier 10-10, beholding a tropical paradise. Yet, before we could partake of a frivolous spree on Honolulu, word reached us that Admiral Husband Kimmel, the commander at Pearl Harbor, wanted to welcome us aviators with a formal greeting. LCDR Smith appeared, telling us to appear on the tarmac in our dress whites. And what a greeting it was! After keeping us standing in the hot sun for what felt like hours, sweating through our uncomfortable clothes, Kimmel drove up in his limousine. He barked out a caustic welcome speech, one that made clear he wanted nothing to do with pilots. Kimmel finished with, "You're entitled to stay here at Pearl Harbor, provided you do not request me for any communications, transportation, or *anything else!*" After that, he clomped off toward his limousine. When asked about Kimmel nowadays, I say that he never gave us anything else, except trouble.

After Kimmel's prickly greeting, we changed into our khakis

and began moving all of our equipment to the naval air station at Ford Island, a flat, square-mile slab of land in the center of Pearl Harbor. Immediately upon arrival, each member of my squadron "donated" a portion of our pay to purchase a flatbed truck—for something less than fifty dollars—and converted it into a kind of "bus" capable of holding crucial airplane parts. It could also carry all of the squadron's officers, provided that four or five reckless ensigns hung from its sides. Naturally, such danger did not rattle us, although it put great pressure on me. Since I was one of the expert automobile drivers, the others expected me to drive the "bus" without flinging the hangers-on onto the tarmac.

The day after our arrival, we went to work training for war. For us pilots, "working" first meant getting qualified in our plane, the SBD Dauntless. This aircraft had joined the Navy about one year earlier, right after the first production models, the SBD-1s, arrived off the assembly line at the Douglas factory in El Segundo, California. The Scout-Bomber-Douglas (SBD) was a two-seat dive bomber, 9,300 pounds heavy fully loaded, thirty-three feet long, with a wingspan of forty-one feet. It boasted three weapons: two forward .50-caliber Browning machine guns mounted in the nose and a swiveling .30-caliber machine gun that could be operated by someone in the rear seat.* In addition, the SBD-2 carried one of two bomb payloads: a payload consisting of one 500-pound general-purpose bomb under the fuselage and two 100-pound bombs on the wings, or a payload consisting of a single 1,000-pound bomb. The SBD-3, the improved combat model, of which our air station possessed nine, followed the same design, except

---

* Originally, the rear machine gun had only one barrel, but over time, we gradually replaced them with double-barrelled machine guns.

that it had self-sealing tanks and a radio homing system known as the YE-ZB.*

I loved my SBD-2. At the time it was as unique as the first iron-clad ship, the CSS *Virginia,* was during the Civil War. Back in 1862, iron and steam suddenly replaced wood and sail. In 1942, the SBD replaced the battleship. In my opinion, we owe everything to Edward H. Heinemann's plane. I studied the intricacies of the SBD relentlessly. After nine months of training at Pensacola and Opa-Locka, I had flown nine different types of aircraft. All of these planes had followed the same basic construction pattern, and a simple orientation sufficed to acquaint a new pilot with each plane's cockpit. After a few minutes of "pointing" from an instructor, a trainee could be ready to fly any unfamiliar plane. Not so with the SBD. It had a complex arrangement of controls, and its expensive hydraulics required pilots to be trained to fly it blindfolded. We had to read a half-inch-thick booklet covering all the new equipment, and then we had to be blindfolded to identify seventy different controls and instruments. I studied the SBD's operating manuals during *Enterprise's* three-day trip across the Pacific. I wrote Jean facetiously, "it could be more complicated—only 70 controls and instruments to watch (not counting navigation and radio). Actually, the ships darn near fly themselves." I passed my blindfold test on May 14, just eight days after my unexpected transfer to Hawaii.

Next, we had to prove we could navigate. To accomplish this,

---

* By May 1941, the Douglas factory in El Segundo had completed eighty-seven SBD-2s, the only versions before Douglas upgraded to the SBD-3. Scouting Six received a portion of the SBD-2 batch and the first of the SBD-3 batch, and it took these planes during *Enterprise's* voyage to Pearl Harbor. The SBD-3s attached to the squadron were Bureau Nos. 4521, 4522, 4523, 4524, 4525, 4527, 4570, 4571, and 4572.

each pilot received a map showing the various airfields around Hawaii and instructions to land at each one of them, flying by latitude, longitude, and magnetic course. The Navy made things simple for us, devising clever mnemonic devices to help us remember our navigational lessons. After setting the directional gyroscope from the magnetic compass, the phrase "Can Dead Men Vote Twice?" rattled through my brain. This acronym translated meant "Compass plus Deviation equals Magnetic plus Declination (or Variation) equals True course." There was a companion jingle: "When correcting, Easterly errors are additive." All this mess translates into the direction you are heading (pointing) and the path you are making over the ocean.

I loved flying the Dauntless. During my first two months, as I familiarized myself with the controls, I flew seven SBD-2 models and one SBD-3 model. Although exceedingly noisy and drafty, it soared like a dream. It was wonderfully stable, not like a fighter. With trim tabs set I could fly using only the rudder pedals with only an occasional "bump" against the control stick with my knee. Soon I mastered it so well that I could fly with both hands free. I could land in a pinch, stopping on small runways or in open fields without any trouble at all. The plane's dive control impressed me most of all. I could shift the airplane's dive brakes—known as split flaps—to any degree, and regardless of diving speed or g-force, the brakes stayed in place. The only major problem I noticed involved the SBD-2's vulnerable hydraulics. Part of the tubing went through the cockpit and if it sprang a leak, fluid sprayed out in a nasty stream. I had to replace my trousers a couple of times because there was so much gunk on them.

Still, it was always unwise to push a plane's capabilities beyond its intent. I found this out the hard way. One day, during one of my navigation tests, I piloted my plane over a tiny island. Below, I noticed a circular asphalt runway, something that looked similar to the biplane runways back in Kansas. Sensing a chance for an impromptu landing, I angled my dive bomber for approach. As I neared the landing pad, the air temperature rose to scalding and my plane dropped like a rock. I realized my error: I was trying to land on a lake of lava! I gave the plane more power, barely managing to avoid an unsightly death. I shook off the jitters. Luckily, no one had seen my blunder.

Not every pilot was so lucky. In fact, we lost our skipper only a few days after I passed my qualification examination. On May 21, LCDR Smith led a group of qualified pilots over a remote area several miles from Oahu's Marine Corps airstrip, Ewa Field, to drop smoke bombs over a target. Smith made a perfect dive, but for some unexplained reason, he failed to pull out. His plane struck the target and smashed into bits. Our squadron commander was dead and we were astonished. At noon on the day of the accident, I accompanied eleven other men to the crash site to secure "essential items" from the wreckage, which was now half-submerged in a three-foot-deep swamp.* On May 25, we held Smith's funeral. His untimely death reinforced the notion that we had to sharpen our focus. We were, after all, preparing for war.

Writing to Jean, I reflected on the sobering dangers of being a naval aviator. I wrote, "The commander of our squadron . . . has just answered the last call. Perhaps flying isn't as safe as I'm convinced it is. But you know how I feel about it—that there's a job to

---

* The "essential items" included the SBD-2's navigational booklets, control handles, and ship identification booklets. I've always wondered about the cause of Smith's crash. He was an excellent pilot, with many dives, but his accident was never solved while I served with Scouting Six. Later on, we assumed he crashed because our SBD altimeters always showed 1,000 feet too high. He might have relied on his instruments and attempted to pull out of his dive too late.

be done, and since I like it and let the govt. spend thousands of dollars to train me for it, I'll more than gladly take the risk."

With LCDR Smith's death came a sequence of promotions. Hal Hopping received a promotion to LCDR, and he took control of the squadron. LT Gallaher became the new XO, and another man, LT Clarence Dickinson, became the new flight officer (FO). I also received a promotion. On June 2, 1941, Hopping elevated me to lieutenant (junior grade). With this promotion, I received several collateral duties, operating as assistant personnel officer, educational officer, and welfare officer.*

Although Smith's death was a tragic shock, it did not halt Scouting Six's intense training schedule. During the first two months, I logged fifty-eight hours in the air, sometimes flying three missions in a single day. LCDR Hopping put us to work, making us fly day and night. By midsummer, I wrote to Jean, "We've been flying so much lately that we've been considering putting coffee pots in the planes and bunks in the 'ready room.'" The breakneck pace of training tested our ability to keep track of our complicated schedule, for each day brought with it a flight to a different island. Somedays I had meals in three different places. Hopping's main goal was to prove to the doubting "battleship admirals" that naval aviation was here to stay.

For leadership, however, I often looked to LT Gallaher for advice. Gallaher possessed several important, inspirational talents. Whenever he entered a room full of chatter, he commanded attention within a few seconds. We loved to talk a lot and we were hard to control, but he'd walk into a room bellowing, "Quiet! Quiet! Quiet!" Everyone silenced reverently to hear what he had to say. Gallaher

---

* Officially, LCDR Hopping signed my oath of office on October 3, 1941, backdating the promotion to June 2.

had a keen intellect, and he conveyed vital information quickly and cogently, without any pretense of arrogance. He was great in this regard and always knew what he was talking about. Gallaher also recognized our talents and encouraged us to present our specialties to the squadron. He discovered the experts in engines, gunnery, navigation, ship identification, aircraft identification, and bombing and had each of us present our findings. It was like a college classroom, but with room for jokes and humor. I never had more fun learning about aircraft than with Gallaher. He loved to share knowledge with a close friend in Bombing Six, LT Richard Halsey Best. When one of them would learn anything, the other would soon know the same thing. Because of those two officers, the pilots in Scouting Six and Bombing Six respected each other and we mutually improved our abilities.

By May 22 I was ready for my most daunting challenge, landing on a carrier. As a matter of tradition, nothing worried us more than landing on deck for the first time. I spent hours agonizing over this important event. After receiving my briefing, I ran out to an SBD-2 (Bureau No. 2170), eager for the chance to show what I could do. When I reached my plane, I saw one of Scouting Six's enlisted sailors sitting in the rear seat. This was Aviation Machinist's Mate Third Class Bruno Peter Gaido. Normally, when a pilot made his first landing, he did not take along any passengers. If the pilot botched his landing he did not want to risk the life of an innocent gunner. To simulate the weight of a gunner, the ordnancemen normally placed sandbags in the rear seat. Before I reached my plane, Gaido had removed these sandbags and stood in their place. He waved hello and said, "Can I go with you?"

I replied, "This is my first carrier landing and I am supposed to have only sandbags."

Gaido snorted and pointed, "You got wings, don't cha?"

"Yeah."

Gaido continued, "You can fly, can't cha?" He sat down in the gunner's seat, strapping himself in.

I couldn't budge him. He seemed confident in me and because of that, I became confident in myself. We took off, and when it came time to land, I experienced no trepidation. I found *Enterprise* cruising slowly, its deck clear. Flying past the bridge structure, I signaled my intent to land. *Enterprise* turned into the wind and the green "landing light" came on. Putting my speed at five knots above stalling speed, I leveled off at the height of the deck—about sixty-five feet—and made a semicircle, watching the landing signal officer (LSO) wave two large, colored paddles. Ideally, I wanted to get "in the groove," to use aviators' parlance, which meant setting the plane with the appropriate speed, direction, and angle of descent. If I missed the "groove," the LSO would deliver a "wave-off" signal and I would have to go around again. Otherwise the LSO waved a "cut" signal, which meant cut the engine and land. As it happened, on this day, buoyed by Gaido's confidence, I made a perfect landing. I put my hook and wheels down, cut the throttle, and then pulled back on my stick after my plane's nose dropped.

I knew I had landed well because no one got active on "Vulture's Row," an open deck at the rear of *Enterprise*'s island structure. The ship's photographer sat there, and he had orders to film each and every bumpy landing or accident. The name "Vulture's Row" emerged because we only saw activity when someone was in danger of crashing. As a rule, if the photographer looked bored, we were okay. If he stood up, we had to do something quickly. No such worries today. My plane screeched to a halt, catching one of the seven arresting wires stretched between *Enterprise*'s second and third elevators. Gaido and I felt the jolt of the wire—a force of about 2 g's—and then we let the wire slowly pull back the plane. The taxi director issued a "brake" signal and then two crewmen came forward to unhook the wire. With that, the taxi director issued another signal, waving me forward and clearing the deck for another landing. I exited the cockpit, all smiles.

I performed five more perfect landings over the next week, all without fault. I wrote to Jean, "Am getting accustomed to these carrier landings and am almost at home 'in the groove' (as we call the approach to the ship) as at an airport." After my sixth landing, I shouldered an important squadron tradition. To train the pilots and gunners, allowing them to practice their aim, one SBD pilot had to drag in flight a long white fabric sleeve used as a target. The other planes would attack it, firing bullets of colored paint. Through this method, LCDR Hopping assessed our marksmanship.

I pulled the tow sleeve for the first time on May 27. This resulted in an important incident in my life, the episode that earned me my nickname. After target exercises, I decided to land at the nearest field, Ewa Field, so that my gunner, Milton Wayne Clark, could haul in the tow sleeve and pack it away before we flew back to the air station. My plane wafted in at about 110 feet, about thirty feet higher than the trees surrounding the field.* I radioed the tower but received no response; however, I noticed the green landing light was turned on. Thinking I had been given permission to land, I approached the runway, making a gentle turn, just as if I were landing on *Enterprise*. As I made my descent, I looked up to discover two squadrons of Marine fighter planes lined up for their own approach, apparently intent on using the same runway. "Oh, nuts, they're coming right at me!" I said to myself. I had to make a quick decision: should I give my plane some gas and climb out of the way, or should I bring it to a quick stop on the runway and then taxi to the side so the Marines could land? I knew that Marine pilots always used the entire runway, so it seemed best to bring my

---

* I was flying an SBD-3 (Bureau No. 4524).

plane to a quick halt. That way we could achieve both our purposes on the same field.

I landed my plane, pulling my dive bomber off into a red clay field, clearing the way for the incoming marines. Little did I realize that the field was not solid clay, but layered with six inches of dust! The moment my plane's prop blast hit the dust, it sent up a mushroom cloud a mile high, preventing the marines from safely landing. I shouted to Clark, "We're in deep trouble here! Get that tow sleeve as fast as you can! We got to get out of here!" Comically, Clark jumped out of the rear seat and disappeared into the maelstrom, following the towline to its terminus.

Meanwhile, I received a message from the furious tower control operator: "Unknown dust cloud, who the hell are you?" I didn't respond. Clark returned to the rear seat in less than a minute. I shouted frantically, "Hurry up! Hurry up!" My gunner jumped into the backseat and gave a thumbs-up and I navigated my way back onto the runway, a near impossibility as nothing could be seen inside the swirling, dusty vortex. Using only my compass to guide me, I taxied back onto the strip. I peered out of the cockpit and looked down. I said to myself, "Yeah, that's asphalt." I decided to drive another fifty feet to get to the center of the runway. I spun my plane ninety degrees, and with all possible speed, I took off, making sure to take off low so the operator in the mooring mast tower could not identify my SBD's telltale Navy markings.

Behind me, the furious Marine aviators shouted obscenities into their radios. "Who caused that — dust cloud?" Rather than head directly for Pearl Harbor, I made a sharp left turn and flew out to sea, taking a long, circuitous route to get back to Ford Island. I landed safely, parked my plane, and then walked over to *Enterprise*. As I came up the gangway, I saw Cleo Dobson standing there, grinning. "Welcome aboard, Dusty," he joked. Apparently

Dobson had seen the whole incident, circling above the dust storm from 15,000 feet, listening as the marines' colorful conversations choked the radio. Even before I returned, Dobson had told everyone on the ship—or so it seemed—describing the comical event in detail. The story of "Dusty" Kleiss spread like wildfire. Within an hour, everyone on *Enterprise* knew the tale. Within the week, all the sailors in every harbor knew the story. From then on, no one ever called me Jack. I was always Dusty.

Finally, I had my own nickname.

CHAPTER 8

SCOUTING SQUADRON SIX, PART 2

June–November 1941

Once all eighteen pilots in Scouting Six passed our various examinations, we started training as a unit. In standard formation, my squadron consisted of eighteen SBD-2s and -3s arranged into three divisions of six planes each. LCDR Hopping commanded the whole squadron in addition to the first division. LT Gallaher directed the second division, and LT Clarence Dickinson directed the third. Each division, in turn, consisted of two three-plane sections. Each section leader flew at the head of an inverted-V formation with two wingmen, one to starboard and one to port. I started out as a wingman in the second division. On June 2, I received official word of my promotion to LTJG. My rank entitled me to become a section leader. If I impressed my superiors, I believed I might advance into one of those important spots.

Squadron drills began about mid-June, and they gave me a chance to see our aircraft carrier in full operation. *Enterprise* had an admiral on board, one with a storied reputation. Most of us young aviators who came on board *Enterprise* dreaded to be around admirals. They seemed to assume they should be treated like gods. We wondered if we would be able to survive him. However, *Enter-*

prise's task force commander (and hence the senior officer on the ship) was Vice Admiral William Halsey, whose leadership style was not at all what I anticipated. When sailors boarded *Enterprise*, we ascended one of two gangways, one for enlisted and one for the officers. Halsey always stood on a platform between the two gangways and turned his body accordingly to greet new sailors. I expressed surprise to see him so chatty with the enlisted men.

Halsey wore a big grin: "How's Elsie? Has she had the baby yet?"

"No, sir, that's next week."

"Well, how's your dad doing?"

"He's just fine, sir."

I marveled that Halsey could remember the personal lives of all 2,200 sailors. He never forgot anything, or so it seemed. Halsey had a different approach with the officers. If he saw a khaki-uniformed officer, he saluted and said, "Welcome aboard." However, he confronted white-uniformed officers, asking them, "You're in whites. Why is that?" If they offered a reasonable excuse, Halsey grunted and let them pass. If they said something like, "I thought that was the proper uniform, sir," he'd snarl, "This is a working ship! Go back and change!" I instantly liked his command style. He got right to the point and noticed everything. Halsey wasn't an easy mark. Ne'er-do-well sailors found it impossible to put anything past him. I used to think that admirals were horrible people and they should be avoided like crazy dogs. But Halsey had the habit of appearing everywhere, and he looked out for us pilots. Once he watched while a SBD was being launched by the hydraulic catapult on the hangar deck. During the launch, the catapult malfunctioned. The pilot received no "jolt" but stopped his plane before it reached the edge of the ship. The next day the catapult had been removed for repairs under Halsey's orders.

Under Halsey's leadership, *Enterprise*'s four squadrons practiced day and night. In July and August, I logged fifty hours of flying time each month. Halsey focused on quick takeoff and landings. The best squadrons could take off or land their eighteen planes in nine minutes, or thirty seconds between each aircraft. Halsey demanded that *Enterprise*'s air group land a full squadron in four minutes, thirty seconds, or fifteen seconds between each aircraft. For takeoff, we usually managed thirty seconds between each aircraft. Under Hopping's determined leadership, my squadron managed to meet Halsey's demand before any of the air group's other squadrons.

We also practiced at night with glide bombing, a dangerous drill. On moonless evenings, my squadron practiced taking off and forming up. When the planes left the deck, we took off without lights, a dangerous task, but necessary if we should ever take off in nighttime waters patrolled by submarines. Then, once we gained altitude, we turned on our wing lights. Every plane had three lights, one on each wing and one on the tail. Each light was colored, with wing lights indicating the plane's section number and the taillights denoting its position (one, two, or three) within the section. Naturally, this required each of us to memorize the light arrangements of each plane in the squadron and then identify them at night, all so we could form up without causing a midair collision. Once formed for drill, Hopping led our planes in a mock attack. One plane dived low, dropping a flare. Then the others came in at a shallow, forty-five-degree dive, throwing our bombs at the target. Next, each section turned on its wing lights again, formed up, and returned to Ford Island, navigating the treacherous mountains, which loomed ominously in the darkness. Amazingly, we never lost an airplane while performing those maneuvers.

When it came to combat drill, my squadron focused on two important tasks: dive bombing and scout bombing. With dive bombing, we had to learn how to cruise in formation at an altitude of 20,000 feet and then peel off, one by one, against a chosen target.

We practiced against bull's-eye targets on the ground or targets towed by ships out on the water. From start to finish, the process of dive bombing offered a death-defying display of aeronautical control and accuracy. Compared to learning to dive bomb, a roller coaster was a ticket to Dullsville. We started four miles up. From this altitude, the target appeared to be about the size of a ladybug on the tip of a shoe. When ready to dive, the squadron commander waggled his wings and each plane peeled off, one by one, plunging downward toward the target. Inside each cockpit, we pilots armed our bombs, adjusted our instruments, and set our plane's dive brakes, the perforated flaps on the back of each wing. Then, when our turn came, we "pushed over"—that is, dropped the stick forward—and down we went.

At full dive speed, an SBD dropped at 240 knots, or 275 miles per hour. Even a typical, "perfect" dive was hard to endure. Air resistance buffeted the plane and deafened our hearing. We had to keep our cockpits open during a dive, so the noise of the wind drowned out nearly all other sound. With one eye on the bomb scope, we adjusted the dive so our target was centered and had no tendency to drift up and down, or left or right. Our other eye glanced at airspeed and other instruments, assuring us that our dive brakes were working. Mainly we watched the altimeter, which spun like a top but was inaccurate by 1,000 feet. If it spun past 5,000 feet we knew it just passed 4,000. We required 1,500 feet for normal pullout and another 1,000 feet to stay above bomb fragments. A quick pull on the manual release handle gave each pilot a jolt as the undercarriage bomb—either a 500-pounder or a 1,000-pounder—pivoted "downward" (really behind the plane) to clear the propeller. To pull out, we pulled smoothly on the stick, which resulted in 6 to 8 g's worth of pressure. (At 6 g, this means that if a pilot, his parachute, and his flight gear met the design weight of 200 pounds, then he pushed down on the seat with a force of 1,200 pounds.) Once we had pulled out into a level flight, we closed our dive brakes, swinging those big perforated flaps flush with the trailing edge of the wing, accelerated to full throttle, set high RPM (rotations per minute) on the engine, and headed for home.

If we followed the standard rules, after releasing our bombs we had no idea if we hit our target. We had to rely upon the report of the pilot who dived behind us, or perhaps the word of our rear-seat gunner. Only then, after we had returned to the ready room, could we learn where our bombs had hit and what adjustments we had to make to improve our aim. Some of the bolder pilots, me included, chose to bank high on our pullout. That way we might see the explosion—that is, if we practiced with live bombs, which we rarely did. The senior officers, Gallaher in particular, warned us not to do this. If we got too curious, he cautioned, enemy fighters would certainly pounce on us. High banking at pullout was against all rules and common sense but almost all of us did it. We just *had* to see if we made a hit or miss.

For scout bombing, we trained at lower altitudes, about 1,000 to 1,500 feet. Scout bombing required us to train in pairs. Two-plane teams flew in pie-shaped wedges radiating outward from the carrier. In these teams, we learned to identify targets and report contact information—meaning number, ship type, latitude, and longitude—through Morse code. Our radioman-gunners sent the information back to the carrier, and then, once we received confirmation of receipt, our two-plane teams made a quick attack, damaging the enemy target while the carrier rushed the bombing squadron and torpedo squadron to our location. Usually we used 500-pounders for scout bombing because they lightened our plane's load, allowing us to carry more fuel and increase our search range. Naturally, scout bombing drills involved close attention to navigation, which required memorization. To navigate the Hawaiian Islands, each Scouting Six pilot carried a detailed terrain map, but as we discovered, this map proved too delicate and too large to open inside the cockpit. (Additionally, it showed no radio information for the various Hawaiian airfields, making it virtually useless in flight.) I simply took to studying the map while I was on the ground, memorizing the shapes of the various mountains. That way I learned to navigate by sight alone. However, when my plane was out over open water, I had no alternative but to use my magnetic course and nautical mile training, which meant plotting my plane's movements on a chart board, recording my location at regular intervals. If pilots belonging to a two-plane scout bombing team failed to do this task, we could easily get lost.

The drills exposed a few glaring problems with our dive bombers. One of the most troublesome malfunctions regarded our planes' wing-mounted airbags, flotation devices that inflated whenever a plane made a water landing. Inexplicably, several SBDs crashed because their airbags inflated spontaneously in flight. Usually only one airbag inflated, but that was a disaster, for it ruined the plane's ability to fly. When the airbag deployed, it was so big that the airplane was uncontrollable. It went sideways and then vertically, crashing into the ground. At first no one could explain why the airbags inflated prematurely. In theory it would take the resistance provided by a foot of seawater to place enough pressure on the quarter-inch aperture to set off the airbag inflator. Only after intricate exploration of the apparatus did our maintenance crews discover the problem. Hawaiian wasps had entered the apertures, building their nests next to the pressure-sensitive device that inflated the bags, and whenever a pilot slipped his plane to the side, the nest jostled loose and triggered the device. After vociferous complaining, we convinced our support crews to rip out the airbags altogether. We understood the implicit risk involved in our request. If we landed in the water, we had only a few seconds to exit the plane before it became a submarine.

Training exposed the flaws in some of *Enterprise*'s other aircraft. Notably, our torpedo planes failed to impress. On July 25, Scouting Six and Torpedo Six planes participated in a combined attack. During these operations, one or two SBDs dropped from the sky and skimmed above the water. As we did so, we deployed smoke tanks, filling the air with a thick cloud. The torpedo planes, Douglas TBD-1 Devastators, deployed behind the smoke screen, burst through it, and released their torpedoes at the target. In theory, under combat conditions the TBDs would not be exposed to enemy fire for more than a few seconds before retreating into the smoke. I remember this particular drill because I served as one of the torpedo recovery planes. I shadowed several TBDs and dropped smoke markers so the torpedoes could be recovered and reused. (During these practice missions, the torpedo warheads were filled with water. When the torpedoes stopped, the warhead expelled the water with air and the empty noses held the torpedoes afloat.)

During this combined attack, I found it hard to track the torpedoes because none of them came anywhere close to the target. Most of them sank or veered off in the wrong direction. I saw two or three spinning in a circle like a dog chasing its tail. I was no expert in torpedo technology, but I could see the problem clearly. Whenever the torpedoes hit the water the shock of the entry caused the guidance system or the propeller to malfunction. I assumed at least one of them would have reached the target. This news was terribly disappointing. Shortly after I returned to the carrier, an officer (I don't remember who) accosted me, telling me I wasn't to breathe a word of the failed torpedo test to anyone. We always had fears that the Japanese had spies in Hawaii, and we wanted to keep our torpedo problems secret.

The constant fast pace of training allowed me to judge the effectiveness of my squadron mates. In particular I got a good sense of the abilities of the gunners, and used this knowledge to select my permanent rear-seat gunner. I was pretty harsh on those who tried out for gunner positions. My notebook—which I still possess—has a bunch of critical comments such as "missed almost every question," or "does not know boats, ground tackle, naut. terms," or "must hate to study, has nautical knowledge of a good corporal." Somehow, I found one man who impressed me. Toward the end of July, I chose twenty-year-old John Warren Snowden, a newly minted radioman, as my gunner. I selected him because he had a quick, discerning mind and a strong sense of initiative. For instance, on July 26—the first time we flew together—Gallaher led a group to a remote island to practice carrier landings. Because Gallaher's plane had experienced engine trouble that day, in accordance with standard practice he took the closest operational plane, which happened to be mine. It was up to me to repair Gallaher's plane and fly it home. Any other rear gunner might have complained at being downgraded to a damaged plane, but John Snowden was different. Even before I had figured out which cylinders were failing, John had already gathered up spare sparkplugs and started inserting them into their proper places. In a few minutes we had fixed the faulty plane and we flew it home to Ford Island, triumphantly.

John was an excellent gunner. As the squadron's education officer, I was first to know the scores of the enlisted men as they vied for top ranking on the gunnery sheet, which entitled them to higher pay. Although younger than the other aviation sailors, he was far ahead of all other enlisted men. I snatched him up before the other pilots noticed his abilities. He scored number one in all categories for promotion, the highest ever recorded in my little black book. At the time, I wrote proudly to Jean that, "My gunner is . . . one of the best dead shots in the Navy (which is saying a lot)." John became a close friend. Normally, officers and enlisted men tried not to fraternize, but John and I broke that mold. When Jean sent me a load of candy bars in the mail, I believed John should get his fair share, and I let him take the first bite. (John loved candy bars!)* Our friendship blossomed because I always appreciated the danger gunners faced. Years after the war, I wrote this to a woman whose relative had been a gunner in our squadron:

> Just imagine sitting in the back seat of an SBD during combat. You would face to the rear, holding twin .30 caliber machine guns, scanning the sky for Zeros, ready to shoot them down before they shoot you. Then, suddenly, you are plunged downward vertically at 250 miles per hour, pushing downward on your seat with a force of eight "Gs" after the pilot dropped his bomb. . . . We pilots always received medals when our airplane and crew did something important. The enlisted man in the back seat was rarely mentioned. I would have been killed long ago had it not been for the skills of my RM 3/c, John Snowden.

Over the course of the next few months, John and I got to know the various planes attached to our squadron. Usually we got assigned to an SBD-2 designated 6-S-5. (All of Scouting Six's planes bore Navy insignia, indicating the air group, plane type, and position in the squadron. This SBD-2, 6-S-5, was commonly known as "Sail-Five.") The pace of drill required us to put our faith in our maintenance crew to refit and keep Sail-Five well tuned. At every takeoff, a pilot had the option of rejecting an airplane if he considered it unfit. However, if a pilot rejected a plane too often, he earned a poor reputation among the mechanics. I tried not to be

---

* There was another team in our squadron as close as John and me, ENS James Dexter and RM 3/c Donald Hoff. Don Hoff was not only good as a Radioman Gunner, but he had keen eyesight and a fantastic memory. After a battle, he was able to tell exactly what numerous airplanes had done. James Dexter was a superb pilot.

a perfectionist; I never turned down a plane, except on one occasion. During a training mission, I jumped into a plane that wasn't Sail-Five. As I came into takeoff position, I revved up the throttle and then got a funny feeling. I looked at the takeoff officer, who gave me a thumbs-up. In response, I gave a thumbs-down, a signal that something was wrong with the plane. Immediately, Chief Dodge came over to determine the problem. Dodge looked over the cockpit, checked the engine and gauges, and gave a thumbs-up. Again I shook my head and gave a thumbs-down. Totally baffled, Dodge looked over the plane a second time and again found nothing wrong with it.

By now the deck crew had become impatient. Other planes were waiting to take off. I rejected the plane, as per my right. The crew pulled my SBD-2 off to the side and let the rest of the squadron get airborne. When I dismounted the aircraft, a furious lieutenant came over to me, snarling, and said, "If you're afraid to fly, we'll just find someone else." Another member of Scouting Six, ENS Walter Willis, came on deck and took over the plane. Willis got airborne, but he flew no farther than one hundred yards before the engine quit. The SBD-2 crashed in the ocean, and a destroyer had to rescue Willis and his gunner. To this day, I don't know exactly what it was, but I knew that engine just wasn't right. I never complained about it; I had no need to say, "I told you so." The crash vindicated me. Of course, I just wonder how I'd have been regarded if that plane had made it safely. Don't ask me what was wrong with that plane. I just had a funny feeling about it.

For the most part I liked my companions, the other pilots in Scouting Six; however, I developed rivalries with a few of them. My biggest competitor was Scouting Six's new flight officer, LT Clarence Earle Dickinson Jr., or "Dickie," as he was known to the other pilots. Twenty-nine-year-old Dickinson came from a small town outside Raleigh, North Carolina. Like me, Dickinson had gradu-

ated from the Naval Academy. We knew each other from Pensacola, but not very well. In fact, a small incident had already driven
a wedge between us. Upon graduation, I had received temporary
duty in New York City, where I had friends. When Dickinson heard
about my assignment, he insisted upon going in my place, based on
his seniority. Dickinson took my spot on the plane leaving to New
York, and I was left, bag in hand, on the ground.

Our careers crossed paths again in 1941 when Dickinson reported to *Enterprise* just a few weeks ahead of me. Dickinson had
a quick, discerning mind, a stunning love of naval history, and a
high-pitched, squeaky voice to explain all his forthright opinions
to everyone. He was prone to heated outbursts. For instance, during our training in Hawaii, Dickinson lost favor with the maintenance crew when he nearly crashed his plane after lapsing into
a panic. At one of the outlying fields, we were practicing rapid
takeoffs and landings. On this particular day, Dickinson led the
group. LCDR Hopping had tasked him with encouraging the other
pilots to engage our "emergency power," that is, to train in high-
speed takeoffs, pushing our engines to maximum thrust during
a climb. Dickinson took off first and I followed two planes behind
him. As per Dickinson's instructions, we ascended quickly using
maximum thrust, but each plane had to come off that "emergency
power" after only a few minutes' flying or risk damaging the engine or propeller. Dickinson's dive bomber roared off the runway
and made a beautiful ascent, and soon the next three SBDs joined
his plane, each climbing steadily.

Suddenly, before the whole squadron had gotten airborne,
Dickinson shouted into the radio, "Clear the field! Clear the field!
Emergency!" I leveled out, watching as the other planes on the
ground gave way so Dickinson could make his emergency landing.
His plane rumbled back onto the runway at full power, just barely
managing to stop before he ran out of track. I circled patiently for

a time, and finally, Dickinson took off again, leading the squadron in its practice flight. Later, after I landed, I asked Chief Dodge what had gone wrong.

"What's the story?" I asked, pointing at Sail-Four, Dickinson's SBD-3. Chief Dodge explained how Dickinson's plane had made its abrupt landing, taking the whole of the runway to come to a screeching halt. "Yes," I said, "I saw that; was there something wrong with the engine?"

Chief Dodge grimaced. "No! The engine was perfect. There wasn't a thing wrong with it. He engaged emergency power, but even so, the engines and propeller took it."

I was still confused: "Well, how come he made an emergency landing?"

Dodge replied, "It had to do with his tachometer," the device that reported the rotations-per-minute of the propeller, something that every pilot had to watch carefully when he put his plane into an emergency power climb. Dodge continued, "His tachometer was stuck at zero. It's clearly broken. However, Dickinson thought the problem was his engines. He thought he had lost power."

I was befuddled. I asked, "Wait, so he thought his engine was slowing down even though he was clearly speeding up?"

Dodge shook his head. He grumbled, "Talk about a stupid person!" The incident left the engine crew properly miffed, for Dickinson's frantic cry for an emergency landing made them appear negligent, as if they had failed to tune his engine properly.

I might have forgotten about this incident had not a more serious one occurred weeks later. On September 21, 1941, Dickinson nearly killed me. That month, a Hollywood film crew arrived on *Enterprise* to acquire footage of carrier planes in action. The script required us to fly toward a camera at an altitude of about 5,000 feet, and then one of our dive bombers had to simulate getting shot down. On this day, Dickinson led the group with each plane flying tightly—only a few yards apart, slightly to starboard and slightly astern of the preceding plane. As usual, I piloted Sail-Five. I held a position closest to Dickinson's SBD, the lead plane in the formation. Due to safety concerns, the whole scene had to be regulated by signals from *Enterprise*. When the carrier gave its signal, Dickinson was supposed to dive and, once clear of the formation, open his wing canisters, releasing hydrofluoric acid into the air, which gave the illusion that his plane had been shot down and was on fire. After that, I was supposed to take over the squadron and engage the fictitious enemy.

As the scene unfolded, *Enterprise* delivered its signal, shooting up a flare, but instead of diving and then releasing his hydrofluoric acid as he had been ordered, Dickinson did the reverse, opening his tanks first and then diving. At point-blank range, Dickinson waggled his wings, spraying a heavy dose of the corrosive acid into my plane. Immediately my plane's paint flecked off and the cockpit windshield fogged up. The toxic cloud streaked in and blasted me full in the face. My gosh! It stung! I cannot begin to describe the pain it caused, like thousands of needles dancing across my face. My goggles fogged up and cracked. Had I not been wearing them, the acid cloud would surely have blinded me, perhaps permanently. Even so, corrosive mist fogged my goggles so I couldn't see at all. My eyes started squirting fluid and they burned as if someone had rammed a lit match into them. My helmet, clothing, and gloves melted, and my fingers, frozen white, wrinkled and splintered. In icy pain, my hands gripped the stick as if they were lifeless hunks of meat.

Unable to see, I put my plane into a dive to get below the gas cloud. I tried to feel my way back to land as best I could. I didn't want to stall or go into a spin, so I kept my engines going at cruising speed and piloted with my eyes closed. At this point, I thanked God that all SBD pilots had to pass a blindfold test. I wonder if I would have survived if I hadn't learned all the controls blindfolded. Once below the gaseous, corrosive cloud, using my nerveless hands, I raised my goggles to see where I was, but my cockpit window was scarred and opaque. I tried to look through the windshield, but it was all fogged up. Blinking furiously, I poked my head out of the cockpit and looked downward. Providentially, I had leveled my plane only fifty feet above the waves. I kept my head outside, squinting and squinting, trying to nullify the pain in my eyes. I saw an island ahead and put down for an emergency landing. I cannot tell you how I did it, but blinded and burned, I managed to land Sail-Five perfectly. My plane and I were saved.

As this drama unfolded, the ground crew at the airfield watched my smoldering plane gliding inbound, and as soon as it stopped, they started spraying it with water. Burned and itchy, wearing only shreds of a uniform, I climbed out of my cockpit, receiving a healthy dose of hose water. I must have looked awful; skin flaked off my face, chest, and hands. In a letter to Jean, I said that I "came forth from the fray with the appearance of a first class chimney sweep." In truth, I had sustained serious physical injuries. My hands were a solid mass of fissured flesh. My skin was just falling off. The ground crew secured me and put me in an ambulance, while the officers at the airfield contacted the naval air station at Pearl Harbor, telling my squadron mates that someone needed to pick up Sail-Five, and that it could no longer fly, at least not until it received a whole new set of glass and plastics.

I remained in the hospital for nine days. The burns got worse over the next few days, but somehow I endured it. That was my worst experience as an aviator. It could easily have been the end of me. Of course, I did not tell Jean any of that. When I wrote to her on September 22, I explained the incident lightheartedly, not even mentioning Dickinson or my death-defying landing. I concluded, "Oh yes—the rugged part of it was that the scene had to have a retake and since I [have] to be exactly in the same place for blending of scenes, I . . . [will probably start] coughing and sputtering before the smoke hit[s] me, I'll betch'i."

Dickinson never apologized for the accident. He stopped by the hospital to see me but refused to say, "I'm sorry." He said, "I'm sorry it happened." He did not say what I wanted to hear: "I'm sorry I caused this." I became perturbed. When I pressed the issue, Dickinson shrugged it off, saying that he had simply tried to follow the movie script and that he should not be faulted for it. I grew furious, accusing him of trying to weasel out of an apology. He snapped back, saying that he was only following orders. Our argument got ugly, and I ended up throwing him out of my hospital room. This drove a wedge between us, one not easily mended. We tried to bury the hatchet by hosting a cocktail party for the other pilots and their wives, but our friendship—if one had even existed—was permanently broken. The other pilots in Scouting Six split over the incident, and I think Dickinson lost friends because of it. During a picnic held by the squadron at Barbers Point, I showed up still bearing the nasty burns on my face and hands. Some of the junior aviators and gunners sneaked up behind Dickinson and simulated the act of pouring their beers on his head. They took pictures of it, with Dickinson blissfully unaware of the high jinx going on behind him.

Angry as I was, I didn't need their mockery of Dickinson to make me feel better. I was glad to be alive. However, when accidents like this occurred, I truly wondered if we were ready for war. In two months, I had my answer.

|||||||||||||||||||||||||||||||||||||||||||||||||||||||||||||||||||||||||||||||||||||||||||||||||||||||||||||||||||||||||

CHAPTER 9

THE PACIFIC WAR BEGINS

November 1941–January 1942

On November 28, 1941, *Enterprise*'s task group—Task Force 2—set sail from Pearl Harbor, bound for Wake Island, home of a 450-person Marine Corps garrison. Our force consisted of the carrier, three cruisers, and nine destroyers. Admiral Halsey had obtained orders from Admiral Kimmel to deliver two squadrons of marines to Wake Island. Tensions between the United States and Japan had escalated all month and we anticipated the possibility of war breaking out at any moment. Admiral Halsey announced to *Enterprise*'s captain that he planned to set *Enterprise* at "Battle Condition Three," the third-highest state of readiness, and that we had to be on the lookout for Japanese vessels during our trip to Wake. If we saw any submarines, we had orders to bomb them immediately. If we saw any surface ships, we had orders to report their location.

I was equally on the lookout for marines, for as it turned out, the Marine force scheduled to land on *Enterprise* included VMF-211, one of the two squadrons I had frustrated at Ewa Field six months earlier during the infamous "dust cloud" incident. When Halsey told his bridge crew about Battle Condition Three, he said that VMF-211 would be landing on the deck shortly. Immediately a concerned officer left the bridge, ran down to Scouting Six's ready room, and warned me to expect a bunch of angry marines. Members of my squadron rallied to my bunk, for they expected a brawl. Hours later, the marines bounced aboard, all of them making perfect carrier landings, an act that impressed and chagrined us naval aviators. Major Paul Putnam's F4F-3 came to a stop, and an *Enterprise* officer ran over to welcome him. Scarcely out of his flight gear, Major Putnam roared, "*Where is Dust Cloud?*" The nervous officer feigned ignorance. Shrugging, he asked, "Whatever do you mean?" Other marines stormed into our ready room. There they found me sitting quietly in one of the chairs.

One of them blared, "Hey, buddy, can you introduce me to that unknown dust cloud?" With a straight face I shook my head.

I replied, "What is 'dust cloud'?"

The marine grumbled something unintelligible and went on, interrogating every *Enterprise* pilot he encountered. More marines came to me throughout the day, asking the same question. I indicated that I'd never heard of that name or event. The marines went from ready room to ready room, interrogating pilots, but no one ever gave up my identity.

Despite the humor involved in keeping the marines from their quarry, *Enterprise*'s cruise to Wake carried somber overtones. Admiral Halsey issued "Battle Order Number One," instructing the crew to operate *Enterprise* as if we were at war. Halsey explained, "The ENTERPRISE is now operating under war conditions. At any time, day or night, we must be ready for instant action. . . . It is part of the tradition of our Navy that, when put to the test, all hands keep cool, keep their heads, and FIGHT. Steady nerves and stout hearts are needed now." Commencing on December 5, our carrier began deploying our dive bombers and torpedo bombers as scout planes, searching out nearly 600,000 square miles to find any trace of Japanese ships. I flew scouting hops on December 5 and 6 that extended for 150 miles or more, and as it happened, the two back-to-back flights spared me from early duty on Sunday, December 7. Nothing worthy of note happened during the cruise. We delivered the marines to their destination, and then turned back toward Pearl Harbor. Task Force 2 was scheduled to reach the harbor on December 6, but foul weather delayed our arrival. Luck intervened. By happenstance, my shipmates and I would not be in port when the Japanese air raid occurred.

On December 7, I arose at 4:00 A.M. and received my mission assignment. That day, *Enterprise* planned to launch eighteen SBDs at 6:00 A.M. in order to scout a region west of Oahu, covering the islands of Nihau and Kauai. The eighteen-plane formation consisted of nine two-plane sections. LCDR Young led one of the sections, as did LCDR Hopping. Twelve other Scouting Six pilots and four Bombing Six pilots constituted the rest of the formation. Because I had flown two days in a row, I was scheduled to remain on board *Enterprise* along with seven other Scouting Six pilots, including two pilots whose SBDs experienced engine trouble that morning. We were to remain as a reserve force in case the eighteen scout bombers made contact. If they made no contact, we would still fly on "inner air patrols," short scouting hops that circled the task force. On schedule, the eighteen Dauntlesses thundered off the flight deck and scattered on their search vectors. As I watched them, I had little idea that I would never see some of these squadron mates again.

At about 8:10 A.M., two hours after takeoff, a strange transmission blasted over the radio: "Please don't shoot! This is Six-Baker-Three, an American plane!" I ran to the yeoman in the ready room, trying to listen in. I asked, "What just happened? Who was that?" The northernmost search team, consisting of two Bombing Six planes, had crossed paths with a wave of attacking Japanese planes, the air strike bound for Pearl Harbor. ENS Manny Gonza-

lez, the pilot of Baker-Three, had been shot down, and the ensuing crash killed him and his gunner, RM 3/c Leonard J. Kozelek.
A host of other garbled messages wafted through the receiver. I
strained to listen in. I recognized the voice of Clarence Dickinson:
"For Christ's sake, shoot that son of a bitch on our tail! He's shooting real bullets!"

At first I could not believe that the Japanese had attacked Pearl
Harbor. None of the radio transmissions made any sense to me. I
thought the supposed "attack" was actually a drill and the messages
coming in over the radio were part of an elaborate game designed
to test our readiness. If the attack were real, so I supposed, surely
one of our planes would have given a position report, or given his
call letters or name, or one of the messages would have made sense.

Of course the Japanese air strike was indeed real, and in fact
it had savaged Scouting Six. In all, the Japanese had shot down
five planes. In addition to Gonzalez's plane, swarms of Japanese
fighters—A6M2 "Zeros"—had also taken down Sail-Three, Sail-
Four, Sail-Nine, and Sail-Fifteen. A Japanese fighter pilot killed
LT Dickinson's gunner, RM 1/c William J. Miller. He continued
to hammer Sail-Four with machine gun fire, forcing Dickinson to
make a daring parachute jump. He landed on a road near Barbers
Point. There he hitched an automobile ride from a civilian couple,
arriving safely at Ford Island.* ENS Mac McCarthy, who was Dickinson's wingman, was also shot down. His plane went down in
flames, crashing on a beach. McCarthy bailed out, but his gunner,
RM 3/c Mitchell Cohn, did not. McCarthy parachuted into a tree,
but upon dismounting it he broke his leg, an injury that kept him

---

* Dickinson's plane crashed at 8:23 A.M., slamming into a wooded area east of
Ewa Field and a short distance north of the beach. Five Zeros pounced on Dick-
inson and his wingman, ENS McCarthy. The civilian couple proved to be Otto F.
Heine and his wife, who were out motoring, heading to a picnic at Fort Weaver.

out of the squadron for three months.* Sail-Fifteen, with pilot ENS Walter Willis and gunner Coxswain Frederick J. Ducolon, mysteriously disappeared. Although no one ever found out what happened, no doubt a Japanese fighter finished them off.† Finally, we lost ENS John H. L. Vogt, whose plane, Sail-Three, dueled with a Japanese dive bomber south of Ewa Field. At some point, one of the Japanese fighters intervened and collided with Vogt's plane, killing him and his gunner, RM 3/c Sidney Pierce.‡ In addition to these losses, Japanese fighters shot up two other planes, a Bombing Six plane and a Scouting Six plane, wounding the pilot and gunner in the latter plane.§ One final plane, Sail-Sixteen, piloted by LTJG Frank Patriarca, had to make an emergency landing in a Kauai pasture, but Patriarca and his gunner survived.¶ The remaining ten planes all reached Ford Island. Somehow they managed to land, even though the furious battle raged around them.

Of course, at 9:30 A.M., when I received orders to take off, I knew none of this. All I grasped was that most of my squadron had disappeared. Officially we had twenty-two pilots on the roster, but now fifteen of them were missing in action. If all of them were dead, I

---

* McCarthy's SBD-2 crashed on Ewa Beach, just one mile south of Ewa Field's southwest runway.

† Zeros attacked Willis's SBD-3 around 8:25 A.M. His wingman, LTJG Patriarca, lost contact with Willis's plane after the battle began.

‡ ENS Vogt's plane likely collided with Zeros from IJN *Kaga*. The wreckage of Vogt's SBD-2 slammed into a shrubby field one block from the intersection of Belt Road and Ewa Beach Road.

§ This latter plane was an SBD-3 (Bureau No. 4572), 6-S-14, piloted by ENS Edward T. Deacon. His gunner, RM 3/c Audrey Coslett, received a bullet to the arm that knocked out two inches of his ulna.

¶ Patriarca piloted his SBD-3 to the Army auxiliary field at Kauai, landing at 11:45 A.M. The army surgeon grounded Patriarca, worrying that he might have suffered from combat fatigue.

was the commander of Scouting Six. That's how my first wartime orders came to me. I had to lead six planes on an inner air patrol and protect Task Force 2 at all hazards. As I ran onto the flight deck, sailors hoisted *Enterprise*'s battle flag and an announcement came over the loudspeaker that we were at war with the Empire of Japan.

I took off, leading two other Scouting Six ensigns and three Bombing Six planes on a patrol to protect *Enterprise* and its escorts. After circling the task force several times, we headed to an area southwest of Barbers Point. We found no enemy ships or planes, but we heard plenty of garbled messages on the radio. Even at this point, I was still unsure if the attack was real or imagined. I checked the radio station at Honolulu. I heard "Sweet Leilani" playing; no mention of an enemy attack. Eventually *Enterprise* radioed my little six-plane division, telling us where we could find an enemy tanker supposedly near our carrier. We shifted course but once again found nothing. This whole thing struck me as absurd. Why send six bomb-laden dive bombers to attack an enemy tanker if enemy aircraft carriers were supposedly in the area? Clearly, those officers issuing the orders were stunned by the news and acting erratically. When my comrades and I returned to the carrier at 11:00 A.M., I still doubted that an attack had occurred, but I now noticed that Halsey had ordered the ship to fly its battle ensign, something our task force commander had never done during drill.

Only as the afternoon wore on did I comprehend the reality, that Pearl Harbor had been bombed and the battleship fleet had sustained heavy casualties. My squadron, Scouting Six, could not account for twenty-six pilots and gunners. Perhaps they were all dead and I was truly in charge. I had little time to dwell on this heavy possibility.

At dusk, Halsey ordered a second bombing mission. Now the admiral wanted the six operational SBDs to escort Torpedo Six's

TBDs on a mission to sink the Japanese carriers. Although I did not yet know it, the six Japanese carriers that had launched the air raid in the morning had already turned around and were headed back to Japan. Nevertheless, amid this fog of uncertainty, Halsey decided to use the TBDs as his main strike force. Accordingly, the six Dauntlesses did not receive bombs, but 1,000-pound smoke tanks. If we found a carrier, our SBDs had to provide cover so the TBDs could drop their torpedoes safely. This flight was a near catastrophe. I flew in Sail-Eighteen, one of the planes that had suffered from engine trouble that morning. Its cockpit lights and its navigational instruments did not work. Flying in darkness, our six dive bombers flew at only three hundred feet, at seventy knots—just above stalling speed—whipping back and forth with sharp S-turns so we did not stall or outpace the slower TBDs. Eventually all of the planes returned to the carrier, having found nothing. The whole air strike had gone on the wrong heading because a Bombing Six SBD with a faulty compass had navigated the mission.

The next day, December 8, I launched again in an SBD, this time flying on a scouting hop. Right away, things went wrong. First, I discovered that my plane had been painted incorrectly. Overnight, the maintenance crew had prepared a spare SBD-3 from the "overhead"—the area where the chiefs kept the planes yet to be tested—and marked it "6-S-18," or Sail-Eighteen. Unfortunately, a plane designated Sail-Eighteen already existed—the one I had flown the previous day—and ENS Earl R. Donnell now flew it. The new Sail-Eighteen was in poor condition. The mechanics rushed it into battle-readiness and I feared they might not have checked all of its instruments. I didn't complain. In an emergency, I figured it best to fly the plane assigned to me.

My plane got off the deck and I proceeded on course to cover the leftmost scouting sector. I had instructions to fly a wedge-shaped path and scour the ocean for enemy ships. At the time, *Enterprise* was cruising southwest of Pearl Harbor, and if we expected to find enemy ships at all, they would have been west of our flagship. As I flew my outbound leg, I noticed Donnell's SBD drifting too close. One or both of us must have been in the wrong sector, I thought. Using hand signals, we compared our compass readings and noticed a three-degree difference. Suddenly, after listening to his headphones, Donnell pulled sharply to starboard and flew out of sight. I figured Donnell must have received a transmission from *Enterprise*. For some unknown reason, I did not hear it. I worried my radio might not be functioning. I completed my search and returned to my rendezvous point with *Enterprise*. I flew inbound, hitting heavy clouds at three hundred feet. It was exceptionally foggy. I dropped my plane low, as far as I dared because I didn't really trust the altimeter on my plane. When I got close enough to see the waves, I knew I had lost *Enterprise*.

Whenever we left our carrier, we expected to rendezvous with it at a preset location called "Point Option." Unfortunately, or so we pilots quipped, *Enterprise*'s skipper emphasized the word *option* because it was optional for the carrier to be there. That seemed to be what happened to me on December 8. Someone on *Enterprise* decided to move "Point Option" to a different spot. The folks on the ship radioed those of us on the scouting hop—and Donnell had clearly received that message—but because of my plane's nonfunctional radio, I had not gotten the same message. Realizing that my plane was running low on gas, I called to the backseat, telling John Snowden to radio the ship. Snowden confirmed my fears: the radio did not work. I felt a tremor of worry. I could not find the ship, and I had no means of contacting it. Worse, *Enterprise* had launched two Sail-Eighteens. If Donnell's plane returned, would the air group commander realize that there was another Sail-Eighteen still flying? Not willing to take that risk, I increased altitude, trying to get above the clouds. I climbed to 12,000 feet, but found solid overcast.

Then I climbed to 22,000 feet. Still, I saw nothing. I didn't panic. I took the next logical step. I performed a "box search." As a rule, if a pilot became lost, he had to increase altitude and go around in a square, adding five additional miles in each direction. I began flying outward from my position, going revolution after revolution, until finally I was going about forty miles in my square. This was a pilot's worst nightmare, to be utterly lost over the open ocean with dwindling fuel and no means of radioing for help.

After hours of circling, I noticed a tiny break in the clouds, no larger than a few yards in diameter. In the middle of the breach I saw a wake. It was *Enterprise*! Low on fuel, I put my plane into a steep dive, plunging downward as fast as possible, trying to plummet through the hole before it closed. I careened vertically at 440 knots. At about 5,000 feet, I gripped the stick to pull out, and my plane leveled off at 1,000 feet. Without our dive flaps open, John and I endured tremendous pressure, possibly 11 g. I used everything I had to pull back on the stick. I thought I was going to break it. I was on the verge of blacking out. Briefly, I sustained tunnel vision, but my plane handled the dive better than I did. It pulled out and sustained no damage to the wings. All honor to the good folks at Douglas, they constructed their SBDs superbly. I think a well-made SBD could safely pull 13 g with no damage.

I slowed my plane and drifted toward the carrier. Suddenly the escort destroyers—nine of them—began shooting. "What's going on?" I shouted to myself. "Are we in a battle?" I didn't see any Japanese. I looked behind and noticed waterspouts splashing half a mile away. Then I realized it. They were shooting at me! They thought I was a Japanese dive bomber and I was attacking them. Thankfully, once the destroyer skippers saw my plane's tail markings and realized that I was an American, they stopped firing, letting me go on my way. I reached *Enterprise* and landed with only twenty-five gallons of gas remaining.

As soon as I dismounted my cockpit, the officer of the deck accosted me. He had an ill look as he declared, "Admiral Halsey wants to see you in his stateroom." I swallowed hard. My sudden dive had no doubt frightened the destroyer skippers, and they had reported it to Halsey. I trembled. What drastic thing would he do to me? I had caused a hell of a lot of trouble and the destroyers had wasted plenty of ammunition on me. I was sure I was about to be kicked out of aviation.

Without removing my flight gear, I went to Halsey's quarters. The stern-faced admiral greeted me. Strangely, when Halsey spoke, he conveyed no anger. He said, "Now sit down a minute and have a cup of coffee." Too tired to chitchat, I immediately launched into a long narrative about my scouting hop, describing my malfunctioning plane, how I had lost the carrier, how I had found it again, and how I dived through the clouds, avoiding the destroyers that shot at me. I told him everything I did. I sat back and wondered what was going to happen next. Halsey calmly replied, "That's all." Worn out and uncertain, I departed the admiral's stateroom, fretting. Halsey was so angry with me that he couldn't even find words to say! This wasn't good at all.

The next day, my worries subsided. I had misread Halsey's demeanor. He wasn't angry with me. In fact, he was impressed. Halsey wanted to see if I had the makings of a squadron commander. He told me he wanted to test me out on the air group commander's plane. (I didn't fly it until December 21.) Further, he went to LCDR Hopping, telling him that if a vacancy opened, he should move me to Scouting Six's first division, as that unit—usually slated to attack first when we went on a dive bombing run—required the best pilots. Essentially Halsey wanted me to fly as the number-two section leader behind the squadron commander. Halsey's recommendation, which came to fruition five months later, had dramatic reverberations, and as it turned out, perhaps saved my life.

After my return to *Enterprise,* the other Scouting Six pilots who had flown into Pearl Harbor returned as well. They bore the sad news that six men—two pilots and four gunners—had been killed. Moreover, we got to see what the Japanese had done to the rest of the fleet. That evening, as *Enterprise* sailed up the narrow channel and neared its dock, we could see the wreckage of the battleships, eight hulks sitting ruined on east side of Ford Island. The Japanese pilots had sunk or damaged all of them. I could see USS *Oklahoma* (BB-37) overturned with its keel jutting strangely in the air. Three torpedo hits had capsized it. Farther down the line, the mangled superstructure of USS *Arizona* (BB-39) lay half-submerged, victimized by a bomb blast that detonated its forward magazine. The ship was now a metallic tomb for 1,177 brave sailors. Further, the Japanese air raid had damaged or sunk nine smaller vessels, destroyed more than 180 aircraft, cratered our runways, and left 2,400 Americans dead. When I learned how the Japanese had killed my friends from Scouting Six, I was shocked. By comparison, seeing the fleet splintered and smoldering, that was just surreal.

More than a few wanted vengeance for the death toll at Pearl Harbor. In late December, a sailor drew up a fifteen-stanza poem titled "The Galloping Ghost" (a reference to *Enterprise*'s nickname, "The Galloping Ghost of the Oahu Coast"). The fourth stanza proclaimed:

They had their first choice, at the pride of our fleet,
But never again, shall it ever repeat.
We're out for revenge, to even the score,
A thousand to one, and even much more.

Retaliation came quickly. On December 9, my squadron struck the first blow. That day, Perry Teaff spotted a Japanese submarine, *I-70,* and bombed it. Perry's bomb did not sink the submarine, but it did damage it enough that it could not move or submerge. The next day, Clarence Dickinson piloted his SBD (a new plane assigned to him) out to that location and finished it off. For his act of valor, Perry eventually received the Navy Cross, the first member of Scouting Six to earn such a distinction. Dickinson received a Navy Cross, too, albeit for sinking a submarine that could not move, submerge, or shoot back. While I fully acknowledge my prejudice against Dickinson, I stand by my belief that it cheapened Perry's valor for the Navy to give Dickinson the same award.

At this point, I contacted Jean to let her know I survived the attack on Pearl Harbor. I could tell she was worried about me. The newspapers had told her all about the surprise attack and she knew that my carrier was normally stationed in the harbor. By December 13, she still had not heard from me and she wrote me a letter that admitted, "You must be all right or I, no doubt, would have heard by this time, but darling, I still don't know. I've reached the point where people talk to me, and I don't even hear them, I'm so absorbed with my own thoughts. . . . The only thing I can think about now is someone who's somewhere on the Pacific."

I finally wrote her a short note on December 15. My letter did not arrive until December 21. She did not know my fate until two weeks after the treacherous Japanese attack. Jean suffered indecision as to what she ought to do in such a time of strife. I'll say this: she bravely contemplated joining the armed services so she could be near me, but I would not have it. I could not bear to have another reason to worry. With war assured, the future was suddenly uncertain enough.

The war did not wait for the U.S. fleet to recover from the shock it received at Pearl Harbor. That same week, the Japanese began a series of offensives to expand their empire and weaken the Allied nations in the Pacific. On December 8 they invaded Thailand, Malaya, and Hong Kong. They also assaulted U.S. possessions. They

subdued Guam on December 10, and on December 23, they overwhelmed American-held Wake Island, where we had just dropped
off that squadron of fighter planes. Finally, they commenced an
invasion of the Philippines, coming ashore at Lingayen Gulf on December 22. Unable to extricate themselves, more than twenty thousand Americans surrendered to the Japanese by May 1942. Day by
day, it seemed as if defeat loomed closer and closer.

There was some good news. None of our aircraft carriers had
been damaged by the various Japanese attacks. At the time of the
December 7 onslaught, our two carriers in the Pacific—*Lexington*
and *Enterprise*—were sailing for Pearl Harbor. Only a portion of
Enterprise's air group got caught in the fray and *Lexington* was
spared entirely. When it became obvious that none of the damaged battleships could be repaired within the year, the Navy sent
three additional carrier battle groups to our assistance, those of
Saratoga, Yorktown, and *Hornet. Saratoga* didn't last long. On January 11, 1942, it suffered critical damage when a Japanese submarine torpedo struck it, flooding its boiler rooms. Barely involved in
the fighting, *Saratoga* headed to Bremerton, Washington, for repairs. Meanwhile, *Yorktown* and *Hornet* had to sail from the Atlantic coast. They didn't arrive until January and March, respectively.
Until then, *Enterprise* and *Lexington* had to fight the war without
them.

The Japanese offensives of December and January had weak-
ened our strength in the Pacific. They had hoped to knock us out
of the fight before we could declare war and threaten them with our
land, sea, and air forces. Prior to December 7, we had a sizable fleet
with many anchorages and a large army in the Philippines. Now, at
the end of the month, we had a devastated fleet with precious few
defensible ports and an army starving on the Bataan Peninsula.
By the New Year, the Japanese held nearly all the islands on the
west side of the International Date Line and they threatened one of

our allies, Australia. We possessed only a handful of islands in the South Pacific and only two territories in the Central Pacific: Midway Atoll and Hawaii. Thankfully, our Pacific Fleet still had some fight left in it. In addition to our carriers, we had more than fifty submarines and about 110 surface ships: light and heavy cruisers, destroyers, tenders, and minelayers. However, the Japanese had more than 200 ships, including six colossal aircraft carriers: *Akagi, Kaga, Soryu, Hiryu, Shokaku,* and *Zuikaku.* We knew what most of these ships looked like and respected their capabilities. The Office of Naval Intelligence provided us with scale models of every known class of Japanese vessel and we kept half-sheet slips that listed the length, tonnage, armament, protection, and propulsion of each vessel. We held no illusions. The Japanese navy was hard to beat.

USS *Enterprise* went on four patrols after the attack on Pearl Harbor, on December 9, December 19, January 3, and January 11. The first three war patrols turned up nothing, but the fourth turned out to be a major operation. Accompanied by three heavy cruisers, a tanker, and seven destroyers, *Enterprise* set sail, first for Samoa, where the task force expected to reinforce an American base with a load of marines, and next for the Marshall Islands, where Admiral Halsey expected to find a Japanese base loaded with ships and planes.* This was part of our navy's first task, to weaken the Japanese-held bases closest to Hawaii. According to plan, *Enterprise*'s new task force—Task Force 8—constituted part of a large combined strike against two of the easternmost Japanese-held island chains in the Central Pacific, the Gilberts and the Marshalls. One carrier task force, under Rear Admiral Frank Jack Fletcher,

---

* Task Force 8 consisted of twelve ships: one carrier (USS *Enterprise*), three cruisers (USS *Northampton, Chester,* and *Salt Lake City*), seven destroyers (USS *Dunlap, Balch, Maury, Ralph Talbot, Blue, Craven,* and *McCall*), and one oiler (USS *Platte*).

planned to attack Jaluit and Mili in the Marshalls and Makin in the Gilberts. Meanwhile, our task force planned to raid Wotje, Maloelap, Kwajalein, and Roi-Namur in the Marshalls. Both admirals hoped our strikes would be the first in a series of naval battles to roll back Japanese expansion in the Pacific. At the time, none of us pilots knew our task force's final destination. Only Admiral Halsey and his staff were privy to that information. Still, we guessed Halsey expected to use us in battle.

On January 24, 1942, just two days before leaving Samoa, my squadron assembled on the flight deck to have a group photograph taken. We understood this might be our last opportunity to commemorate our eight months of training. All eighteen pilots lined up in front of Sail-Ten. I was seated in the front row. Little did I know that within a week's time, four of my friends would be dead.

We learned of our destination on the day we took the group photograph. The plan to strike the Marshalls came from the new commander of the Pacific Fleet, Admiral Chester W. Nimitz. Initial intelligence reports placed a large number of enemy submarines there, and a Japanese submarine fleet commander headquartered at Jaluit. Nimitz feared that Japanese forces in the Marshalls—and also in the nearby Gilberts—could strike at American-held Samoa, one of our only footholds in the South Pacific. As our task force bore down on its destination, Admiral Halsey and his chief of staff, CDR Miles Browning, selected targets for Enterprise's air group. Initially they chose Wotje Island and Maloelap, but reconnaissance information radioed from a submarine induced them to add Kwajalein Atoll to our list of targets, an irregularly shaped cluster of ninety-seven small islands dotted with palm trees.

Halsey and Browning envisioned the raid to consist of a morning attack of three elements. Once in range of the islands—about 175 miles—Enterprise would launch its air group against Kwajalein. This would be the main attack, which would consist of thirty-six

SBDs from Scouting Six and Bombing Six and nine TBDs from Torpedo Six (all armed with 500-pound bombs). I was scheduled to be part of this assault.

Our air group had several objectives. We had to scour Roi Island, bombing any ships there. If we found no ships, we were to proceed to Kwajalein Island and attack the anchorage. We had orders to strike hangars, fuel tanks, and other installations on Roi and Kwajalein. The other two elements of the raid consisted of a group of Fighting Six planes sent to strafe Wotje and Maloelap and nine TBDs from Torpedo Six (armed with torpedoes) as an attack flight for use against heavy ships if the opportunity arose. Our senior staff expected plenty of action. *Enterprise*'s executive officer, CDR T. P. Jeter, issued a report of prospective operations that placed five enemy capital* ships, three submarines, and seven auxiliary ships at Kwajalein's various anchorages. Jeter reminded us of the importance of our mission: "We can all take pride in being privileged to participate in the first offensive engagement of the Pacific Fleet, and in the first naval action in which an American aircraft carrier has taken part. 'Remember Pearl Harbor.'"

I went over all this information in my head over and over again, wondering how I would experience my first combat situation. I experienced no nervousness, none that I can recall, anyway. In my quarters, Perry Teaff and I whiled away the hours with humorous stories and I tried to express my feelings by writing letters to Jean. This was difficult. Because of censorship, I couldn't tell her about my creeping anxiety that *Enterprise* was cruising toward a target. On January 17, I wrote, "Wish I could tell you some of the places we've been and some of our experiences, but of course I can't." Nev-

---

* A blanket term for warships of significant importance, including battleships, cruisers, and destroyers.

ertheless, my heart poured out in these letters. I told her how much I loved her and how I wanted to be with her forever. I explained, "Jean, darling, I believe you're beginning to find out something I knew the moment I met you and have known ever since. . . . I love you. And to me those words have always held a special meaning, just like your idea of 'forever' on that first day when we called on the Coverdales. I hope you never change."

More than ever, I regretted how I had broken up with Jean a year earlier and broken her heart. I had missed my opportunity to marry her when Annapolis's two-year nonmarriage requirement expired. The night before the battle, in my bunk, I cursed myself for my foolishness. How could I let such a wonderful woman slip away? She had finally come back to me, but now I was on a war cruise in the belly of an aircraft carrier. I could die tomorrow.

A cold chill crept up my spine. I worried I had forever missed my chance at love.

||||||||||||||||||||||||||||||||||||||||||||||||||||||||||||||||||||||||||||||||||||||||||||||||||||||||||

CHAPTER 10

THE BATTLE OF THE MARSHALL ISLANDS
February 1942

At 3:00 A.M., Sunday, February 1, 1942, the crew of *Enterprise* arose to an announcement calling "all hands." I flopped out of my bunk and headed off to an early breakfast. Only dim, ineffective blue lights illuminated the darkened passageways. We kept the ship purposefully dark so as not to disturb our night vision or needlessly make the carrier prey to Japanese submarines. When I finally found my way to the officers' wardroom, it was filled to the brim with khaki-uniformed men, a scene I had never seen before, some young officers arriving at breakfast, abuzz with anxiety, clawing their way through a jittery predawn meal. I joined my Scouting Six companions, dining on a rare, hearty meal of steak and eggs, a telltale sign that a battle was in the offing. Some of the pilots were filled with anxiety. I remember eating my breakfast without any apprehension of going into battle.

I know it sounds like bragging to say I experienced no fear that morning, but it was the truth. I'm not sure why, but I don't think I get scared, at least not the same way as other people. Perhaps my Kansas childhood had something to do with it. In the open prairie,

we learned to live with the presence of death. Maybe I became in-
ured to the prospect of dying. Also, I had a lot on my mind. I still
fretted about missing my chance to marry Jean. Additionally, my
mind turned over the day's impending tasks. I ran through every
possible contingency. What would I do if my squadron encountered
antiaircraft? What about enemy fighters? What about enemy ships?
I had plenty to think about. I was deep inside my own thoughts.

If anything, I was eager. I wanted an opportunity to fight back
against the Japanese. At the time we felt outnumbered, cornered by
a gargantuan foe. Believe it or not, I thought about some of my favorite childhood stories from Coffeyville's Carnegie Library, "Jack
and the Beanstalk" and "Popeye," tales that involved a little guy
working over a big bully. Now, decades later and thousands of miles
away, these stories suddenly resonated with me, for they served as
convenient metaphors for the two warring fleets, our diminutive
American task force and the impressive Imperial Japanese Navy. I
couldn't fathom being afraid. It seemed illogical to stand back and
do nothing. It was the time to fight and I felt ready for it. Worry
and fear were deadly in a "do-or-die" situation like this. They could
prevent a sound night's sleep and cause physical ailments. Fear
numbs the mind, and it's as bad as taking alcohol or drugs. A warrior cannot function by harnessing fear. I think most of my squadron mates understood this also. With one or two exceptions, I saw
no evidence of fear in their countenances. In short, I swallowed my
eggs hungrily; I didn't choke on them.

After breakfast, I ascended the ladder leading to Scouting Six's
ready room, a small chamber inside *Enterprise*'s island superstructure. Twenty-one chairs, arranged in seven rows of three, were now
filled with the bodies of my squadron's eighteen pilots. Off to the
side, a yeoman called out reports, and as the agonizing minutes
wore away, we intently studied our charts. Each of us possessed a
square-foot Plexiglas board with a circular slide rule in the lower

right-hand corner. As the yeoman talked, I recorded wind speed, wind direction, and magnetic declination, plotting the course to our targets. I checked and rechecked the data. With radio silence, this chart board might be my only ticket home. A five-mile error (about one-eighth of an inch on the chart board) could give a pilot real trouble.

The latest intelligence of the Japanese positions still placed five capital ships, three submarines, and seven auxiliary ships at Kwajalein's various anchorages. We also learned that any number of bombers and fighters might be present at the airfields. At our briefing, we were told it was "reasonable to expect" surface ships, land-based aircraft, seaplanes, antiaircraft batteries, hangars, docks, and a fuel storage depot; however, our report told us nothing exact about the atoll's defenses. I was a little perturbed we didn't know more, but I didn't really care. I was chomping at the bit, ready for a chance to attack our enemy. In a recent letter, I indulged in some of the anti-Japanese hatred prevalent among Americans at the time. I claimed I was ready to "speak the language those little men can understand."

I remember one strange thing during the briefing. My squadron's gunnery officer, LTJG Carleton Thayer Fogg—or Foggy, as we called him—started lecturing us about the necessity of activating our guns safely. He said, "We should activate our forward guns only a couple of seconds, just a couple of seconds, before firing." Foggy had explained this lesson to us before, over and over again in fact, explaining that when a pilot switched his guns from "safe" to "fire," there was always "one chance in a hundred" that the guns might fire automatically. This was the last thing I heard before the show started. At 4:30, the yeoman barked, "Pilots, man your planes!" I clutched my chart board and raced out of the ready room and onto the flight deck with the others.

It was still dark when we received the order to occupy our planes.

I weaved through the labyrinth of parked planes and found mine, Sail-Seventeen, the eighteenth plane slated for takeoff. I would be flying in the second three-plane section attached to LT Gallaher's second division, and would be one of two wingmen with LT Reginald Rutherford, an officer who had joined Scouting Six the day after the Battle of Pearl Harbor. As always, John Snowden occupied the rear seat of my dive bomber. My plane carried three bombs— two 100-pounders under the wings and one 500-pound contact bomb under the fuselage. Snowden, who had just finished double-checking our plane's twin .30-caliber machine guns, helped me onto the wing and into the cockpit.

Once I strapped in, the deck's sailors wound and engaged the plane's inertia starter. My eyes scrolled over the assortment of instruments in the cockpit, making sure each functioned properly and that all locks, cages, and battens had been removed. Looking at one of the signalmen, I gave a thumbs-up. My plane had barely started its engine before the first planes began roaring off the deck. At 4:45, the takeoff signal director gave a motion, and six F4Fs from Fighting Six climbed into the air and took position as the Combat Air Patrol (CAP), that is, the fighter swarm designated to provide cover for the task force. Next, CDR Young received a signal from the bridge: "Commence the airstrike." The takeoff director pointed at Young, who engaged his throttle, and his plane raced down the deck. One by one, my squadron's planes followed, throttling their engines and getting airborne.

Urgent signals of lighted wands guided me to takeoff position. The signal officer pointed at me and spun his hand round and round above his head, directing me to turn up full power. I glanced at all my plane's instruments and nodded. Sail-Seventeen was ready to go. I was ready to go. The signal wands came down and forward. My plane rolled forward into the thirty-knot wind. I had to accelerate to 105 knots within the space of a football field, all the room I had available to take off. I followed a few hooded lights marking my "runway." Ahead of me I could see a flicker of exhaust denoting the previous plane as it ascended into the darkness like a firefly. Everything else was black as ink. Using the lights, I cleared the bow, raised my wheels, and felt the "settling" sensation the moment my plane left the flight deck.

Taking off from a carrier at night was tricky business. Each pilot had to accelerate quickly, lest he lose sight of the plane in front of him. The only way to rendezvous in the air was to watch the blue exhaust flame from the preceding plane and follow it to cruising altitude. If a single pilot delayed too long, then the whole squadron could be strung out and unable to gain formation until sunlight. Conversely, if a pilot accelerated too quickly, then he might risk a midair collision, or worse, a crash on the deck. I jotted down the time of takeoff, 4:50, keeping my eyes glued to the exhaust lights ahead of me, particularly those belonging to our group and squadron commander. CDR Young and LCDR Hopping each executed a gentle turn, allowing the trailing planes to catch up. Hopping flashed his pale blue wing-mounted recognition lights, indicating that I had joined the correct formation. In turn, I flashed yellow lights to my wingmen, allowing them to join me. I fishtailed until my section leader and wingman caught up and we formed our three-plane V with wingtips only ten feet apart. After a single, gentle turn around the carrier, all but one of the Scouting Six planes had joined the formation, and then Hopping signaled "lights out."

The whole process proceeded ungracefully. During the ascent, Bombing Six passed through the third section of Scouting Six, nearly causing a midair accident. Additionally, ENS Daniel Seid's scout bomber missed its takeoff opportunity due to engine trouble. It took off later and had to trail after the rest of the group. Altogether, it took about fifteen minutes to get two dive bomber squadrons—thirty-six planes—airborne. At 5:00, nine TBD Devastators—all of them armed with 500-pound contact bombs—got airborne and trailed after us. Together the predawn strike consisted of forty-six planes. We were in the pitch-darkness at 14,000 feet, but I could hear the rumbling engines of our planes. I was part of a massive, potent strike, one intended to give the Japanese defenders at Kwajalein a rude awakening.

After the takeoff our errors didn't cease. About fifteen miles from the atoll, just as the first rays of light doused the horizon with an orange haze, a great roar resounded from LTJG Fogg's plane. Apparently Fogg had charged his guns too early—and then nicked the trigger. Because of an apparent electrical defect, the very one he had been carping about in the ready room, his forward machine guns fired on automatic, a process that he could have stopped had he pulled back on the charging handle, but in the heat of the moment, he didn't do it. I watched helplessly as Foggy shot away his fixed-gun ammunition. The noise spooked the other pilots flying close to him, for he nearly shot some of them. Luckily, no one was hurt.

If Foggy's error had not alerted the Japanese defenders, LCDR Hopping's navigational errors surely did. According to our plan of action, Hopping was supposed to begin the attack precisely at 7:00, taking Scouting Six down against two conjoined islands, Roi and Namur, the northernmost islands of the atoll. Due to an error in the wind data, Hopping flew over Roi fifteen minutes early. When the air strike had launched two hours earlier, the weather balloon had failed to indicate a heavy tailwind. Thus we arrived on the scene well before sunrise, before we could initiate our diving attacks. Flying in the dark and utilizing outdated maps, Hopping failed to identify Roi-Namur from the air, and our noisy engines alerted the Japanese defenders. Hopping eventually realized his mistake, so he made an abrupt course correction, returning us to the north side of Roi-Namur; still, we had to circle for about fifteen minutes until it became light enough to attack. At 7:05, Hopping finally signaled that it was time to begin. Unfortunately, by this time the Japanese airmen had already begun scrambling their single-seat fighters. These were Type-96 Mitsubishi A5M fighter planes, which mounted two machine guns in the fuselage. Although not as fast as their better-known cousins, the A6M "Zeros," they were incredibly nimble and promised to give us a hell of a fight. The enemy fighters came at us just as we began our attack. So much for the element of surprise! The only positive outcome of this whole miscalculation was that the delay allowed ENS Seid's plane time to catch up.

When Hopping finally called for the attack on Roi, breaking radio silence, he let us know that we had discretion in choosing our targets. Hopping called for the first division's planes to follow him down. He put his plane into a shallow dive, at about forty-five degrees instead of the usual seventy-five.* All of the antiaircraft gunners on Roi-Namur trained their sights on our skipper's plane. It looked like a red fountain of fireworks. The air was full of antiaircraft fire. In fact, it was practically choking, and down below it looked like myriad flickering lights. I snorted. This "little undefended island," as our superiors called it, was tossing plenty of ammunition.

Hopping's plane made an easy target, coming in slow and at such a low altitude that it was silhouetted against the rising daylight. All the enemy guns were trained on him; he didn't have a chance. One of the first Japanese fighters rose up and found itself right on Hopping's tail. The enemy pilot fired a few short bursts, and seconds later, our gallant squadron commander's riddled plane

---

* For various reasons, dive bombing doctrine recommended going into dives at sixty-five degrees. Our squadron preferred about ten degrees steeper.

plummeted into the ocean, killing him and his gunner, RM 1/c
Harold Thomas. Thankfully, the other five planes from the first division dived through the antiaircraft fire and the fighter cover and
began dropping their 100-pounders, pockmarking Roi's airfield,
lighting up the dimly lit battlefield with brilliant sparks of flame.

LT Gallaher called out to the planes from our division, telling us
to delay our attack and circle back around for a steeper dive. As we
circled, we came nose-to-nose with the same Japanese fighter that
shot down LCDR Hopping. Gallaher broke to the side and rotated
his plane, giving his gunner, RM 1/c Thomas Merritt, a perfect
shot at the passing plane. Merritt fired a burst from his .30-caliber
machine gun, sending this enemy fighter plunging into the water.
No one saw a parachute. It was the first kill of the day.

High above Roi, Gallaher signaled the next wave of the attack. He nosed over, followed by his two wingmen, Foggy and Bill
West. Here I witnessed another crash. Foggy made a perfect dive
over the airfield, dropping all three bombs atop a set of barracks
from an altitude of 500 feet. His bombing attack resulted in ter-
rific damage, probably killing the base commander, but after the
pullout, his plane began to fly erratically. It turned northeast, back
toward *Enterprise*, so it seemed, but after traveling one-half mile, it
crashed into the sea and submerged. It had either been hit by antiaircraft fire or damaged by shrapnel from Foggy's own bomb blast.
In any event, Foggy and his gunner, RM 3/c Otis L. Dennis, were
never seen again.

After Gallaher, Foggy, and West dropped their bombs, LT Rutherford nosed over with his two wingmen, ENS Earl R. Donnell and
me. Because we knew so little about Roi's installations, we chose
our own targets. I could see a runway, so I aimed for it. We attempted a "by the book" dive. Prepping an SBD for a diving attack
required several steps. First, I called over the interphone to John
Snowden, letting him know that we were about to dive and that he

should take his dose of ephedrine, a nasal spray that prevented an aviator's eardrums from bursting due to the sudden change in altitude. Second, I reached under my seat to pull out my bombs' arming pins so they would detonate after release. Third, I switched my plane to low blower and low prop pitch.* Then I engaged the full split flaps, which allowed me to zero in on my target. Next, I opened up the pilot's cockpit hatch in order to prevent the window from fogging up due to the change in temperature. Finally, I took my dose of ephedrine. When my plane was ready, I "pushed over," throwing the stick forward and putting the plane's nose down.

My plane screamed out of the atmosphere like a banshee, descending from 14,000 feet to 2,000 feet in about thirty seconds. As the cool air roared around my open cockpit, I peered through the Mark-3 bomb scope and surveyed the runway. Fires already speckled the field. I sighted a parked plane. With my other eye I glanced at my altimeter, watching it spin wildly and counting down the seconds to release altitude. All the while, Japanese antiaircraft gunners plied their work of death, filling the sky with puffs of shrapnel. At 2,000 feet I gripped the bomb release on the left side of the cockpit and wrenched the lever, releasing my two 100-pound wing bombs. When I was certain these bombs had dropped clear, I executed a snap pullout, and for a brief instant, the pressure of 8 or 9 g's squeezed my body. With long, heavy breaths, I kept the world in front of me as it tunneled because of all the blood rushing out

---

* The SBD contained a mechanism in the cockpit called the "blower," or "supercharger," a compressor that increased air density, allowing the engine to draw more fuel and increase its performance. At high altitudes, engine performance declined because air density and air pressure decreased. The blower had two settings, "high" and "low." Usually we used low blower only during takeoff and landings, but on this occasion I wanted good engine performance when I reached my pullout, so I switched to low blower because it served the engine better at sea level.

of my head, and rolled out of my dive with another ninety-degree turn. Below and behind me the parked enemy plane disappeared in a ball of flame. As I leveled out, I opened fire with my .50-caliber forward machine guns, strafing the airfield.

I pulled hard on the stick to regain altitude. I knew I had to form up with my wingmen in order to survive. We tended to be at our most vulnerable immediately following pullout, that is, right after we reduced speed. In a few seconds I picked up the locations of LT Rutherford and ENS Donnell, but so had the Japanese. A Japanese fighter slid underneath my plane, targeting Donnell. He did not ascend quickly, so his plane made an inviting target for the hotshot Japanese fighter pilot. A quick burst of machine gun fire perforated this unfortunate SBD-2, releasing a yellow-orange cascade of burning aviation gas from the destroyed fuel tanks in the wing roots. Donnell's plane rolled over in flames, hitting the water, killing the young pilot and his gunner, AMM 2/c Alton J. Travis. Donnell was gone; if I survived, I knew I would have to inform Donnell's parents about it.

The Japanese fighter that shot down Donnell pulled out of its pass, climbing above my plane, and then it dived on me from behind. For a few seconds it looked as if I would be splashed, too, but John Snowden swung the rear guns into position and let loose a hail of fire. Snowden's well-aimed volley hammered the enemy fighter and it plummeted past without returning fire, missing a midair collision by about twenty feet. I pitched forward and let him have it with my .50-caliber machine guns. After I ceased shooting, the out-of-control fighter spiraled downward. For a moment I lost sight of it, until I noticed flames burning brightly against the dark water. The stricken fighter arched northward, over Roi-Namur, and it crashed one thousand feet out to sea, nearly hitting the spot where Donnell's plane had gone down. No one bailed out of it. I breathed a sigh of relief. There was no doubt that John's marksmanship had saved our lives.

I pulled back on the stick to regain altitude. I still had my 500-pound bomb, and I wanted to use it. We had expected to find enemy surface ships at Roi's anchorage, but intelligence had proven incorrect on that point. I headed to the next logical choice, Kwajalein anchorage. Kwajalein Island, the largest island in the atoll, was about forty miles to the southwest. A flight to that location would test my fuel supply, but I was willing to risk it. As I regained diving altitude, I noticed two other SBDs heading in the same direction, Sail-Four and Sail-Eight, flown by LT Dickinson and ENS Dobson. I joined Dickinson and Dobby, and soon CDR Young's voice echoed over the radio, "Targets suitable for heavy bombs. Targets for heavy bombs at Kwajalein anchorage." We needed no further encouragement.

With my plane on the right, Dobby's in the middle, and Dickinson's on the left, we made haste for the anchorage, arriving there at 7:45. By now broad daylight bathed the atoll. We could see the enemy vessels clearly, but of course, the Japanese antiaircraft gunners had eyes on us as well. Below, in the calm water of the lagoon, I viewed an assortment of targets, including a dozen auxiliary ships: tankers, seaplane tenders, submarines, and oilers; however, the most noticeable target was the 5,800-ton light cruiser *Katori*, anchored at the end of a pier. The gunners on the immobile cruiser sighted us and started shooting.

When I spied *Katori*, I looked around for fighters. I saw none. I said to myself, "Oh boy! This is great!" For a second time in an hour, I went into a combat dive. I picked up *Katori*, watching it enlarge in my sights, and at 1,500 feet I released my 500-pounder, which slammed square amidships. I didn't see the blast, but John Snowden did, and he said I really clobbered it. The detonation tore a hole in the side of the ship and seawater began rushing in. I thought I had sunk it; however, I later learned the Japanese managed to sail it out of the lagoon and back to Yokosuka for repairs. Meanwhile, Dickinson and Dobby dived at other targets, two tankers making their way to the channels that led out to sea.

As I pulled out of my dive, I noticed a radio station on Enubuj Island, a landmass on the southeast side of the atoll. As I careened toward it, I realized I was in extreme danger. Like a hot dog, I had taken a flight path directly between the twin towers and realized too late that I could not fly between the antennas because thick wires connected them. My heart raced. If I hit that cable or struck one of those towers I knew it would be the end of me. Instinctively, I squeezed the trigger on my forward machine guns and blasted apart one of the towers. It fell, clearing a path above the treetops. The way open, my plane wafted over the island and headed out to sea. I never collided with anything. Strange as it is to say, I worried more about the tower falling on me than I had with the cruiser shooting at me moments earlier. As I headed east, toward daylight, I caught sight of Dickinson's and Dobby's planes, both cruising at 155 knots about ten miles ahead. It took us about two hours to return to *Enterprise*.

My companions and I landed at about 10:00 A.M. John Snowden and I had precious little time to report to LT Gallaher and learn the results of the attack. In a few short minutes I learned that four Scouting Six aircraft had not returned. I already knew the Japanese had shot down the planes piloted by Hopping, Fogg, and Donnell, killing all six crewmen. Additionally, I now learned that Sail-Six, the plane piloted by Daniel Seid, had also crashed north of Roi. No one knew why it went down, but Seid and his gunner, AMM 3/c David F. Grogg, were dead.

I followed Dobby and Dickinson into the wardroom and there we devoured a hearty meal of sandwiches, pineapple juice, and coffee. In sharing stories from the attack, I learned we had done well. At Roi we destroyed six planes on the ground, in addition to two hangars, two buildings, and six storehouses. At Kwajalein anchorage we damaged four ships: two tankers, a supply ship, and the cruiser I had bombed, which later received a second bomb hit courtesy of Earl Gallaher. One of the most important strikes, though, was the bomb hit delivered by Dobby, who dropped his 500-pounder on the bow of a tanker attempting to make its way out to sea. The tanker stopped dead in the Carlos Pass, one of the few deepwater channels that allowed ships to escape the lagoon. When news of Dobby's bull's-eye reached Admiral Halsey, he determined that *Enterprise* should launch another strike. We needed to go back and finish off the trapped Japanese ships. This would also be an excellent chance to test the TBD crews. If their torpedoes could not sink stationary transports in calm waters, it would definitively prove the Mark-13 torpedo would never work under combat conditions—something that our torpedo plane pilots already feared after long experience.

Despite the impressive damage inflicted upon the enemy, I should point out that Scouting Six was the only squadron from *Enterprise* to lose planes. In addition to the four planes lost in combat, six were so badly damaged that they had to be sent below, kept for parts on the hangar deck. Further, Bill West had received a wound through the right shoulder, having been hit by gunfire while tangling with an enemy fighter. This wound knocked Bill off the flight schedule for a full month. By comparison, all nine TBD-1 Devastators returned, as did all eighteen SBD-2s belonging to Bombing Six. All of Fighting Six's Grumman F4F-3 Wildcats returned, except one that had crashed during the predawn takeoff.

As we snacked, word of the second air strike came down to the wardroom. After only a half hour of rest, I learned that the repair crew had refueled and rearmed my plane. LT Gallaher told me that, for this mission, I must fly with Bombing Six. Shortly after Halsey ordered the second strike on Kwajalein, he ordered two additional missions. Now he also wanted *Enterprise*'s dive bombers to hammer the Japanese bases on Maloelap Atoll and Wotje Island. Accordingly, I had orders to accompany eight rearmed Bombing Six SBDs. Our target was Taroa, a small island on the eastern rim of Maloelap. LT Dick Best led our contingent. At 10:40, ten minutes after learning of the new mission, I joined John Snowden on the flight deck. We mounted Sail-Seventeen for a second time, and within minutes we were roaring down *Enterprise*'s deck, again on our way to enemy territory.

LT Best led us to 13,000 feet and headed south, flying past Wotje—the target of a contingent of planes led by Gallaher—arriving at Taroa from the north. At about 11:30, as our planes came within ten miles of the island, I noticed three Japanese fighters patrolling the eastern waters. This was ill news. Would they see us? LT Best considered it wise to fly underneath them and not draw any attention. We cruised under them, as ordered, and reached a point just east of Taroa. There we lined our planes up for a diving attack. However, just as we completed our maneuver, the three Japanese planes spotted us. LT Best had to make a quick decision: continue with the diving attack or abort the mission? Best was a brave, bold man—utterly unflappable. His response was predictable. He ordered us to form into column and begin the attack at once. Best realized that our rear-seat gunners would have to sacrifice their mutual protection once we were strung out into a line, but we—the pilots—would have more time to choose our targets on the ground. I flew in the first three-plane section, on Best's wing, so I had first choice of what to hit.

As we sped toward the "push over" point, I turned my head, watching the three Japanese fighters swoop down from above my starboard bow. I engaged my split flaps and my plane slowed so rapidly that all of the Japanese fighters dived past me. One Japanese plane came close. I can still remember the sound it made. WHOOSH! When I close my eyes, sometimes, I can visualize the pilot's goggled face looking up at me. Safe for the moment, I followed Best into his dive, careening through a barrage of antiaircraft fire. During my dive, flak burst near the rear seat of my plane, sending a piece of shrapnel glancing off John Snowden's buttocks. Dutifully, John thought it unwise to mention his minor injury until we returned to *Enterprise*. At 1,500 feet, I released two bombs—my 500-pounder and one of my 100-pounders—striking a hangar. As I swooped out of my dive, bearing west over the atoll, the three Japanese fighters closed for another attack. I swung my plane to give John his favorite firing angle, but nothing happened. My eyes widened, and I said to myself: "He has never taken more than five seconds to do his thing!" I leaned over the side to see if John had been hit, but just then a bullet whizzed above my head, striking the framework. For a few terrifying seconds, machine gun fire rattled my plane. Holes opened up in my plane's starboard wing tanks and one shot bounced into the cockpit, glancing off the antenna post above my headrest. Had I been taller, I would have been killed. John looked back at me and signaled that he had shot away most of his ammunition. He had targeted enemy antiaircraft gunners when we strafed the island. I had to use my forward machine guns to chase away these bandits.

Pulling a tight wingover, I flew straight at the nearest fighter. I made some sort of snap turn. I don't know what it was. I had never done it before, but it got me in position to get a burst at the fighter, and it went down, apparently headed for a crash. Later on, I discovered that I couldn't claim him as a definite kill because I never saw him hit. He either limped home with his friends or he died when his plane slammed into the waters around Maloelap. My plane was not in great shape. Both starboard wing tanks were filled with holes and I could see the gasoline billowing out in a cloud. Amazingly, the wing tanks did not catch fire, and I knew immediately that I had escaped with a bit of luck. My number-six cylinder, however, was spewing oil onto the windshield from a bullet hole. I was flying an SBD-2, not an SBD-3. There was a big difference between the two. The latter possessed self-sealing fuel tanks; the former did not. As we discovered, whenever an SBD-2 took machine gun fire to the fuel tanks, it usually caught fire. This was what happened to Donnell earlier in the day. For some reason, my ordinary fuel tanks—the non-self-sealing kind—didn't catch fire. I thank God every day for that. Somehow, I was spared a fiery death. Even better, the other two Japanese fighters decided not to pursue. Had they pressed their attack I would probably have been a goner.

I turned north, flying back over my inbound path. Of course, *Enterprise* had changed position by then, so when I reached open water—where it had once been—and when I was certain that no enemy planes had tracked me back along this path, I turned west. I found our carrier at 1:15 P.M. and landed safely on the flight deck, catching wire number three. Of the nine planes under LT Best, eight had made it back, and of those, four, including my own, had been damaged. One plane, Baker-Fifteen, had been shot down, killing ENS John J. Doherty of Bombing Six and his gunner, AOM 3/c William Hunt.

I dismounted my plane and surveyed the damage. The line chief reported that my plane had five gallons of fuel remaining and was too shot up to fly. A Japanese bullet had penetrated one of my engine cylinders. More surprising, I learned that John Snowden had been wounded, indicated by a bloodstain on his backside. He apologized to me profusely for shooting away all his ammunition at the antiaircraft gunners on Taroa. He admitted he should have reserved some for the fighters. Gosh, what a modest man! I replied that no apology was necessary. I was just glad John was okay. I remarked to myself, "He'll pay for this by his daily visits to sick bay, between flights, of course, where shrapnel will be removed from his ass."

I sauntered across the flight deck and entered Scouting Six's ready room. There, for a second time, I began swapping stories with my comrades. I learned that six of them had just returned from a second bombing mission of their own, the one over Wotje Island. There at the anchorage, they had damaged two cargo ships. Our conversation had lasted only ten minutes when the deafening clangor of the Klaxon sounded general quarters. LT Gallaher walked into the ready room and announced, "Enemy planes have been sighted. They are approaching." We buzzed with excitement. Somehow the Japanese had found our task force! About 3,500 yards off the starboard bow, coming out of a cloud, five twin-engine bombers charged at *Enterprise*. LT Dickinson idly opened a battle port cover. There, framed in the porthole, we could see the flight of enemy planes closing in.

"My God! Here they come!" Dickinson shouted and hit the deck, hiding behind a row of chairs. He was the only member of Scouting Six to take cover. Another member of the squadron asked him why he did that. He replied that flat like that was the safest place to be when a bomb hit. We all laughed at him and took turns at the porthole, narrating events just to make him more nervous. The moment was therapeutic for me. I was still angry at him because he had not apologized for the movie fracas back in September, the incident that nearly killed me. It was soothing for me to see Dickinson in a comical moment of weakness. Months later, when I finally had an opportunity to read his serial memoir, I was shocked to see it bearing the brazen title, "I Fly for Vengeance!" *I Fly for Vengeance*? Would you believe it, that's the name of his book! When I arrived at the moment where Dickinson narrated the attack by the twin-engine bombers, I noticed he failed to mention how he took cover on the floor of the ready room. Maybe I shouldn't be so vindictive. When we tell war stories, we veterans unconsciously leave out all the details that embarrass us. I wonder what I've unconsciously left out now.

I didn't waste any more than a few minutes toying with Dickinson; I wanted to see the action firsthand. Along with other Scouting Six pilots, I ran onto the flight deck and watched awestruck as *Enterprise*'s starboard gunners opened up, unleashing fury at the five planes. They struck the lead plane and it began streaming gas. All five enemy bombers flew over the carrier and dropped their payloads from about 3,000 feet. Happily, all their ordnance splashed harmlessly to port. Having expended their bombs, all the Japanese bombers charted a course for home—all except one. The damaged lead plane turned around and dived toward *Enterprise* from port. It became clear that its pilot—who I later found out was a man named Lieutenant Kazuo Nakai—intended to crash his plane onto our carrier's deck. It looked like *Enterprise* was about to take a mortal hit.

At that moment, I saw one of the most amazing things I've ever seen in my long life. A sailor jumped into the rear seat of a parked SBD-2. He raised the twin .30-caliber machine guns and commenced firing. His shots perforated the incoming suicide bomber, and at the last second, the smoking Japanese plane pitched to the right, causing the starboard wing to graze the flight deck. The wing clipped the tail of the parked SBD-2, severing its stabilizer and spinning the plane and its intrepid occupant in a half circle. Incredibly, the rear-seat gunner kept firing, pumping more bullets into the doomed Japanese bomber, even as it careened over *Enterprise*'s starboard side, spewing gasoline over the deck. The next instant, the Japanese plane exploded and the wreckage sank. *Enterprise* had been saved by the action of a single sailor.

But that was not all. The puddle of gasoline caught fire. Grabbing a fire extinguisher from the rear seat of his plane, this super-hero-sailor leaped onto the deck and quelled the blaze. By the time the damage control crew reached the scene, the fire was subdued and the brave sailor had vanished. Shocked by what we had seen, my squadron mates and I inched our way to the damaged plane, gawking at the hole caused by the missing stabilizer. I looked at the markings. It was none other than Sail-Five, my old SBD-2. It was a sad moment for the plane, but Sail-Five's career ended in glory. One thing was certain: whoever had manned its rear-seat guns must have been a member of our squadron.

From above, I heard a great bellow. "Bring that man up to me!" I beheld the grim visage of Admiral Halsey peering over the rim of the port bridge wing. He demanded the name of the sailor who had saved his flagship. At first no one could answer Halsey's request. About twenty people had been on deck when the suicide attack occurred, but no one came forward to claim credit for shooting down the bomber. Six officers went onto the flight deck and asked around, but they returned no useful information. One of them admitted to the admiral that the sailor could not be found. Halsey snorted, "You can't find him?" He glowered, his face making it clear that he would not accept another "I don't know" report. Halsey now sent ten officers, instructing them to seek out various sailors known to have been on deck. After an hour's worth of interviews, the crew finally nailed it down. They identified the man as AMM 3/c Bruno Peter Gaido, same man who had tagged along on my first six carrier landings back in May 1941.

Halsey said, "Send him up here!"

Gaido reported to the bridge, and Halsey asked him point-blank why he acted so boldly.

With the same calm demeanor I had witnessed months earlier, Gaido replied, "Well, nobody else was shooting at him and he was going to hit the carrier, so I just got out there and shot at him, and that's all there was to it."

Halsey was incredulous. "There was a fire out there," he said. "Nobody can explain who was carrying the fire extinguisher and put the flames out."

Gaido replied, "I guess I grabbed the fire extinguisher and did that."

"Why didn't you tell someone about this?"

Gaido looked a bit embarrassed. "Well, I was supposed to be on watch. I left my post because I thought the attacking plane was more important. After I put out the fire, I put on my uniform and went back to doing what I was supposed to be doing."

Halsey's furrowed brow softened a bit. "What are you? What's your rating?"

Gaido replied, "Machinist mate, third class."

"You are now machinist mate, first class!"

Gaido received a battlefield promotion. Whenever we saw him, we gave him a cheer and a pat on the back. I think I gave him more praise than anybody. Whenever he explained why he jumped into the back of Sail-Five, he said, "Well, what else would I have done? Anyone could have done that!" To him these actions were something anyone should be expected to do, and therefore they merited no praise. I disagreed. Not everyone had the guts to do what Gaido did. He had shown impressive valor. In fact, he was the bravest man I ever met. I admired his approach to duty. It was one of boldness and modesty. I hoped that if the chance ever came my way, I could emulate it.

Before my carrier wrapped up its combat operations in the Marshall Islands, I learned some disappointing news. I spoke to Tom Eversole about his experience in the battle. He told me that none of the nine torpedoes had hit their intended targets.

Eversole had been part of the second wave. At 7:31, his squadron's XO, LT Lance E. Massey, led nine torpedo bombers armed with Mark-13 aerial torpedoes. They had orders to attack the Japanese transports trapped in the lagoon at Kwajalein. Although the torpedo bomber pilots expected their targets to be virtually immobile, they knew it would be a risky mission. They had to go in without a fighter escort and without a smoke screen. Further, LT Massey told his pilots they had to fly slow and low to the water, so as not to disrupt the delicate systems on the Mark-13. At 9:05, after cruising 180 miles, the nine torpedo bombers made their attack and dropped their torpedoes. When they returned to the carrier at 11:30, none of the pilots were certain they had done any damage. The after-action reports specified that one torpedo detonated prematurely on a coral outcropping. They also claimed four hits and two possible hits against the enemy ships, but these reports are in variance with Japanese damage assessments, which specified only one torpedo explosion. And the official reports are also in variance with what Tom told me.

Call me a "conspiracy theorist" if you wish, but it's my humble opinion that someone altered *Enterprise*'s action reports, covering over the fact that the torpedoes almost always failed. I don't know why anyone would want to hide the fact that our planes deployed torpedoes that had only a minuscule chance of success, but I think it is a great shame they did so. I also don't know why the Mark-13 aerial torpedoes usually failed to explode. Perhaps their exploders misfired or perhaps they ran too erratically under the water. But I know this: if our pilots could not sink stationary tankers in calm waters under ideal weather conditions, what chance did they have if they confronted armed warships on choppy seas while dodging antiaircraft fire and enemy planes? If the torpedoes detonated only 11 percent of the time under ideal conditions, any fool could see they would detonate zero percent of the time under horrific combat conditions. If anyone ever decided to deploy the torpedo bombers, they had better arm them with bombs.*

All in all, I was pleased with the battle. We had struck the Japanese and made them pay for what they did to our fleet at Pearl Harbor. I was pleased with the bravery of my squadron, even Dickinson. When he was in the air, he displayed the same stern stuff as everyone else.

I wrote to Jean, "I wish I could tell you some of the places I've been and what we've been doing. Someday, perhaps, I can. But just now all I can say is that our men have got more guts and our gun-

<hr />

* Although I didn't find out any of this until later, the Bureau of Ordnance didn't conduct satisfactory tests on the Mark-13 until 1943. During a test at Newport, bureau officers cataloged 105 torpedo drops, recording satisfactory runs out of only 31 percent of them. Even so, every torpedo suffered from at least one defect. Some failed to arm, some sank, some ran crooked, some ran too deep or too shallow, and some had weak propellers, meaning they couldn't run fast enough to reach an enemy ship. Nearly all of these defects occurred because pieces of the Mark-13 destabilized during the torpedoes' rough entry into the water. Even if a torpedo plane flew at the slowest possible speed, 100 percent of all drops resulted in some kind of defect, even if it didn't lead to an unsatisfactory run. Eventually the Bureau of Ordnance corrected these problems by developing wooden drag rings and shroud rings to stabilize the torpedoes' entry into the water. With these alterations, by 1944 the Mark-13 became a reliable weapon. Of course, this was poor consolation to the torpedo squadrons that operated in 1942. They routinely experienced misfires. For instance, on March 10, at Lae and Salamaua, Torpedo Two dropped thirteen torpedoes against fourteen Japanese transports, scoring only one hit. On May 2, at Tulagi, Torpedo Five dropped seventeen torpedoes (in two separate attacks) and scored only one hit. The only aberration came at the Battle of the Coral Sea. On May 7, 1942, Torpedo Two and Torpedo Five dropped twenty-two torpedoes and claimed nineteen hits. The next day, both squadrons attacked again, dropping twenty torpedoes, claiming another eight hits. Many of these "confirmed" hits were exaggerations. Japanese reports indicated that Torpedo Two and Torpedo Five scored, at most, seven hits on May 7 and no hits on May 8. So even when the torpedoes appeared to function, they still underperformed.

ners have a better eye than those of any other country." I couldn't tell Jean about my brushes with death, but I let her know that a battle had occurred, that I'd fought in it, and that all her prayers had helped. I commented, "Here I am again. You and God did a splendid job, but I'll admit that for a while I was worried. Snowden, my radioman, got a nick in one leg (or rather, a scratch) and I got nothing worse than a torn shirt . . . and that, my love, is the extent of my injuries in a good many months of flying."

On February 3, *Enterprise* set sail for Hawaii. I had fought my first memorable battle in the Central Pacific. This was but a taste of what was to come.

CHAPTER 11

WAKE AND MARCUS ISLANDS
February–March 1942

Task Force 8 returned to Pearl Harbor on February 5. For three days we had liberty and a free stay at the Royal Hawaiian Hotel. I had a chance to recharge, pause, and reflect on the direction my life had taken. The grim warrior spirit brought on by the war and my longing for Jean were in conflict with each other. Exhilarated by the rush of battle, I wanted to fight my nation's enemies, but at the same time, I longed to return home and live a life of love and peace. After our stay at the Royal Hawaiian came to an end, I wrote this to Jean: "I want to say beautiful things to you tonight, m'love, but I just can't. I got a couple of days of liberty a short while back—got to walk on soft grass, look at stars and clouds and mountains—and then I could have. But tonight my mind's so full of thinking how to bump off Japs there isn't much room for anything else. Life's so mixed up and so unreal that I could use a lot of your optimism tonight."

My window of personal reflection closed quickly. My squadron had to rebuild. During our brief period in port, Scouting Six received some new planes, "dash-threes," that is, SBD-3s to replace the "dash-twos" lost in the Battle of the Marshall Islands. The changes made to the "dash-three" model were important. First, they had no wing-mounted flotation bags. We had been complaining about the flotation devices so much the Navy finally listened and decided to remove them from the new combat model. Second, as mentioned earlier, all SBD-3s had self-sealing fuel tanks. After the Marshall battle, LT Gallaher made it clear that self-sealing tanks were essential to combat operations. His report contained this warning: "It is believed that the loss of airplanes would have been less had the planes been equipped with leak-proof tanks." Now, if perforated by enemy fire, an SBD might not break out into flames, as had happened to ENS Donnell's plane over Roi. Importantly, the new SBD-3s brought with them a special gadget, the YE-ZB homing system, a radio device that allowed us to home in on our carrier. This system consisted of a high-frequency transmitter (the YE) attached to a carrier's antenna array and a coded receiver (the ZB) installed on the plane. Each carrier's antenna emitted a signal in Morse code—one of twelve predesignated letters—accounting for every thirty degrees' arc around the ship. A returning carrier pilot entered in the code for his home carrier—in my case, USS *Enterprise*—and by listening for the Morse-coded letter, he instantly knew the direction of his ship. Under ideal conditions, we could follow the beam to within 500 yards of our home base. The first ZB receivers did not arrive until February 1941, and during the first months of the war, only three Scouting Six SBD-2s had them installed. Now, thanks to our feedback, YE-ZBs came standard issue in the SBD-3s. During our first carrier takeoffs with an SBD-3, John Snowden practiced relentlessly changing the radio coils; as gunner, it was his responsibility to prepare the ZB device in flight, and after a battle, to help me navigate our way home.[*]

---

[*] My new plane was an SBD-3 designated Sail-Eleven (Bureau No. 4665). Nine days of tinkering finally prepped it for battle.

New pilots—temporary transfers from other squadrons—arrived. With Hopping dead, LT Gallaher received command of the squadron. LT Rutherford assumed command of the second division and Dickinson retained command of the third division. We all felt gut-wrenching sadness at losing Hopping. He was a wonderful, attentive leader, but Gallaher was a superb replacement. He led us by example. He demanded perfection and he got it. On February 13, Gallaher warned us to stow our gear. Halsey had another adventure for us. The next day, *Enterprise* departed Pearl Harbor and set sail on another war cruise, heading westward. Halfway into the voyage, we learned we were going to assault Wake Island. Weeks earlier, on December 23, that island's Marine contingent had surrendered to an overwhelming Japanese assault. Everyone in the United States knew the heroic story of the outnumbered defenders of Wake. Now we had orders to hammer the Japanese occupants. Essentially, Halsey and Nimitz wanted us to repeat our performance in the Marshall Islands. To clear out the Central Pacific, we had to start by eliminating the Japanese planes, runways, and hangars on all their outlying bases. We needed to remind them that their island possessions weren't invulnerable.

Poor weather marred our voyage. *Enterprise* sent out reconnaissance missions every day, and on February 18, Tom Eversole's torpedo bomber crashed. A storm rolled in during Tom's return trip and his plane didn't have enough fuel to make it back. After setting down in the water, Tom and his two crewmen, AMM 2/c L. C. Pederson and RM 3/c J. M. Blundell, inflated their rubber life raft and started paddling east.

Back on board the carrier, everyone was worried, particularly me. I considered Tom my best friend on the ship. Would Poseidon swallow Tom and his two companions? Admiral Halsey brightened my dour disposition when he ordered the entire task force to alter heading to go after the missing crew. The next day, one of the replacement pilots for Scouting Six, ENS Robert K. Campbell, spotted the life raft and reported its location. When Campbell landed aboard *Enterprise* he told us an interesting story. He had seen Tom sitting calmly in the back of the raft, navigating his way to Midway Atoll, about 250 miles east, while his two enlisted men rowed like fiends. The whole scene, as Campbell described it, was hilarious to us, and now that we knew Tom was safe, we had some fun at his expense. A ship cartoonist drew up a caricature that depicted Tom as an old sea captain, hand in coat, watching serenely as his two crewmen rowed exasperatedly from their sinking plane. He labeled it, "Eversole gets a command afloat." I was overjoyed when a destroyer reported that it had picked up Tom. The morale on the whole ship went way up. We all thought to ourselves, If Halsey would turn the whole fleet around to look for just one aircrew, he might well do the same for me. We felt confident that if we had to ditch, the fleet would come looking for us.

By February 23, our task force still made no contacts with enemy ships or planes, making it abundantly clear that our air group would fly the next day. If everything went according to plan, our air strike would take off one hundred miles north of Wake. The February 24 launch followed the same pattern as the air raid of February 1. We had instructions to bomb and strafe Wake's landing strip, barracks, seaplane ramps, hangars, planes, and fuel storage, and then wait until four surface ships (two cruisers and two destroyers) arrived to bombard the island. The hours leading up to the assault were worrisome for me. Like many, I expected Wake to be heavily defended. After rising at an early hour, eating breakfast, and reporting to the ready room, I scribbled a single letter to Jean, one that might have been my last if things had gone differently. I concluded: "Wish me luck, Jean darling, because these days, now, I especially need it. You know that you have all my love and nothing else do I have to give. If anything should happen to me you will always know that I send my last thoughts to you. Love, always, Jack."

Not much longer after signing off, at 5:30, the yeoman cried out, "Pilots, man your planes!"

Running onto the flight deck, I entered a shroud of misty rain, ugly conditions for a morning launch. When we revved our engines we discovered we couldn't see the horizon. When our spinning propellers slapped the moist air, it created a halo effect, making it impossible for any of us to see straight ahead. Despite the danger, ten F4Fs got airborne, right on schedule, four of them slated for CAP and six others assigned as our attack group's escorts. Thirty-seven SBDs launched next, to be followed by nine TBDs armed with contact bombs. LT Gallaher piloted the first Scouting Six plane. He got airborne all right, but the second plane, Sail-Two, flown by my roommate, Perry Teaff, took off forty-five degrees to the bow, veering to port and slamming into an antiaircraft gun on its way into the ocean.

A brand-new signal officer had caused the accident by giving an incorrect motion. Instead of gesturing "make forty-five-degree turn to the right," he gestured, "Immediate takeoff," indicating that Enterprise's bow, invisible to the pilot, was dead ahead. In fact, Perry's plane was crooked, and in the fog he could not see more than forty feet in front of his plane. When his dive bomber hit the water, the impact smashed Perry's face against the bomb scope, destroying his left eye. One of the escorting destroyers, USS Blue (DD-387), arrived on the scene to rescue him. They picked him up and took him to sick bay. Perry's gunner, RM 3/c Edgar P. Jinks, was glimpsed climbing out of the sinking plane, but could not be found after that. The destroyer crew could hear Jinks shouting for help, but in the fog they failed to locate him. At some point his frantic shouting suddenly ceased, and he drowned. Perry's career as an aviator was over, even though he recovered quickly. As soon as he received his glass eye, he used his commercial license to show that he could fly, with one eye, as well as Wiley Post. The Navy wouldn't buy that argument. It refused to take him back. Of course, at the moment I had to set aside my worries. I had a job to do, and the loss of a single SBD crew could not halt the air strike. With the F4Fs and Gallaher's lone SBD circling patiently, we had to get the rest of the air group off *Enterprise*'s flight deck as soon as possible. The launch continued, and by 6:15 all planes were in the air.

CDR Young led our group south, circled it around to a rendezvous point five miles south of Wake, and then turned it north to strike the island on our way back to *Enterprise*. The attack began at 7:50, with the various dive bomber divisions fanning out in different directions. Scouting Six's three divisions had orders to strike three specific regions of the island labeled "Critical Areas A, B, and C," which included the two channels leading north and south out of the lagoon, the southeastern landmass, and airstrip. Scouting Six's second division, to which I belonged, had orders to deal with Critical Area B, the airstrip. We had five planes in our division. We dropped from an altitude of 11,000 feet, sweeping due north across the east edge of the airfield. I dropped my 500-pound bomb atop an ammunition depot, causing a tremendous explosion. In general, we had little to cheer about. We damaged plenty of buildings, but we found no enemy aircraft—except two twin-engine bombers that fled at the onset of the attack—and only one ship in the harbor, a small auxiliary vessel. In short, intelligence had failed us again. Furthermore, we lost another dive bomber, Sail-Eight, shot down by antiaircraft fire. This plane crashed east of the island. Both crewmen—ENS Percy Forman and AMM 2/c John E. Winchester—got out. The Japanese took them prisoner, but sadly,

they died later when an American submarine unknowingly torpedoed the transport ship that carried them.

Little else occurred, except at our rendezvous point, about a half
mile north of the spot where Sail-Eight had crashed. When I arrived, I noticed a 150-foot, 400-ton patrol boat circling the waters.
Wasting little time, I nosed over and tried to sink it with my 100-
pound fragmentation bombs. As I wrote in my logbook, my bombs
missed because "of the violent maneuvering and because I rushed
the job too much." It's not so easy to hit a small target when you're
making a shallow dive and the target is a moving ship. The path
of your bombs covers too much horizontal distance, and the target
can change course.

I still had my forward-facing machine guns and had yet to fire
them, so I swooped in and gave the patrol boat everything I had
left. According to John Snowden, who counted, I wafted back and
forth above the patrol boat about nineteen times. By the time I had
finished, it was spinning madly in a circle and sinking. The panicked Japanese sailors figured it was better to jump into the water
than remain on board their helpless patrol craft, and into the ocean
they went. Soon our fighters showed up and joined the brawl, strafing the crippled boat, chopping up the water and the swimmers.
At 10:54, USS *Balch* (DD-363), one of the destroyers sent to bombard Wake Island from the north, circled to the east side of the
island, finishing off the boat. It picked up four prisoners, three of
whom had minor cuts and bruises. The fourth had been wounded
by strafing fire.

We returned to *Enterprise* at about 10:00. Altogether it was another thrilling experience, a successful surprise attack. However,
the whole thing had been far too easy. We had not hit any impressive targets, leaving many of us to wonder whether the raid had
been worth the lives of Forman, Winchester, and Jinks. The bomb-

ing raid was akin to target practice. We found no surface ships and no airplanes except three four-engine flying boats. If we had been seeking a big victory, we did not get it at Wake.

The campaign was not yet over. Halsey had another target for us. The day after the strike on Wake, our task force set course for Marcus Island, nine hundred miles from Japan. This would be our closest raid yet to enemy territory. That same day, *Enterprise* received Perry Teaff. Surprisingly, even minus his eye, Teaff was in high spirits. He joked with me that he planned to get a sporty glass eye for weekdays and a bloodshot one for the morning after. "He really is taking it fine," I jotted in my logbook. "He was certainly a nice lad."

Fog and foul weather continued to plague us as our task force inched closer to our destination. The air group had to postpone searches for the next three days and then, when the scout bombers started flying again, we lost another plane, Sail-Sixteen, which crashed trying to land in bad weather. A cruiser rescued the crew, LT Charlie Ware and RM 2/c William H. Stambaugh, but with no new information, we wondered about our ominous target. By March 3, the day before the attack, we still knew next to nothing about Marcus Island, nor did we learn anything of its defensive capabilities. I jotted in my logbook, "Tomorrow is the big day at Marcus. Wish we knew how many fighters and AA they have there . . . or if they have a landing field. Wish we had a spy system." Anxiety might have gotten the better of me. Before I went to bed, I wrote yet another "last love letter" to Jean, in case the worst were to happen. I wrote, "How are you tonight? Still as beautiful as I remember you? I hope so because that's the way I'll always see you. If anything should ever happen to me my biggest regret would be not getting to see you again. Maybe you could swoop down from Heaven much later—I wouldn't mind waiting—and I could tip toe my way up through Hell—'cause that's where I'm sure to go—and then I could see you again. . . . Night and happy dreams, Jean, and always my last thoughts and words will be to you."

For the third time in five weeks, I rose before dawn. I enjoyed the hearty pre-battle breakfast and endured the uninformative pre-flight briefing. When we heard the clarion call to arms—"Pilots! Man your planes!"—I bolted onto the flight deck and found it basked in moonlight. Providentially, the foul weather had finally broken. At last, we had no rain and fog with which to contend. We powered up our engines, and at 4:45, with the flight deck illuminated by a full moon, six F4Fs roared off the flight deck. Next, CDR Young sallied forth in his plane, followed by fourteen Scouting Six planes. Seventeen SBDs belonging to Bombing Six brought up the rear. It took considerable time for the air strike to collect at the outbound rendezvous point because heavy clouds intervened at 4,000–6,000 feet. Eventually, at 5:25, our thirty-eight-plane air strike marshaled its numbers and proceeded to the target. We had no idea what to expect. If we found anything, we could bomb at our discretion, but we knew the basics. We ought to privilege aircraft, ships, and radio stations as our primary targets.

It took about one hour to find Marcus Island. The solid overcast forced us to rely on chart board navigation. At 6:30, a fortuitous break in the clouds appeared, and 17,000 feet below, Marcus Island appeared like a tiny triangle, brightened by the moonlight. CDR Young gave the order to attack and we went to work. Marcus Island's defenders rushed to their antiaircraft guns and began shooting through the break in the clouds. The diminutive island was no more than six miles across at its widest point, but even so, it sent up a barrage of flak, the best shooting I had seen yet. Even at 17,000 feet, eight antiaircraft shells burst near my plane with frightening accuracy. Approaching from the southern beach, I put my plane into a dive and aimed for a barracks on the south side of the runway. I plunged to 5,000 feet and released my bombs at that cautiously high altitude. My two 100-pound bombs hammered the buildings, causing immense fires, but my 500-pounder failed to release. When I realized it was still attached, I broke to starboard, crossed over the east beach, and waggled my wings until my sticky bomb cradle broke loose, casting the bomb harmlessly into the sea.

As I redirected my plane to the inbound rendezvous point, I noticed that my squadron had lost yet another plane. The pilot of Sail-Seven, LTJG Hart Dale Hilton, reported his plane was afire and that he had to ditch. Hilton's SBD-2 made a flawless water landing ten miles east of Marcus Island, and he and his gunner, RM 2/c Jack Leaming, escaped into a rubber raft. As I roared overhead, Hilton gave a thumbs-up to let me know that he and Leaming had survived. Although the two crewmen tried to row to safety, the tide washed them ashore, and there the Japanese captured them. Both men spent the next three and a half years as prisoners of war.

At 8:45, I returned to *Enterprise*. Without even a moment to pause and eat a sandwich, John Snowden and I received orders to go on a scouting hop. By 10:00 we were in the air again. Our two-hundred-mile search turned up nothing.

I'm not sure what we accomplished by our raids against Wake and Marcus. We destroyed structures on these islands, but in the aftermath, we didn't feel much beyond the thrill of hitting our targets. Our commanders told us to take heart, that our strikes had inflicted a psychological defeat upon the Japanese. A few days later, I read War Information Bulletin No. 68, written by CDR T. P. Jeter, our carrier's XO. It read:

> Our Air Group has again struck a blow whose effect cannot be completely determined in terms of material damage. It cannot but make the Japs stop and consider when we strike one of their bases only 1015 miles from TOKYO and only 660 and 705 miles respectively from their powerful island bases at

CHICHI JIMA and SAIPAN. The enemy can have no doubt that the U.S. Navy is maintaining its traditional policy of offensive action. Perhaps the "Son of Heaven" is wondering how many "partial eclipses" the "Rising Sun" will experience before it completely and permanently sets.

We set sail for Pearl Harbor, another mission complete. We believed we had won three back-to-back-to-back victories at the Marshall Islands, at Wake, and at Marcus, but nothing decisive. Although we did not yet know it, the decisive battle we longed for was just around the corner.

|||||||||||||||||||||||||||||||||||||||||||||||||||||||||||||||||||||||||||||||||||||||||||||||||||

CHAPTER 12

RETURN TO THE CENTRAL PACIFIC
March–June 1942

On March 9, my ship, USS *Enterprise*, returned to Pearl Harbor, and for the next week we took time to rest. Altogether the war had inflicted a terrible toll on my squadron. Since the war began, Scouting Six had lost nineteen men: eight pilots and eleven gunners. Of the original nineteen pilots who traveled from San Diego in May 1941, only eight—including me—still served with the squadron.* After we returned to Pearl, three more veterans departed. Cleo Dobson and Edward Deacon both transferred, becoming assistant landing signal officers. They remained on board *Enterprise*, so we still saw them, but now they helped us with our final approach. Also, LTJG Ben Troemel mysteriously disappeared. I don't know the particulars, but the rumor—and I must stress that this was only a rumor we heard—was that the Navy decided to investigate him because of his German surname.

Troemel left the squadron but stayed in the Navy, serving at

||||||||||||||||||

* The others were Earl Gallaher, Clarence Dickinson, Norm West, Cleo Dobson, Benjamin Troemel, Edward Deacon, and Frank Patriarca.

naval air stations in the continental United States. I'd probably dismiss the stories about the Navy investigating him as mere hokum, but the Navy questioned my loyalty as well, as my surname is German in origin. Eventually officers who I didn't recognize began asking me questions, trying to see if I had ties to the "Fatherland." For whatever reason, they asked me subtle questions to see if I had a vast fortune or if I went to opulent parties. I don't know why they tried to connect wealth to German sympathy, but I was asked all sorts of leading questions to see if I gave off a whiff of disloyalty. I endured multiple visits from personnel officers, who asked me detailed questions about my family history and my personal travels. They checked and rechecked what I had to say, and then they just stopped coming. I don't know what I said, but I must have passed their test. As a result, I stayed with the squadron.*

After that, we lost five other pilots, all replacements who joined Scouting Six after Pearl Harbor. To fill the vacancies caused by transfers, promotions, and casualties, we received twelve new pilots. We also got two veterans who returned from injuries. Bill West had been wounded in the shoulder during the Marshall Island strikes. He was now healed and ready to fly. Mac McCarthy had broken his leg during a parachute jump at the attack on Pearl Harbor. He returned to us as well. We were elated to see them again. Dickinson became the new XO, taking command of the second division, and LT Charlie Ware—a Naval Academy graduate—commanded the third division as flight officer.

Meanwhile, I became a section leader. I now commanded the second section attached to LT Gallaher's first division, which meant

---

* Troemel remained in the Navy, retiring as captain in 1959. The third-to-last surviving pilot of Scouting Six, Troemel died on September 29, 2008, at age ninety-three.

I was responsible for my own plane and those of my two wing-men. "Number Two" section leader was an important position. As "Number Two," the other pilots in the squadron would watch my bombs fall, making corrections based on where they landed. Dive bomber squadrons followed this basic principle: the more accurate the dives of the "Number One" and "Number Two" section lead-ers, the more accurate the dives of the rest of the squadron.

My squadron remained at Ford Island NAS for fifty-one days, missing *Enterprise*'s next cruise, the one that took it on the famous Doolittle Raid. (The rest of the air group accompanied the carrier on that raid, and Bombing Three took our place.) But we had plenty to do at Pearl Harbor. First and foremost, we had to train new pi-lots, not only our own but also the new pilots assigned to Scout-ing Five (VS-5) of USS *Yorktown* (CV-5). Next, we had to ensure discipline among the air group personnel. In mid-April, I received an assignment to a court-martial case involving a rear-seat gunner from Torpedo Six. Drunk one night, this particular gunner had slugged a shore patrol officer, and after his arrest he broke out of the paddy wagon. I got tired of this case pretty quickly. By April 30, I lamented in my journal, "The stupid court martial and training of new pilots, and alerts have worn us out, although this was sup-posed to be a [period of] rest." During the last days of April, we worked feverishly to prepare a new batch of SBD-3s. After the Mar-cus Island raid, only four of the original batch of SBD-2s remained operational. On April 27 we received fourteen replacement planes, and we labored mightily to get them into battle-ready condition. After tweaking these new dive bombers, the Navy reassigned them to another squadron. The next day we received another batch of eighteen SBD-3s, worked all night to prepare them, and then lost them to yet another squadron. On April 29 we received a third batch. We kept this group. After all the nonsense passed, I received an SBD-3 that we designated Six-Sail-Seven.

Our short respite in Hawaii offered me additional opportunities to connect with Jean. Ordinarily I communicated through letters only, but once ashore, I had opportunities to call her on the telephone. Telephone calls had to be short—just three or four minutes in length—and they occurred sporadically. It was great to hear her voice. It gave me a much-needed boost. I don't remember much about our telephone conversations, but according to my letters, I was starting to sour on the war. I knew it needed to be fought and won, but I was starting to doubt that I had the stamina to stay on for the duration. "I can't last six or seven years doing the things I'm doing," I wrote her. And it was true. I was feeling physically drained and emotionally tormented. I wanted to go back to California and marry Jean—that much was certain. Thankfully, Jean felt the same way. Living in far-off California, she had once assumed a sense of naïveté about the war, believing what I had told her, that my job was not terribly dangerous. But now the reality began to seep in. On her own, she comprehended the hazards of my line of work and she worried she might never see me again. On St. Patrick's Day, she wrote a sentimental letter to me:

> I wonder if our future will ever take a turn toward the brighter side? Sometimes, you seem so very, very near. This afternoon was one of those afternoons. You seemed so close that had I turned around to say something to you, I'm sure I could have heard your answer. I'm trying "awfully" hard to stay cheerful, but when I let myself think that there's a possibility of never seeing you again, I wanted to cry until I can't cry any more. I'm sorry, dear, that I have to be such a "cream puff," but I just can't help it. You see my life will always be centered around you, whether it be five years, ten years, or fifty years from now. . . . I probably shouldn't be telling you how I feel way down on the inside, but I've kept it so long. I can't keep it any longer.

Here I am at age three, riding atop my aunt's mule in Lincoln, Illinois. Seconds after this photograph was taken, the mule bucked, sending me on my first "flight"—and nearly killing me. (Norman J. Kleiss)

A young sailor: age six, wearing my favorite outfit. (NJK)

(Below) My first shipmates: the Lincoln Street children of Coffeyville, Kansas, showing off our boat, the *Punkin' Creek Special*. The crew includes my brother Louis (second from right), my sister Katherine (far right), and me (second from left). (NJK)

Here I am as a midshipman at the U.S. Naval Academy. I'm wearing the uniform of the Academy's wrestling team. (NJK)

My beautiful girlfriend and future wife, Eunice Marie "Jean" Mochon. This photo captures how she appeared when I first met her in 1939. (NJK)

Pensacola, 1940: I'm giving a "thumbs-up" in preparation for my first solo flight. (NJK)

A pair of photographs showing nine SBDs from my squadron, Scouting Squadron Six, the first taken on October 17, 1941, and the second taken on October 27, 1941. In the top image, we are in "step up" formation; I'm probably piloting the second plane, 6-S-18. (NJK)

A calm before the storm, October 1941. Top: This image shows five gunners from Scouting Six attending the Air Group Six picnic at Barber's Point, Hawaii. My gunner, John W. Snowden, stands at right. Bottom: Here's another image from the Barber's Point party. Most of these men died during the war. RM 1/c Harold Thomas (third from left) was killed at the Battle of the Marshall Islands. RM 3/c Mitchell Cohn (third from right) was killed at the Battle of Pearl Harbor. RM 3/c Edgar P. Jinks (second from right) was killed by accident at the Battle of Wake Island. ENS Bill West (right), who was one of my closest friends, died on May 20, 1942, when his SBD crashed during a windy takeoff. I had the misfortune of watching him drown. (NJK)

These are the pilots of our sister squadron, Torpedo Six, taken in January 1942. My best friend from USS *Enterprise*, LTJG Tom Eversole, is in the front row on the left. (NHHC)

The pilots of Scouting Six, taken May 12, 1942. Back row, left to right:
ENS John Q. Roberts, ENS Carl D. Peiffer, ENS James A. Shelton, ENS
William R. Pittman, ENS John C. Lough, ENS Vernon L. Micheel, ENS
Eldor E. Rodenburg, ENS Thomas F. Durkin, Jr., ENS Richard A. Jaccard,
ENS Franklin W. O'Flaherty, ENS Clarence E. Vammen, Jr., ENS James C.
Dexter, ENS Reid W. Stone, ENS William P. West. Front row, left to right:
LTJG Norman West, LT Frank A. Patriarca, LT Charles R. Ware, LT Wilmer
E. Gallaher, LT Clarence Dickinson, LTJG N. Jack Kleiss, ENS John R.
McCarthy. (NJK)

Scouting
Six's patch

The indispensable gunners of Scouting Six. They are, back row, left to right:
Jack Leaming, Joseph DeLuca, Joseph Cupples, Thurman Swindell, Edgar
Jinks, L. A. Hoss, Joseph Winchester, Thomas E. Merritt. Middle row, left
to right: E. G. Bailey, William H. Stambaugh, Floyd Adkins, W. H. Burgin,
Bruno P. Gaido, Milton W. Clark. Front Row, left to right: John W. Snowden,
Alfred Stitzelberger, Louis D. Hansen. (NJK)

The flight deck of USS *Enterprise* in late April 1942. The SBD in front is 6-S-7, the plane I flew at the Battle of Midway. Presumably, I'm at the controls, about to take off on a routine antisubmarine patrol.

Ordnancemen from USS *Enterprise* load a 500-pound bomb onto the undercarriage of an SBD. This photograph was taken in August 1942—after I left the squadron—but it shows a former Scouting Six SBD that flew at Midway, now assigned to Bombing Six. Note the V-shaped bomb cradle, which prevented our bombs from going through our propellers. (NHHC)

An SBD Dauntless delivering its payload.

On May 27, 1942, I received the Distinguished Flying Cross on the deck of the USS *Enterprise*. My commander, Earl Gallaher, had recommended me for gallantry during the Battle of the Marshall Islands, February 1, 1942. In this image, Admiral Chester Nimitz (foreground) presents the Navy Cross to Messman Doris Miller (center). I'm standing second from the right, the shortest man in the lineup. My friend Cleo Dobson is the tall officer at the far right. (NHHC)

Wearing my Distinguished Flying Cross, just a few minutes after Nimitz pinned on the award. (NJK)

USS *Enterprise* steaming into the wind during the Battle of Midway, at 7:25
A.M., June 4, 1942. At this point, both dive bomber squadrons had launched,
but Torpedo Six had not gotten airborne. There are several TBD Devastators
on the rear of *Enterprise*'s flight deck. (NHHC)

A screen capture from a film reel taken from USS *Enterprise*'s bridge
camera. It depicts me and John Snowden taking off in 6-S-7. Although
positive identification of this reel is uncertain, this could have been taken on
the afternoon of June 4, 1942, in which case, this is the mission that led to
the sinking of *Hiryu*. (NARA)

This is *Dauntless Courage,* aviation artist David Gray's depiction of my diving attack on *Kaga*. The smoke at the stern represents the damage from Earl Gallaher's bombs and the explosion on the bow represents the damage from my bombs. (David J. Gray)

Famed designer Norman Bel Geddes's diorama of the morning of June 4, 1942: depicted here are *Enterprise* and *Yorktown* dive bombers attacking the Japanese carriers *Soryu, Akagi,* and *Kaga.* (NHHC)

Here, on the afternoon of June 4, USS *Yorktown* is struck by an aerial torpedo delivered by a Japanese plane from the carrier *Hiryu.* My squadron and I would exact revenge on *Hiryu* soon enough. *Yorktown,* however, would sink on June 7. (NHHC)

The Japanese carrier *Hiryu* at 8:00 A.M., June 4. This photograph was taken from a B-17 launched from Midway Atoll. Although it does not show *Hiryu* when *Enterprise*'s SBDs attacked it, the scene looks similar. Note the circle at the front of the flight deck and the wake coming from the carrier's high-speed turn. (NHHC)

A later view of *Hiryu*, the second carrier I bombed at the Battle of Midway. Note the hole in the flight deck. My bomb tore out the front of the flight deck and rolled it over like a taco shell. (NHHC)

This photograph shows the last hours of *Mikuma*, the cruiser I bombed on June 6. My bomb exploded just astern of the slanted smokestack (or, in this perspective, just to the left of the smokestack). My friend Cleo Dobson flew the SBD that was used to take this photograph. (NHHC)

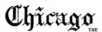

Chicago Sunday Tribune

THE WORLD'S GREATEST NEWSPAPER

VOLUME CI—NO. 23

JUNE 7, 1942

A ✳ PRICE TEN CENTS

JAP FLEET SMASHED BY U. S.
2 CARRIERS SUNK AT MIDWAY

13 TO 15 NIPPON SHIPS HIT; PACIFIC BATTLE RAGES ON

News of the Battle of Midway spread like wildfire across the victory-starved United States. Here, the *Chicago Sunday Tribune* made the battle its headline. As you can see, our Navy's attention to secrecy made it hard to get correct information. The newspaper reported two enemy carriers sunk instead of four.

Yank Flyers Exact Heavy Toll; Enemy Loses Many Planes.

PEARL HARBOR, Honolulu, June 6 (AP).—United States armed forces have sunk or damaged 13 to 15 warships and transports of the repulsed Japanese invasion fleet at Midway Island and "a momentous victory is in the making." These include the sinking of two, and possibly three, aircraft carriers.

Adm. Chester W. Nimitz, commander in chief of the Pacific fleet, enumerated enemy losses tonight in his third communique on the great and continuing battle in the Pacific.

"Pearl Harbor has now been partially avenged," he said.

That Midway Punch

This cartoon celebrates the victory at Midway. You'll notice how it uses racist imagery to lampoon the Japanese. Today, we regret the way we depicted our enemy, but back in 1942, our government and the media encouraged every American to think this way. (*Sheboygan Press*)

On July 3, 1942, less than a month after Midway, Jean and I had a speedy wedding in Las Vegas, Nevada. This picture was taken shortly after the ceremony. (NJK)

Receiving the Navy Cross, the highest honor I have ever received in service of the United States. The officer at right is reading the order from Secretary of the Navy Frank Knox. (NJK)

Here I am, a dive-bombing instructor, watching my ACTG squadron practice its dives at Cecil Field, Florida. If one of them missed— which was often—I'd have to hop off my SBD and run for shelter. (NJK)

On March 7, 1952, I celebrated my thirty-sixth birthday with a party at Lockheed, an aircraft manufacturer in Burbank, California. I supervised three hundred engineers and test pilots for the Bureau of Aeronautics. Jean is to the left, and I'm at the right. Those are my children in the middle. They are, left to right: Nancy, Roderick, and Jack, Jr. (NJK)

Observing an aircraft engine alongside one of my test pilots at Lockheed. I held the rank of commander at this point. (NJK)

This image was taken on 1962, when I was a captain on the verge of retirement. (NJK)

A snapshot from a reunion of USS *Enterprise* families in 1999. At left is my trusty gunner, John Snowden. Next to him is his wife, Fay. Second from the right is my wife, Jean. I'm at the far right. (NJK)

At work on *Never Call Me a Hero* inside my San Antonio apartment, showing my co-authors a photograph of my carrier, USS *Enterprise*. I am ninety-five years old in this photograph. (TJO/LLO)

Just a lucky fool—with my love, Jean. (© William Luther/*San Antonio Express-News*, ZUMApress)

My letters to Jean were equally romantic. I've always been a cautious man when it comes to sharing my feelings, but for some reason, those days after the Battle of Marcus Island awakened my romantic ardor. I wanted Jean to know that I loved her, truly and deeply.

Seriously, though, do you know you are my biggest mystery (every man should have one—and you can't say I haven't tried). You're several distinct persons (or images?) to me. You're the girl I kissed goodbye (but not forever—by any means) on the dock that moonlit night. And next you were the girl who arrived just in time to keep me company for Christmas dinner (she's standing on top of my desk now, right on top of a lot of paperwork she won't let me touch). And then she is an entirely different lady beckoning me within her mansion and eager (??!!) to be kissed stately, reserved and not reserved, and beautiful (no more need be said! Except that when she lifts both eye brows and starts to worry about something which might happen or something that might not happen [and in either case, so what?] then her beauty isn't quite). . . . And again my Jean is the maiden fair who would knit me a pair of socks (10½ please) but who I hope doesn't send them to me soon because the moisture on this paper is easily earned sweat and because I'll probably freeze if and when I get to sunny California and finally she is the girl who likes perfume, and bright silver, and order and planning (too dog-gone much!) and likes the Rockies, and deer, and maybe once a year a beer, and pictures, and clubs (I don't but I should), who is the optimist of the family (and the worst poker player), who likes big name hotels (which mean little to me), who wears riding boots like a gunny sack and much too big (but looks plenty good except for the boots—and probably can't ride a horse anyhow), and who likes (?) to swim but won't go near the ocean (or will she?) or pose in a bathing suit (for me or camera), and, but of all she's the girl who likes attention, though she'll admit it not a bit, hardly even to me.

Yes, she's a problem, probably will take me a lifetime to fig- ure her out and even then it wouldn't do any good because she's not the sort to be changed easily if by that time I wanted to. I've made lots of mistakes wherein you were concerned, like not kidnapping you and taking you to Pensacola just because you said you didn't want to go, and again—although this wasn't my fault—in not kissing you early that Sunday morning to see how (or if) you'd wake up.

At last, we were on the same page.

After fifty-one days ashore, my squadron departed on another mission. On April 30, *Enterprise*—accompanied by another carrier, USS *Hornet* (CV-8)—left on its seventh war cruise since the De- cember 7 attack at Pearl Harbor. The Pacific War hadn't changed much. Our fleet had raided the Marshall and Gilbert Islands, Wake, Lae, Salamaua, Marcus, and Tulagi, but we couldn't claim any kind of pivotal victory. We had damaged many bases, destroying ships and planes, but the battle lines were mostly unchanged. To shift momentum, we needed to cripple the Japanese carrier force. On this mission, we tried to do just that. Our task force—called Task Force 16—made haste for the Coral Sea, where another carrier group, Task Force 17, with *Yorktown* and *Lexington*, had made con- tact with the Japanese fleet. We arrived too late to join in the battle, but while at sea, we heard provocative reports. Pilots from *Yorktown* and *Lexington* had sunk a Japanese light carrier, *Shoho*, but *Lexing- ton* had been sunk due to battle damage incurred in return. Two of the big Japanese carriers, *Shokaku* and *Zuikaku*, escaped with some battle damage. Our fleet had missed an opportunity to take out those important ships and we were now short another carrier.

By May 11, *Enterprise* reached a position near Efate, dispatching a squadron of Marine fighters to that island. For the next week, Task Force 16 patrolled the Coral Sea, and our squadrons conducted scouting operations each day. This routine became somewhat monotonous, and I felt disappointment at not finding any enemy ships. On May 19 I commented in my logbook, "Same old search 200 miles relative, or about 240 out, 190 back. *Atlanta*, a special AA cruiser, joined us, making us much happier. She also brought with her a lot of mail, but I didn't get very much. Gosh, but a year is a long time to be away from home. Wonder if five or six years will be as hard as one year?"

During this cruise my squadron lost several aircraft. On May 14, while on a scouting hop, ENS Thomas Durkin's plane went missing. Near dark, Durkin radioed that he had to make a water landing. Both Durkin and his gunner abandoned their sinking SBD and after fourteen awful days on the ocean somehow made it in their life raft to Espiritu Santo. By the time we knew where they were, *Enterprise* had already turned back for Pearl Harbor. Consequently, they could not be picked up. Then, the day after Durkin went missing, ENS Bill Pittman crashed his SBD on takeoff, but thankfully, a destroyer rescued him and his gunner.

My squadron experienced one deadly crash during this cruise, and I had the unfortunate distinction of watching it happen. Unhappily, this accident involved a close friend, Bill West. The mishap occurred on May 20, just after *Enterprise* had crossed the International Date Line. We launched sixteen planes from Bombing Six and Scouting Six, but during the takeoff, the pilots misjudged the wind. Without sufficient airspeed, Bill's plane started wobbling and stalled. His engine sputtered and quit, sending his SBD careening off the starboard bow, plunging into the water. The ship's "man-overboard" Klaxon sounded, and I ran to the railing. From only two hundred feet away, I witnessed the heartrending drama.

Bill's dive bomber sank like a stone, and he had no opportunity to escape. During the crash, Bill had smacked his head against the bomb sight, much like Perry Teaff had done a few months earlier. The impact left Bill groggy and he sluggishly unhitched his harness. When water poured into the cockpit, Bill broke free. He walked to the rear of the aircraft and held on, but then his plane plunged downward, nose-first. Bill let go, but at the last second, his boot caught hold of the radio antennae wire that spanned the length of the plane. When his SBD sank, it dragged him down with it. In just a few seconds, he was gone. A pool of bubbles remained on the surface. Bill's rear-seat gunner, AMM 2/c Milton Wayne Clark, escaped the doomed plane by a hairsbreadth. He was picked up by a "plane-guard" destroyer, one of two destroyers assigned to recover pilots who crashed during takeoff.

The death of Bill West traumatized me. This was one of the greatest shocks of the war, and this cruise became particularly unhappy for me. Bill was a great guy, and it was sad to lose him, especially to a meaningless accident. Many of my best friends died in the Pacific War. I endured the news easier when I knew they had died in battle. Bill's death felt worse than any of them. Watching a good friend die in a freak accident practically killed my soul. It made human life appear cheap and empty. I wanted to believe Bill was worth more than that.

On May 26, our task force returned to Pearl Harbor. The next day, LT Gallaher came down to my bunk. He told me our ship's company planned to hold an awards ceremony on the flight deck. He told me to look sharp in my dress whites. "Get there a little bit early," Gallaher told me, "You're supposed to be near the front of the group." When I asked why, he replied, "President Roosevelt has decided to award you a medal of commendation for what you did at the Marshall Islands." In fact, the award was the Distinguished Flying Cross. I was shocked and a little disgusted. I had just lost one of my best friends and here I was about to receive an award, one that rightly belonged to him. Bill had flown through that raid in the Marshalls with a shoulder wound. The Navy ought to have recognized him, not me. Also, I wanted to offer my condolences to Bill's wife, Nancy, who was on Oahu that day. Because of this ceremony, I couldn't be where I should have been, consoling her.

As I made my way to the flight deck, I felt bitter. But when I saw the white-clad rows of sailors standing rigidly at attention, the assemblage of gold-plated officers reviewing their notes near the podium, the camera crews intending to mark this moment for posterity, and the wreckage of the battleships USS *Arizona*, *Oklahoma*, and *West Virginia* sitting sadly in the background, my heart started to pound. I recognized the honor the nation intended to bestow upon me. The awards ceremony passed like a great whirlwind. At 1:45, the crew of *Enterprise* assembled on the flight deck to welcome aboard Admiral Chester W. Nimitz, commander in chief of the Pacific Fleet, who intended to hand out nine medals: five Navy Crosses and four Distinguished Flying Crosses. I had never met Nimitz before, so I wasn't sure what to expect. Months earlier, he arrived seemingly out of nowhere, handpicked by Roosevelt to whip our shattered fleet into shape. As Nimitz walked onto the deck, a band played "Ruffles and Flourishes." The nine recipients—including me—stood in line in front of the assembled crew. Nimitz began:

> I am proud to bestow, in the name of the President of the United States, these awards today. Among the citations which will go to these officers and men of the fleet are those for deeds which epitomize the bold warfare our fleet is waging—above, below, and on the surface of the Pacific Ocean. On today's honor list are represented the fleet's several combat elements. Recognition now can come to some of the fliers who participated in the fleet's first important action of the war, that against the

Marshall and Gilbert Islands. . . . May the news of these honors
furnish inspiration to your shipmates and to the rest of the Navy
in the days to come.

Nimitz trooped down the line of officers, pinning medals to our chests and shaking our hands. The first four men in line received the Navy Cross. These included Captain George Murray, captain of *Enterprise;* LCDR William S. Veeder, a destroyer skipper; and two submarine commanders, Lieutenant Commanders William L. Anderson and Charles W. Wilkins. Next, Nimitz handed out Distinguished Flying Crosses to two members of Fighting Squadron Six, LCDR Clarence Wade McClusky and LTJG Roger W. Mehle.

When Nimitz leaned in to pin on Mehle's medal, he whispered, "I think you'll have a chance to earn another medal in a couple of days." Mehle stood right next to me, so I just barely caught what Nimitz had said. I gave a sideways glance. What had the admiral just revealed? Earlier, I had noticed that all three of our carriers were in port, which suggested a big operation was about to happen. Now Nimitz had confirmed my suspicions with his teasing comment. I wanted to swivel my head and say, "What's this now?" but of course, I couldn't. Naturally, my nervousness skyrocketed.

Next, Nimitz came to me. He read aloud my citation: "Lt. (j.g.) Norman Jack Kleiss: As a member of a scouting squadron, he participated in the attacks on Kwajalein and Maloelap atolls, Marshall Islands, on February 1, 1942. His initiative and determination in the execution of these missions, effected in the face of enemy fighter opposition and heavy antiaircraft fire, resulted in heavy losses to the enemy, and enabled him to score a direct hit on a light cruiser."

Nimitz looked at me and said, "Well done!" I remember the moment well. He looked me over carefully, just like LCDR Smith and VADM Halsey had done, and watched my facial expression. I assumed he wanted to see if I was nervous. Maybe he could tell a pilot's personality and trustworthiness just by their facial expression. I don't know how long that look really lasted, but it felt like forever. Nimitz gave me the most careful look I ever experienced in my whole life. His stare jolted me like a shot of whiskey, his eyes penetrating and honest. At that moment I wanted to impress him. When he reached out to shake my hand, I felt emboldened, ready to go back into battle and fight for him, anything to prove that I deserved this hallowed award. I experienced something I never thought possible. A leader had put the fight back into me.

Nimitz pinned the award to my chest and then moved down the line, awarding Cleo Dobson a Distinguished Flying Cross for sinking a Japanese transport at Kwajalein. Finally, he handed out a Navy Cross to Messman Doris Miller, the first African-American sailor to earn that distinction. Miller received this award for his heroics at Pearl Harbor, where he claimed to shoot down four Japanese planes from the deck of the battleship USS *West Virginia* (BB-48). Photographers snapped several images of the event, and they now stand among the most famous images of the Pacific War.

Sometimes, when I have the courage to read a book about those days, it takes me right back to that beautiful sunny Hawaiian day. I can see myself standing there as Nimitz targeted me for that intense personal appraisal. Throughout my life, I've relived the experience over and over. It's a strange feeling, being a twenty-six-year-old lieutenant junior grade all over again. I always wonder what he saw in me. People have often said that Chester Nimitz had a way of knowing his people and getting the most out of them. I can report that ever since he took that sounding of my soul, I demanded the very best of myself forever afterward.

After the award ceremony concluded, we—the nine recipients—entered a makeshift studio inside *Enterprise*'s island superstructure to have our portraits taken. I sat down and gave my characteristic crooked smile. The photograph they snapped is still one of my favorites. The camera crew congratulated me, treating me like some kind of hero. I tried to calm them down, telling them that this was nothing; I was just doing my job. I worried this news was going to spread like wildfire once all the images got published in the newspapers. I did my best not to encourage it. I told no one back home that I had received an award. I mentioned it to Jean only, telling her tersely that I received "a medal for something or other."

Soon after the ceremony, gossip commenced concerning Admiral Nimitz's slip of the tongue to Mehle. We began guessing the location of the next big campaign. Would we finally have our chance to go up against the Japanese aircraft carriers? Three American carriers were in port at Pearl Harbor, and dockyard workers were feverishly at work repairing *Yorktown,* which had been damaged at the Battle of the Coral Sea. With both task forces assembled, we anticipated a big fight. As the gossip spread, Earl Gallaher warned us to keep quiet about news of our imminent departure. He ordered us emphatically to tell no one where we'd been, or what we might do in the future. The skipper didn't usually speak to us that way. We knew for certain that a huge operation was about to happen.

On May 28, Task Force 16—which included carriers *Enterprise* and *Hornet* and fifteen escorts—left Pearl Harbor. Not long after entering open water, Gallaher called together a small group of pilots from Scouting Six. He locked the door to our ready room and revealed to us that our fleet was heading toward Midway Atoll, a remote Marine outpost in the Central Pacific. Although Gallaher did not know the specifics, he said the Japanese planned to invade the islands. Importantly, he believed Vice Admiral Chuichi Nagumo's carrier task force would be present. Nagumo had command of four of the six Japanese carriers that had launched the air raid over Pearl Harbor six months earlier—*Akagi, Kaga, Soryu,* and *Hiryu*—and sixteen surface ships. We knew these carriers well, having studied our enemy ship identification models relentlessly. Thus the next major battle would square our only aircraft carriers against four of the Japanese carriers. This, Gallaher explained, might be the show-down for the Central Pacific. At the time, we did not understand how our leaders knew all this important information concerning the enemy's plans. Only later did we learn that our cryptanalysts in Pearl Harbor had cracked the Japanese naval code, allowing Admiral Nimitz to know the enemy's strength and destination.

Gallaher knew a little more about the upcoming operation than most pilots on *Enterprise*. Years earlier, he had dated Halsey's daughter, Margaret. As a result, he remained close with the admiral and tended to get wind of top-secret discussions between the admirals while the rest of us aviators were left in the dark. Halsey was not with us during this voyage. He came down with chronic dermatitis during our previous voyage and reported to the Navy hospital as soon as we entered Pearl Harbor.

Prior to our departure from Pearl Harbor, I assume, Halsey shared with Gallaher his thoughts on how the upcoming battle would be carried out. Gallaher told us a few details, things that would not compromise our operation if we were captured by the Japanese. First, he told us to practice changing the YE-ZB coils with our radiomen, making sure they could pick up our carrier immediately after an attack. Second, he revealed that the presence of our carrier task force had to remain a secret. If we attacked Japanese ships, we had to fly a forty-mile dogleg toward Midway Atoll before returning to our carrier. This way, the Japanese might think our squadron belonged to Midway's garrison and not to a carrier task force. Third, Gallaher told us that as we approached Midway, we would not launch any scouting missions with our SBDs. Similar to our previous raids, Scouting Six and Bombing Six would be spotted on the flight deck and we would proceed on the mission as soon as we had a confirmed enemy contact. Midway Atoll planned to launch twenty-two PBY Catalina flying boats—giant search planes—and when one of them reported a suitable target, our squadrons would scramble into the air and go after it. We expected to launch against any Japanese carrier targets spotted within 180 miles of our carrier. Finally, Gallaher told us that Halsey wanted only the dive bombers launched on an attack mission. The fighter planes, Gallaher surmised, would likely be held back as Combat Air Patrol and the torpedo bombers—if deployed at all—would only be used for short-range scouting hops.

Even though Gallaher gave us all these details, none of it really seemed to matter because VADM Halsey—the supposed author of this plan—would not be around to execute it. Our fleet was commanded by two other men, RADM Raymond Spruance (who commanded our task force) and RADM Frank Jack Fletcher (who commanded USS *Yorktown*'s task force). We assumed both men knew of Halsey's tactical design, but as the battle unfolded, it became apparent that they did not. Admiral Fletcher, who was senior to Spruance, would have overall command.

Of course, we did not concern ourselves too much with tactical details. We were just pilots, after all. Our commanders had the responsibility of issuing orders. We merely had the responsibility of executing them. For the next six days, our squadron buzzed with excitement. We expected the battle to occur on June 4, the day we reached the waters northeast of Midway, but we prepared for unexpected surprises.

From dawn to dusk we sat in our ready rooms, requiring only a few seconds' notice to hop into our planes. We made only one scouting hop during the week after we left Pearl Harbor. On June 1, I flew on a two-hundred-mile morning search. The other carrier in our task force, USS *Hornet*, launched two scouting missions on May 29 and 31, but otherwise, we relied on reports from Midway's search planes to tell us about the arrival of the Japanese. The days passed with emotions vacillating between eagerness and worry.

Clarence Dickinson had this to say about our feelings during those final days before the Battle of Midway. I'm inclined to agree with him:

> *Each fresh word of information increased our tension. . . . As naval officers and fliers we knew we confronted an opportunity to strike a blow at the Japanese fleet that might well be decisive. . . . There was satisfaction now in everything we had done to prepare ourselves for what was coming in the hours ahead. We had not risked ourselves for nothing. It was a pleasure to exchange wicked grins with all your fellow officers, grins which said more plainly than words how we liked the idea of catching the Japanese at sea near our bases. . . . All of us fully realized that we were getting a chance to change the whole character of the war in the Pacific.*

Dickinson was right. If all of what we were told was true, that the Japanese intended to send four carriers to invade Midway, then Nimitz had taken an incredible risk. He had decided to throw the U.S. Navy's only operational carriers and their escorts—the last best hope for victory—against the pride of the Japanese fleet. Strange as it is to say, the fortunes of the Pacific War appeared to rest on our shoulders. We all understood how the upcoming battle had the potential to become the defining naval engagement of the Pacific War, a battle that could both shift the offensive momentum of the war and demonstrate the capabilities of naval airpower in one fell swoop. We had trained relentlessly for six months, doing everything we could to prove that aviation was a valuable asset to the fleet. All we wanted was to stick around and do our share. Now fate had placed us at the tip of the spear. Dive bombing had to deliver Nimitz his victory. If we failed, the next battle would be remembered as one of the most tragic gambles ever lost by the U.S.

Navy. If we succeeded, and did it decisively, we might stem the tide of Japanese conquest and turn this war in a different direction. I know it's a cliché to say, "The weight of the world was on us," but I cannot think of a better way to describe how I felt. The upcoming battle hinged upon the actions of our air group and those of the other carriers, a handful of aviators. How could this be? Famous battles from our nation's past always relied upon armies of thousands of men. During the Civil War, Generals Grant and Lee dueled in Virginia with legions of dedicated fighting men at their command, but here in the bowels of *Enterprise,* it seemed as if everything depended on a mere sixty pilots and their gunners. I don't know how my companions made sense of it, but I told myself that if I did my duty, and trusted in my training, I might just earn a reunion with my lady love.

Wednesday, June 3, was a particularly awful day, filled with distracting news. We received word that a Japanese task force had attacked Dutch Harbor, Alaska. Then a Navy PBY out of Midway claimed to have sighted the "main body." (In reality, he sighted the Japanese troop transport fleet.) At first it appeared as if we would have to scramble our planes one day earlier than our commanders predicted, sending us off in an unanticipated direction, and at the farthest distance our limited fuel could carry us. We did not launch. Someone up the chain of command determined that the sighted ships constituted the enemy's support force, not the carrier strike force. Barring better information, we had to sit and wait patiently. I wrote in my logbook, "Tomorrow is likely to be a big day."

As daylight faded on June 3, I found repose in writing to Jean, another introspective epistle in which I put my life and naval career in perspective. Although I had survived three battles already, I worried about this upcoming engagement. Would I die tomorrow? I fretted I might not make it home to marry Jean. My earlier reluctance gnawed away at me guiltily. In what might be my final letter to her, I had to make it clear that I loved her deeply and that I was more than just lukewarm to the idea of spending the rest of my life with her. I loved her too much to die and leave her alone in a war-torn world. I could not tell her where I was or what I was about to do, but I wanted to make it clear that I was about to face a battle.

"My darling sweetheart," I began.

> *I love you, I love you, I love you, darling. I only wonder if you will know how much. You mean more to me than anything . . . and I had to make sure that you felt that way about me too. Anything less and I will never be completely happy, and feeling that way I doubt if I could make your happiness complete either. But now I do feel that I love you, and that you love me, so much as is humanly possible, although I wonder if you could ever guess it from my letters. I wonder sometimes [if] they are not too cold, formal, and unreal. . . . But that is only because I'm living temporarily in another world—one I hope you know never. It's a cold and ruthless world filled with hate and incalculable cold-bloodedness. But it is necessary for some of us to live there now and then to protect the other world, the one I'm in when I'm with you. . . . Give me courage, Jean, and luck. Sometimes I need them badly and I know that you can supply them. If when I do something a bit risky—now and then—I feel much better and much safer when I feel that I am doing the thing you would have me do.*

I sealed my letter and then heard the command "lights out." With that, I said a prayer, rolled over in my bunk, and tried to get some shut-eye. Tomorrow would be my day of days.

|||||||||||||||||||||||||||||||||||||||||||||||||||||||||||||||||||||||||||||||||||||||||||||||||||||||||||||||||

CHAPTER 13

THE BATTLE OF MIDWAY, PART 1
The Morning Attack, June 4, 1942

A t 2:00 A.M. on June 4, a messenger tapped my arm.*
"It's time to wake up," he said. The day of battle had come.
I dressed and went to the officers' mess. The delicious smell of steak and eggs wafted through the halls, a telltale sign the cooks

||||||||||||||||||||||||

* Confusingly, the Battle of Midway took place across several time zones. When narrating events from the battle, historians often convert all time-related references to "Midway time," meaning the time zone in which the Midway Atoll was located. However, this was not how I experienced the battle. The crew of USS *Enterprise* kept its records according to a different time zone—two hours ahead of "Midway time"—and consequently, my personal logbook from June 1942 followed this scheme. To put it another way, historians would say that I woke up at 0200, or 2:00 A.M. To me, it felt as if I woke up 0400, or 4:00 A.M., for that is how I recorded it. The same thing can be said about the important events that happened during the battle. Historians say that my squadron attacked the Japanese Mobile Fleet (Kido Butai) in the morning—at 10:20 A.M.—but for me and all the other *Enterprise* pilots, it felt like the afternoon. According to our logbooks, we attacked at 12:20 P.M. Students of the battle might find this confusing. For the sake of continuity—to give readers an understandable frame of reference—I've converted all chronological references to "Midway time," which means I have shifted them backward by two hours. However, please understand that when I experienced these events, I experienced them according to *"Enterprise* time."

expected us to have a bloody morning. Breakfast took an hour, and after 3:00, I returned to my quarters and changed into my flight gear. Recognizing the importance of this moment, I double-checked everything. My upper left arm pocket contained an assortment of soft pencils to plot information on my clear, plastic-covered chart board. My chest pockets contained a pencil-sized flashlight and two lipstick-sized containers that held ephedrine and Vaseline. My leg pockets included a spare flashlight, new batteries, and two wool cloths, one to clean unwanted items off the chart board and another to wipe my windshield. My life preserver, parachute, and helmet completed the ensemble.

I was completely adorned, an aerial warrior ready for action. I walked aft to Scouting Six's office and checked the assignments. I was assigned to my usual plane with my typical bomb load. My SBD-3 carried three bombs: a 500-pound general-purpose bomb and two wing-mounted 100-pound incendiaries. Walking through a passageway, I reached a ladder and descended to *Enterprise*'s hangar deck. Parked planes cluttered the back half. Mechanics feverishly tinkered, making last-minute alterations. The Dauntlesses from Scouting Six and Bombing Six were already on the flight deck, spotted for takeoff. On the hangar deck, where I was, the crews had pushed the Devastators and Wildcats to the rear elevator. I could tell they intended to launch these planes once our SBDs had cleared the deck.

Something caught my eye. I noticed that all fourteen of Torpedo Six's TBD-1 Devastators were fitted with a torpedo attached to their bellies. I was aghast. Why were they armed with the Mark-13s? For a full year, all I had ever heard about these torpedoes was how they malfunctioned. I had seen it with my own eyes during the gunnery test in July 1941. After the Marshalls strikes, the pilots from Torpedo Six had cursed those torpedoes for failing them so spectacularly. Months earlier, I even heard VADM Halsey barking to subordinates, telling them how he didn't want any torpedo-laden TBDs ever to leave the hangar deck. Clearly someone—the admirals, perhaps—intended to launch Torpedo Six and send the TBDs into the fray alongside Bombing Six and Scouting Six. I knew that when the launch came, the flight deck would be cluttered with planes. With all three squadrons launching at once, those of us in the first division of Scouting Six had only 165 feet for takeoff. Of course, I had launched my SBD with only 165 feet of deck before—and done it in complete darkness—but I worried about all the new pilots in our squadron who had never launched off such a short deck with a bomb-laden plane.

I saw my best friend on *Enterprise*, Tom Eversole. He was standing at the aft end of the hangar deck, supervising the sailors as they shoved a Devastator onto the rear elevator. I approached Tom and pointed to one of the planes. I asked him, "Tom, why the hell are the TBDs armed with torpedoes? Do the admirals expect them to go into battle?" He nodded and looked worried. He told me that his unit, Torpedo Six, had orders to accompany the air strike. I asked if any of the SBDs had been equipped with smoke bombs to provide cover for the low-flying torpedo planes as they went in. Tom shook his head and looked away.

I was baffled. From our experience in the Marshalls, at Wake, and at Marcus, I thought our fleet had learned its lessons. We could not send the TBDs into action unless they had adequate smoke protection and torpedoes that exploded more than 10 percent of the time. I never learned who was responsible for ordering the TBDs into action or why they did it. Perhaps the Torpedo Six pilots failed to complain loudly enough. Perhaps no one ever told Admirals Fletcher and Spruance about the deficiencies of the Mark-13s. In any event, the decision set the stage for one of the greatest tragedies of the battle.

I had little time to discuss tactics with Tom. We shook hands and bid each other "good luck." It was a gut-wrenching goodbye. I knew this was likely farewell forever. As we shook hands, a strange thing happened. Tom's image started to blur. I was on the verge of tears! As a young man, I always did my best to hold my emotions in check. I vowed never to show sadness or grief. This was the one moment during the war when I just couldn't hold it back. A flood of memories washed through me as I recalled the wonderful times Tom and I had shared together. I remembered all the high jinx we'd perpetrated at the Naval Academy. I thought of the days we'd spent together as aviation students at Pensacola. Most especially, I remembered our cross-country trip to Kansas City. Even today, it is hard for me to recall that tearful parting. There is nothing quite so dark and terrifying as knowing your friend is about to be killed and being utterly unable to help him. All we could do was put on a brave face and try not to think about it. Oh how I miss Tom.

At 5:30, I entered the ready room and sat down in my chair in the front row. Aside from my squadron commander, LT Gallaher, I was the first to reach the room. I opened a locked cabinet underneath my seat and pulled out my chart board. As the other pilots filtered in, I memorized our task force's position and its bearing. We expected the Japanese carriers to approach Midway from the northwest, but we really had no idea from which direction they'd come. Thanks to the talented codebreaking team at Pacific Fleet Headquarters at Pearl Harbor, our commanders knew that the pride of the Japanese carrier force was headed for Midway. They knew the enemy fleet's first move would be an air strike against Midway, an attack meant to knock out the runway and keep the atoll's surviving aircraft on the ground.*

―――――――――――――

* Midway contained a mix of Navy, Marine, and Army Air Corps aircraft. It possessed thirty-one Catalina PBYs from Patrol Wing Two, a detachment of six

In the ready room, most of the pilots kept silent, listening to the yeoman relaying data, but some of the nervous aviators chattered away. ENS John Quincy Roberts, one of the new pilots, boasted how he intended to put a bomb on a Japanese carrier today even if he had to drag it aboard. My archrival, LT Dickinson, also spoke out, complaining as usual. He reviewed the attack plan and realized that our SBDs would not have any fighter escorts. The F4F-4s had orders to shepherd the TBDs to their target, leaving Scouting Six and Bombing Six to fly high above, away from the protective cover of the Wildcats, alone.* Dickinson had registered similar complaints on previous occasions, and his gripes had gotten old, so I just tuned him out.

Meanwhile, Gallaher wore earphones, quietly printing *Enterprise*'s location on the chalkboard behind him. Our task force started turning east into the trade winds—which was necessary for launch—but it unintentionally took us away from where we expected to encounter the Japanese mobile carrier force. We pilots hoped we might launch about 120 nautical miles from the enemy fleet, but as events started to take shape, it looked as if we might have to launch 210 miles away. I attempted some quick arithmetic. Our SBDs carried 310 gallons of fuel. If we launched now, without closing the distance to the enemy fleet, it would require every drop in our tanks to fly outbound and return. I grimaced. If anything disrupted our outbound flight—if we did not find the enemy carri-

---

TBF Avenger torpedo bombers from Torpedo Eight, twenty-eight Marine Corps fighter planes from VMF-221, forty Marine Corps dive bombers from VMSB-241, four Army Air Corps B-26 Marauders from the 69th Bomber Squadron, and nineteen Army Air Corps B-17s from the 431st Bomber Squadron.

* In March 1942, Fighting Six received a new combat model F4F, the Dash-4, replacing the F4F-3. It had six machine guns instead of four, as well as folding wings. Some of the guys didn't like this heavier version of the Wildcat.

ers at the expected intercept point and had to spend time performing a box search—we might not have enough fuel to return to our carriers. It seemed as if Torpedo Six was not the only squadron set up for a suicide run.

I did not have long to ponder the dangers of fuel exhaustion. Suddenly, at 6:00, a lookout reported that a Japanese scout plane had passed overhead. I dashed outside to get a look. Looking out across the ocean, I noticed a faint wisp of fog and a solid bank of clouds from sea level to several thousand feet high. The gods of the weather smiled upon the American fleet, for the numerous low-hanging clouds made Task Force 16 nearly impossible to see from the air.* We pilots waited anxiously, eyeing a small, three-hundred-foot hole in the clouds, waiting to see if the scout plane appeared. Nothing happened, and everyone presumed the overcast had prevented it from seeing *Enterprise*.

I reentered the squadron ready room and sat down. Looking at my watch, I noted it was a few minutes past 6:00. That was when we received the critical news: our scout planes from Midway had made contact with the enemy. We stared at a telecast screen mounted at the front of the ready room that indicated enemy contact reports. Meanwhile, the yeoman began writing information on our chalkboard based on what he heard in his headphones. He now placed the enemy carrier task force at 175 miles away. I came to a quick realization: the admirals (and the codebreakers who informed them) were correct. The enemy was heading for Midway. We had our chance to strike a decisive blow. Gallaher told us that Spruance and his chief of staff, CAPT Miles Browning, planned to launch all four squadrons, one after another. Scouting Six and Bombing Six

---

* This might have been the heavy cruiser *Chikuma*'s scout plane No. 5, which records show overflew the American task force and reported no contact.

would go first, and once aloft, we would circle at cruising altitude until the other squadrons joined us. After that, Torpedo Six and Fighting Six would take off and cruise with us, albeit at a lower altitude. Meanwhile, the other two air groups—those from *Hornet* and *Yorktown*—would send up everything they had and we'd all proceed to the target together. It was an ambitious plan.

We expected to be ordered to head to our planes right away, but strangely the order did not come. Word soon trickled down to the ready room. We learned that USS *Yorktown* had paused to recover a scouting mission executed by Scouting Five. *Enterprise* had to wait for *Yorktown*, about twenty miles away, to close the distance. Until *Yorktown* reached us, we had to sit tight. To this day, I've never fully understood why we delayed our takeoff. We had a confirmed enemy contact report—albeit not terribly detailed—and that report placed it within range of our dive bombers. If they wanted, our commanders could have scrambled Scouting Six and Bombing Six right away, but they did not. Since the battle, historians have reminded readers how Fletcher sent a message to Spruance at 6:07, telling him to "attack [the] enemy carriers as soon as definitely located," giving *Enterprise* and *Hornet* freedom to conduct their own launch operations without waiting for *Yorktown*. Of course, I didn't learn that fact until after the battle. While I sat impatiently in the ready room, I wondered how long it would take for *Yorktown* to catch up. I also learned that Spruance had turned our task force to the southwest, intending to close the distance to the enemy fleet, hoping to reduce it to about 155 miles, but all the while, we held on to the assumption that, when we launched, we still had to coordinate with *Yorktown*'s air group.

While we waited for the takeoff order, the Japanese made the first move. At 4:30, when still unaware of our presence, the four enemy carriers launched 108 fighters and bombers, sending them to strike the two largest islands in the Midway Atoll: Eastern Island

and Sand Island. Shortly after 6:00, the Japanese planes came in sight of their targets. They overwhelmed the twenty-six U.S. Marine Corps fighter planes that patrolled the skies, killing seventeen brave American pilots. After that, the Japanese had their way with the ground defenses. They destroyed the base's power plant, the water lines, three oil storage tanks, three vehicles, and five other buildings. They killed eight men on the ground. However, the Japanese failed in their mission to render the runway inoperative, scoring only two minor hits on it. By 7:00, the Japanese planes—minus eleven that had been shot down—turned back to their fleet.

Our fleet's first big move came next. At 6:56, after an hour of agonizing waiting, *Enterprise* turned into the wind. Someone on the bridge had decided it was time to turn us loose. The yeoman called out, "Pilots, man your planes!"

As if propelled by a spring, I hopped from my chair and ran out onto the flight deck. Sixteen other Scouting Six pilots followed me and we fanned out, mounting our SBDs. My plane, Sail-Seven, was parked near the amidships elevator. My dutiful gunner, John Snowden, greeted me. He was just as eager to get airborne as I was. I hopped into the cockpit, strapped myself in, and ran through my standard preflight check. Our plane was ready to go in less than a minute.

The dive bombers from Scouting Six and Bombing Six revved up, and what a sound they made, a chorus of thirty-three angry buzz saws chomping at the proverbial bit. The planes were packed tightly, with wingtips practically touching. The ordnancemen scampered in and out and underneath the fuselages, making last-minute adjustments and avoiding our precarious propellers, now churning furiously. Looking backward, I saw John strap himself into the rear seat. He looked at me, giving me his characteristically innocent smile and a jubilant thumbs-up. Behind us, I could see the rest of Scouting Six and Bombing Six ready to go, their blue-gray finish gleaming as the first rays of sunshine shot through the clouds. Behind them, the cigar-shaped TBDs crowded the rear of the flight deck. Every bit of available space was taken by an aircraft. I strained my eyes to see if I could get a last glimpse of Tom. But every TBD looks identical when you stare at its nose. I didn't see him. Pulling my head back inside the cockpit, I adjusted my goggles and looked out ahead to the bow and our beckoning mission.

Enterprise's signal officer gave the go-ahead. Ahead of us, eight F4F-4s took off first, taking position as Combat Air Patrol. Then, at 7:06, our new air group commander, Clarence Wade McClusky, launched in his SBD. McClusky had received the Distinguished Flying Cross standing alongside me eight days earlier. He now led *Enterprise*'s dive bombing group, an odd choice given that, until recently, McClusky had been a fighter pilot. He had logged plenty of flying time in SBDs, but he could not have known our tactics as well as one of our capable squadron commanders, Gallaher or Best. Because of McClusky's seniority, someone on *Enterprise*'s bridge expected him to lead the dive bombers into battle.

After McClusky's plane got airborne, the rest of the air group got underway. Two junior ensigns, Bill Pittman and Richard Alonzo Jaccard, took off next, piloting Sail-Eight and Sail-Eleven. Pittman and Jaccard served as McClusky's wingmen. At 7:10, Scouting Six's planes got airborne. LT Gallaher took off first, with his two wingmen—Ensigns Reid Stone and John Quincy Roberts—following him in order off the flight deck. Then it was my turn. Sail-Seven sped down the flight deck, and with a thunderous hum, it lofted into the air. Only one of my wingmen joined me. ENS Eldor E. Rodenburg's SBD, Sail-Nine, experienced engine trouble at 8,000 feet and returned to the carrier to report a defective blower. My other wingman, ENS James Dexter, who piloted Sail-Eighteen, flew on my port side, for I had just begun circling the carrier. Together Dexter and I formed Scouting Six's Section Two, or "Yellow

Section." Behind us, nine more Scouting Six SBDs took off, forming divisions two and three, and after that, fifteen Bombing Six
SBDs launched, each carrying a 1,000-pound bomb.

At the rendezvous point, I joined a gaggle of thirty-two dive
bombers that were circling in "step-down" formation.* We swiveled
our heads, looking for anything that looked out of the ordinary.
As we circled above the task force, we expected the other squadrons from *Enterprise*—Torpedo Six and Fighting Six—to join us,
albeit at a lower altitude. We also expected four squadrons from
Hornet (the other carrier in our task force) and three squadrons
from *Yorktown* (sailing just over the horizon to the east) to link up
with our group.† That was the plan relayed to us by Gallaher. But
those squadrons never showed up.

We waited and waited, but no additional aircraft ever reached
the rendezvous. Forty minutes passed and we just continued to
circle stupidly above Task Force 16, burning valuable fuel. Duti-

------

* In "step down" formation, the planes were arranged so that each succeeding
wedge-shaped section (three planes) was spaced one below the other, similar to a
flight of stairs. In this formation, the gunners could bring all their fire to bear on
any enemy fighters who dared approach us from above or behind.

† Unfortunately, our three air groups failed to consolidate. We did not know it at
the time, but as we circled above, several problems developed on the flight decks.
First, it took a long time for *Enterprise*'s crewmen to get Fighting Six's ten F4F-4s
up from the hangar deck and spotted on the flight deck. Second, after considering range and fuel consumption, *Yorktown*'s air group decided not to launch
their thirty-five aircraft at 7:00 as planned. Instead, they waited until 8:38, a
full ninety-two minutes after *Enterprise* sent up our dive bombers. As it happened, *Yorktown*'s last squadron, Bombing Three, did not get underway—that is,
consolidated and heading toward the enemy—until 9:07. Finally, even though
Hornet put sixty-two planes in the air, none of these planes joined forces with us.
Hornet's four squadrons—VS-8, VB-8, VT-8, and VF-8—departed Task Force 16
at 8:06, about ten minutes after McClusky's two squadrons departed.

fully we kept off our radios, adhering to the strict protocols of radio silence, performing all communication through hand signals. Terribly frustrated, I rocked angrily in my seat. I wanted to set out in search of the enemy, but some unseen force was preventing us from getting the green light.

Finally, at 7:52, Admiral Spruance, impatient with the delays, sent a message to McClusky. A signalman flashed it in Morse code using a massive shuttered searchlight: "Proceed on mission assigned. Proceed separately." I read the message with satisfaction. Spruance must have understood the urgency of things, and the need to get after it!* Accordingly, McClusky signaled to our squadron and to Bombing Six to follow him. After our final revolution around the carrier, we straightened our rudders, and off we went, speeding urgently to the southwest. The planes from *Hornet* and *Yorktown* were nowhere to be found, and neither were *Enterprise*'s F4Fs and TBDs.†

---

* We set off at course 231°. At this moment, 7:52, both Torpedo Six and Fighting Six were in the process of completing their takeoff and rendezvous.

† So what happened to the other squadrons? Of course, I was not privy to any of this at the time, but *Enterprise*'s squadrons departed in three separate groups. As I stated, McClusky's two squadrons (of which I was a part) left first, bidding goodbye to *Enterprise* at 7:52. Torpedo Six (fourteen planes) departed Task Force 16 a few minutes after we left. It flew on a similar course until about 9:30, when it changed direction sharply. Torpedo Six's commander, Eugene Lindsey, died in the battle, and thus left no after-action report. A junior officer, LTJG Robert E. Laub, filled out the after-action report in his place, although he specified no course of direction. In 1966, author Walter Lord interviewed Laub and received clarification of Torpedo Six's course. It traveled at 240° until about 9:30, when Lindsey spotted smoke from the Japanese carrier fleet and made what amounted to a ninety-degree turn to the right.

Finally, Fighting Six (ten planes) ended up departing even later, and it accidentally followed Torpedo Eight, *Hornet*'s torpedo squadron. The commander of Fighting Six, LT James S. Gray, never submitted an after-action report, either,

We went off on our own, climbing upward to an altitude of 20,000 feet. We had no fighter cover. Since the battle, some historians have hinted that we dive bomber pilots disliked fighting on our own hook. This was not how I interpreted it. When I woke up that morning, I expected our squadrons would fight independently. In terms of entering the battle, this was exactly what I preferred. We did not need fighter cover to do our job. Our rear-seat gunners were excellent shots and more than capable of protecting us. If all four squadrons had set off together, it would have caused us confusion and slowed us down. The only thing that irked me was the tempo of the launch. After Scouting Six and Bombing Six executed a flawless series of takeoffs, we wasted fifty minutes' worth of fuel before Admiral Spruance finally decided to send us on our way.

We needed every drop of gasoline, too, because as events unfolded, our two bomber squadrons burned fuel at an unnecessarily brisk pace. It pains me to say this, but our new air group commander made a decision that had grim consequences for our squadron. LCDR McClusky piloted his dive bomber as if it were a

---

but in 1963, he did write a detailed, privately circulated account, "Decision at Midway," in which he admitted following Torpedo Eight. He wrote, "For a while we tried to cover another outfit [Torpedo Eight] on diverging course, but it was too far behind us to continue. We learned later that Torpedo Six made a considerable dog leg to the southwest, overshooting by an estimated fifty miles then searching to the northwest and finally attacking toward the northeast." Meanwhile, the air groups from the other carriers left on their own hook. At 8:06, *Hornet's* sixty-two planes followed its air group commander, LCDR Stanhope Ring, but even this group did not stay together for long. Sometime around 8:25, *Hornet's* TBD-1 squadron, Torpedo Eight, diverged from the course, going about thirty degrees to starboard. Finally, *Yorktown's* three squadrons—Fighting Three (six planes), Torpedo Three (twelve planes), and Bombing Three (seventeen planes)—took off long after *Enterprise's* and *Hornet's* planes had left the area. *Yorktown's* first squadron, Torpedo Three, did not start takeoff procedure until 8:45. All three *Yorktown* squadrons flew southwest.

fighter. He barreled along at 190 knots instead of the normal cruising speed of 160 knots. McClusky figured the Japanese had probably seen us and the winner of this battle would be the one who
attacked first. His unorthodox cruising speed caused major problems. In each squadron, the trailing planes tended to burn more
fuel because it was their responsibility to adjust and hold fast to the
flight leader's course and altitude. Each time they accidentally fell
off the wing of their section or division leader, even slightly, they
had to increase the throttle to catch up. Our trailing planes burned
fuel faster, and at higher cruising speed the waste was greater than
it should have been.

Our search seemed to continue forever. By 9:20, after flying
about 165 miles, our two squadrons reached the intercept point.*
We expected to find the enemy fleet here, but instead we found
nothing. Looking downward through sparse cloud cover, I had
a clear fifty-mile view in all directions. But all I saw was empty
ocean. The Japanese carriers, after recovering their planes from the
Midway strike, must have changed direction.

Here, McClusky's quick thinking revealed itself. He elected
to make a box search. He turned his plane ninety degrees, and
through hand signals, he directed both squadrons to follow him.
Gripping the stick, I guided my plane into a lazy turn to starboard,
leading my section to the northwest.†

---

* This was about 29°N/179°W.

† This new course was about 321°. Although we dive bomber pilots did not yet
know it, the Japanese carrier force had changed direction at around 9:17. After recovering planes launched at dawn to strike Midway Atoll, the Japanese admirals
turned their carriers northeast, away from Midway, to search for the American
fleet. Had the Japanese fleet continued on its original heading, perhaps we would
have found the Japanese on our outbound leg, but instead, there was nothing in
sight.

It seemed only logical that the Japanese admirals would alter their heading. I am thankful McClusky had the same epiphany. To him goes the credit of leading us in the right direction. If we had mindlessly followed the orders given to us, the Japanese carriers would have slipped away.

As the leader of the second section, only a few yards behind Mc-Clusky and Gallaher, I focused closely on their hand signals, mimicking them for the pilots in the rear divisions. But as we altered our heading on the next leg of the box search, heading northeast, I caught sight of the leader of Bombing Six, LT Dick Best. He was making hand signals, too, and they meant trouble. Best held up his oxygen mask, indicating that his planes were having oxygen problems. He pointed downward. One of Best's pilots, LTJG Edwin Kroeger, had lost oxygen. The whole squadron had to reduce altitude to breathe safely. Accordingly, Bombing Six's fifteen planes dropped to 15,000 feet, and the pilots inhaled normal air. As our squadrons separated, it seemed it just wasn't meant to be that we would deliver a concentrated blow against the enemy fleet.

For the next half hour, I endured a fairly quiet ride. I sat alone in my cockpit, with only my thoughts to occupy me. Occasionally, I chatted with John Snowden over the interphone about the business at hand. I asked John if he had prepared any spare ammunition for the twin .30-caliber machine guns. I quizzed him on the proper procedure when changing the coils for the YE-ZB homing beacon receiver. More than anything, I wanted both of us to stay alert, keeping our eyes moving, looking for anything unusual that might lead us to the enemy fleet.

Then, at 9:55, we had a breakthrough. The morning sunlight was passing through a cascade of mist produced by a waterspout far below us. It produced a spectrum of beautiful color. McClusky seemed to be pointing out the rainbow to Gallaher through hand gestures. All of us could see it. It was gorgeous, perhaps the most glorious rainbow I've ever laid eyes on. But actually, it was some-thing else that commanded Gallaher's professional attention. Fifteen miles ahead, and 20,000 feet below us, a white scar was visible on the solid blue expanse of the sea. Soon it became appar-ent it was the wake of a destroyer going at high speed. It was bar-reling along. I remembered the flare produced by my old ship, USS *Yarnall,* when it traveled at top speed. We had found a destroyer all right, the *Arashi.* Earlier in the day, it had been detached from the Japanese fleet to chase an American submarine, USS *Nautilus* (SS-168), which had attacked the enemy task force. Now the ship hastened to catch up with the four carriers and the other escorts. Since *Arashi* was making a beeline, we figured its course must be pointing in the direction of the enemy carriers. McClusky turned us onto that same heading. Within three short minutes, we found them. There it was: the whole Japanese carrier force, arrayed across the horizon.*

I was worried about our chances of survival. My fuel gauge was already below the halfway point. If we went ahead with the attack, we would certainly use plenty of fuel diving against the ships, taking evasive action, and regaining our altitude. If we survived the attack, we were not permitted to return to our carrier directly. Instead, we had orders to dogleg—flying in another direction for forty miles or so before turning for home—so the enemy would have no idea from which direction we had come. All this flying would consume more fuel. It appeared doubtful that we would ever return to our carrier.

As if to punctuate the gravity of that moment, a Bombing Six plane piloted by ENS Tony Schneider ran cold out of fuel. His engine sputtered and his propeller came to a halt. As I watched

---

* According to my logbook, the Japanese carriers were located at 30°05'N/181°45'W.

Schneider begin a slow glide toward the ocean, I wondered what would lay ahead for him and his gunner, RM 2/c Glenn Holden. What would happen to any pilot who risked an attack and then ran out of fuel? A crashed aircrew could take a chance of being picked up by a patrol plane eventually, but that was one chance in a hundred. I guess any one of us could have jettisoned our bombs and returned to *Enterprise,* but this was unthinkable to me and to my comrades. It would have been cowardice. We had faith in our leader, LT Gallaher, and we were determined to make good on our one shot at the enemy fleet that had inflicted such misery on Allied forces since December 7. We had trained too long and too hard to back out now. We knew we might run out of fuel and die a horrible, lonely death on the ocean, but it did not matter. We made our decision quickly and automatically: we decided to attack. We had to attack. We had to win.[*]

Shortly after Schneider's plane splashed, I saw the Japanese carriers in greater detail. I could see four of them. Right away, I recognized the two closest to us, *Kaga* and *Akagi.* Scouting Six was cruising directly at them. Ten miles out, I spotted a smaller carrier, *Hiryu,* and finally I observed a large dot on the horizon, which I guessed to be *Soryu.* At this point, McClusky finally broke radio silence.

"Enemy sighted!" he announced.

I started hitting switches and pulling levers, bringing my SBD-3 into battle condition. As I have said before, I don't remember having any fear. Perhaps I was an expert at suppressing my worries, but more than likely, my fear subsided when work had to be done. Thankfully, the SBD required plenty of hard work on the

---

[*] A Midway-based PBY recovered Schneider and Holden on June 6, two days after they ditched.

part of a pilot. Before every attack, I was always interested in making sure we got the YE-ZB operational. I called over the interphone to John Snowden, instructing him to change radio coils on the ZB receiver. Once he picked up a homing signal, I recorded the Morse-coded letter showing the exact course back to *Enterprise*. I reached under my seat and armed the three bombs. The new SBD-3s had electrical arming switches, but Gallaher had warned us not to trust them (a wise order, since four SBD-3s from *Yorktown*'s Bombing Three had prematurely dropped their 1,000-pounders about an hour earlier after using these same switches). After that, I recorded the latitude and longitude of our location and made sure I double-checked all the minor mechanical adjustments necessary for the dive, anything to make sure I would not be up for court-martial when I came back—if I came back.

John Snowden and I scanned the horizon. Where were the Zeros? We could not see a single enemy fighter in the sky. More than 19,000 feet below us, I could see *Akagi* and *Kaga*, both cruising into the wind, a perfect position for our dives. So long as the carriers did not make any abrupt turns, no crosswind could throw our bombs wide. I breathed a sigh of relief.

We had found the enemy fleet unprotected.

We were captivated by the sight of the pristine carriers beneath us. Dick Best would tell me that he gawked with fascination at the colors of *Akagi*'s flight deck. It was yellow, with a big red circle painted on the bow, no camouflage at all. It seemed arrogant to him. Why else did the Japanese paint their decks with a bull's-eye, unless they were overconfident? ENS Lew Hopkins of Bombing Six later remembered the sight as "something that is impressed on your mind." Decades later, he claimed he could still close his eyes and picture the Japanese carriers clear as day. My rival, LT Dickinson, who was cruising two planes behind me, later explained, "The target was utterly satisfying. The squadron's dive [position] was perfect. This was the absolute. After this, I felt anything would be just anti-climax." I cannot say that I had similar thoughts running through my head. Only one word repeated over and over: "Survive!" I wanted only one thing in this life. I wanted to live through this and return to Jean.

Historians disagree about what happened next. Some say that McClusky gave orders to our two squadron commanders, Gallaher and Best, directing Scouting Six to take the carrier to port and Bombing Six to take the carrier to starboard. I heard no such order. Perhaps due to his inexperience, McClusky merely shouted into the radio, "All planes attack!" In his haste, he had neglected to assign targets to the different squadrons. McClusky waggled his wings and turned hard to port, leading Scouting Six down over *Kaga*, the nearest carrier. Standard dive bombing doctrine required the leading squadron—in this case, Scouting Six—to attack the carrier farthest away, which would have been *Akagi*. Hearing nothing from McClusky, Dick Best assumed that Scouting Six would take *Akagi* and Bombing Six would take *Kaga*. Then, when Scouting Six came careening downward in front of him, Best realized that McClusky meant for him to dive on *Akagi*. Best turned his plane to starboard, but it was too late—only Best's two wingmen followed him. The other eleven Bombing Six SBDs followed McClusky and Gallaher against the *Kaga*. We had no other choice. McClusky dived ahead of us, so we had to follow. So it happened, our squadron and two-thirds of Bombing Six formed a long string of plunging aircraft, all careening downward at the same enemy carrier.

Our attack began at 10:23. McClusky's plane nosed over, and his two wingmen, Pittman and Jaccard, followed him. Both ensigns expressed shock, no doubt because they expected to act as photographic planes and merely watch the battle. Now McClusky led them into their first combat dives. At first no antiaircraft fire greeted these three plummeting SBDs, but when the Japanese sailors heard the shriek of the Dauntlesses, *Kaga* came alive, spewing a barrage of shells from its antiaircraft guns. McClusky's bombs missed, and so did those dropped by Pittman and Jaccard. This came as no surprise to me. McClusky had never flown a dive bomber into battle, and Pittman and Jaccard had never even seen a battle. Their bombs landed in the same ocean as *Kaga,* but they were not even close to the ship. Earl Gallaher came next, followed by his wingmen, Stone and Roberts.

Gallaher knew we had to hit that enemy carrier pretty soon, or else we might miss our chance. Each succeeding dive bomber pilot made his corrections based on what the preceding bombers had done. If the first dive bomber missed badly, it made it that much harder to make corrections because the whole string would be way off target. We needed to adjust our aim mid-dive, a difficult prospect. In my humble opinion, Gallaher was the best dive bomber pilot in our fleet. He saved the day at that moment, bringing our string of plunging craft back on target. Gallaher dived steeply and he released his bombs as low as our tactics recommended, about 1,500 feet.

I watched as Gallaher's bombs smashed onto the aft section of *Kaga*'s flight deck, just forward of the rear elevator. His 500-pounder landed atop a lone Zero, ripping it to smithereens. The bomb stabbed through the unfortunate plane, pierced the hangar deck, and detonated. His incendiary bombs hit the gas tanks beside the Zero. Immediately, the aft part of the ship was engulfed in a huge mass of flames. As Gallaher pulled out, he rocked his plane sharply, standing it on its tail, so he could get a look at the devastation, something he routinely ordered us not to do. His gunner, ACRM Thomas Merritt, shouted, "God damn! That was a beauty, Cap'n!" Gallaher's two wingmen did not fare so well. ENS Stone's bombs missed, and ENS Roberts's SBD never pulled up from its dive. Maybe it had been damaged, or perhaps Roberts misjudged his altitude. Either way, Roberts's plane plunged straight into the ocean, killing him and his gunner, AOM 1/c Thurman Swindell.

It was now my turn to join the fray. I waggled my plane's wings, signaling my wingman, ENS Dexter, that we were about to push over. I engaged my SBD's split flaps and switched my engine to low blower.

I said to myself, "Here we go," and threw the stick forward.

My plane rolled into its dive and in a few seconds all I could see was the enormous blue ocean coming at me, with the smoking enemy carrier in the middle of it. As I have often said, diving in an SBD makes the scariest roller coaster on the planet seem like child's play. The winds roared loudly around my cockpit. I felt the stomach-sinking feeling caused by the sharp drop. But I was used to it. I had made several combat dives at this point and the disorienting effects no longer bothered me.

My plane knifed downward at 240 knots. The Rising Sun emblem on *Kaga*'s bow made an inviting target, so I used it to sight my bombs. I picked out a spot on the ocean where I expected that big red orb to be in about forty-nine seconds and dived for it. Accurate dive bombing required a precise estimation of the target's lead. Any good dive bomber had to be able to size up a moving target's speed and direction during the first few seconds of the dive and aim for the position where it would be at the end of the dive. Although I had never targeted a moving ship under combat conditions (excepting the patrol boat at Marcus Island), I somehow managed to deduce *Kaga*'s speed perfectly. As Sail-Seven accelerated, I did my best to maintain rudder trim and reduce yaw while diving, all the while monitoring the altimeter.

By now, *Kaga*'s gunners fired everything they had at us. Providentially, not a single nugget of that hellish hail touched my plane. About halfway into the dive—that is, about twenty-five seconds—I could see my target was definitely *Kaga*. It looked just like the identification models we kept in our ready rooms. I wanted to assure myself of a hit, so I released my bombs when the altimeter read 2,000 feet (which meant I was actually at 1,000 feet). This was my lowest dive ever. I jerked the bomb release lever and my three bombs dropped loose. I pulled sharply on the stick. I felt the awful gut-crushing sensation of 9 g's squeezing my body. Sea-spray speckled my windshield. I prefer not to guess how close I had come to plunging into the ocean.

John Snowden saw what happened immediately. My 500-pounder slammed into *Kaga*'s forward elevator, right at the edge of the big red circle where I had aimed. The bomb penetrated *Kaga*'s upper hangar and exploded below the flight deck. My pair of incendiary bombs went in, too, igniting fueled and armed aircraft spotted below. It produced a frightful inferno from which the carrier never recovered.

High above, LT Clarence Dickinson, who was then in the middle of his dive, saw what my bombs had done: "I saw the deck rippling, and curling back in all directions, exposing a great section of the hangar below. . . . I knew the last plane had taken off or landed on that carrier for a long time to come." Once I leveled out, I took a quick look back. I could see the red flames of a huge fire. The inability of *Kaga*'s crew to quell this blaze sealed the mighty carrier's fate. There was a ticking time bomb, deep in the carrier's bowels.

Of course, at the time, I did not ponder any of this. I cared only to get my plane back to *Enterprise*. First, I had to avoid the Japanese fighter planes. Although we didn't see any at our pushover altitude, in fact there were a few of them in the air at low altitude. One spotted me as I came out of my dive. A Japanese pilot swooped at me while my SBD was skimming above the waves. I spotted the Zero and pitched my plane to the side to give John Snowden a good angle. In about two seconds, that Zero was gone, either shot down or unwilling to give chase.

Next, I worked hard to avoid the Japanese surface ships. The four carriers were part of a massive armada. There were seventeen battleships, cruisers, and destroyers encircling them. One of the destroyers opened up with a furious fusillade. I swerved to the right and then to the left. I sped past numerous ships shooting antiaircraft fire at me, and changed course and altitude every second. Once clear of the ring of escorts, I banked in a half circle, putting my plane on a heading toward Midway. As I flew southeast, the dreadful sounds of battle slowly receded into the distance. The thunderous sounds of ships breaking apart were drowned out by the roar of the wind outside the cockpit. I just hoped my comrades were doing as much damage as I had done.

Although I did not see any of the ensuing action, I later learned how my comrades put the finishing touches on the smoking carrier. The remainder of Scouting Six dropped their bombs on *Kaga*, as did the second and third divisions of Bombing Six. Altogether, twenty-one more SBDs went into their dives after I completed my attack. Of course, it was much harder for my comrades to score hits because *Kaga* was obscured in a thick cloud of smoke. I had a much easier dive than they did. Only two additional bombs struck the carrier. LT Dickinson dropped one of these, striking a section of the starboard flight deck near *Kaga*'s amidships elevator. ENS George Goldsmith, of Bombing Six, dropped a fourth bomb, a 1,000-pounder, striking dead amidships. Meanwhile, as *Kaga* exploded, two simultaneous SBD attacks dealt deathblows to *Akagi* and *Soryu*. Three planes from Bombing Six's first division, led by Dick Best, reached *Akagi* less than a minute after leaving our group. Two bombs wrecked the carrier's steering, setting it adrift. Finally, seventeen SBDs from *Yorktown*'s Bombing Three arrived on the scene. These planes descended on *Soryu*, hitting it three times. Between forty-eight attacking SBDs, we scored nine hits, fatally wounding *Akagi, Kaga,* and *Soryu.* All three ships became raging funeral pyres.

At 10:30, when my plane was about five miles from the carnage, I turned my head and gave the scene one long, last look over my left shoulder. Three frontline Japanese aircraft carriers were huge bonfires, flaming like Kansas straw stacks. The fires on *Akagi* reached three hundred feet into the air. The steel was red hot. *Kaga* was in its final death rattle. The four bomb strikes delivered by Scouting Six and Bombing Six had knocked out *Kaga*'s fire suppression system and killed off most of the damage control crews, leaving our incendiary bombs to do their work. *Kaga* was a mass of flames. After seven minutes, the fires, uncontrolled, reached the forward magazine. Suddenly the inferno led to one catastrophic explosion that scooped out the forward part of the carrier. I saw a huge object rocket into the air, smoking and burning. This was *Kaga*'s forward elevator, propelled aloft by the fireball. The blast produced a huge brown cloud of smoke that obscured the dying carrier utterly, and by the time the winds carried the cloud away, the ship was gone.

From start to finish, the attack had taken about four minutes. All that training, all that struggle, to win the greatest battle in naval history in less than three hundred seconds—I have always considered it perfectly amazing. History would not much care which of the victorious pilots made it back to base. For me, just personally speaking, of course, this was a matter of historic importance, too.

After witnessing such a tremendous display of death-dealing pyrotechnics, I hoped my dogleg and return to *Enterprise* would continue uneventfully, but it was not to be. Another Zero made a run at me. Again I banked and my dead-eye gunner, John, unleashed a burst of machine gun fire. For the second time that morning, he scared off a would-be assassin. I breathed a sigh of relief. If I had ever made a wise decision in life, it was picking

John to be my rear-seat gunner. He saved our bacon twice already. Despite his excellent aim, I figured it would be helpful if we joined forces with some of the other retreating pilots. Ahead of me, I saw three Dauntlesses making haste: Sail-Fourteen, Sail-Sixteen, and Sail-Seventeen. I tried to catch up with them, but the three pilots (two of them new) seemed to think I was an enemy fighter. They increased their power and sped away.

I considered it unwise to give chase, as gaining their company wasn't worth the cost in gas. I had to conserve every drop. With about ninety minutes' worth of gas remaining, I throttled back to 110 knots. I did not know the exact distance to *Enterprise*, but I figured I would have to travel more than 150 miles to complete my dogleg and then reach the carrier. Would our fuel hold out? Swallowing hard, I resigned myself to the fact that John and I would probably have to ditch.

After traveling forty miles toward Midway, I took a second reading from the YE-ZB homing system and changed course toward home. Gaining altitude, I reached 3,500 feet, where thick clouds helped shield me from prying eyes. About this time, I saw a plane that was a dead ringer for a German Messerschmitt poking out of the clouds two miles ahead of me and heading directly at me. It must have been *Soryu*'s Yokosuka D4Y1 scout plane, then returning from the mission that had located *Yorktown* and Task Force 17.[*] As I readied my forward guns, the Japanese scout plane pulled sharply into a cloud and disappeared. I entered the cloud and looked around a bit, but when my plane emerged from the cloud, the mysterious plane had vanished. I wasted no more time hunting it. I continued on my path to *Enterprise*.

---

[*] Several *Enterprise* dive bomber pilots reported seeing a single "Messerschmitt," and Earl Gallaher reported its presence in the VS-6 after-action report.

At about 11:30, a new threat emerged. On the horizon I saw a pack of twenty-four Japanese planes, eighteen D3A1 "Val" dive bombers and their six A6M2 Zero escorts. At 10:57 these twenty-four planes had launched off the deck of *Hiryu*, the sole surviving Japanese carrier, and proceeded on their way to bomb our fleet. I came dangerously close to this group of Japanese aviators, and I'll bet that if they knew I had bombed one of their carriers they would have pursued me relentlessly. Three Zeros spotted me and moved to intercept, but they traveled only a few miles toward my plane and then changed direction suddenly, returning to the pack of dive bombers. For whatever reason, the Japanese fighter pilots decided it was not worth it to chase down a lone SBD. I have often reflected on this one moment from the battle and remarked to myself, "How lucky can a man get?"

About sixty-six miles from *Enterprise*, I saw a splash in the water. I called over the interphone, asking John to help me identify it. John called back, telling me that it looked like a Bombing Six SBD that had run out of fuel. I flew in for a closer look. I observed the crew, pilot and gunner, inflating their life raft, and merrily paddling away. (I don't know for certain whom I spotted, but I'm reasonably sure it was LT Joseph R. Penland and his gunner, RM 2/c Harold F. Heard.) I waved at the two Bombing Six crewmen and recorded their position on my chart. I circled the area once to make certain they were okay and then continued on my way to the ship.[*] As my plane sped away from the ocean-bound dive bomber crew, I wondered if John and I would even make it back to report their location. If we ditched, who would be around to rescue us?

---

[*] Presuming I am correct about which plane I saw, my information led to the crew's rescue. USS *Phelps* (DD-360) recovered Penland and Heard the next day, June 5.

Thankfully, that question required no answer. At 11:50, after almost five hours in the air, I found Task Force 16. Out on the horizon, I could see two big brown bars, the flight decks of *Enterprise* and *Hornet*, and all the little wakes of the escort ships surrounding them. I felt greater relief than when I had first spotted the Japanese carriers an hour and a half earlier. I was going to land. I was safe. I could see other SBDs from Scouting Six and Bombing Six trickling in, some in small groups but others flying solo. Many of my squadron mates had failed to return. When *Enterprise* saw us coming, it turned directly into the wind, knowing how low we were on fuel. One by one, we landed on our carrier. When my turn came, the jolt of the wire brought my plane to a halt. My SBD's engine grunted, revealing its thirst for fuel. I pulled up my goggles, giddy with delight. I couldn't have imagined in my wildest dreams that I would survive an encounter like the one we just had.

LCDR McClusky insisted on landing last. Although he was the air group commander and by all rights could have landed first, he begged that the others precede him. As it turned out, McClusky had received a shoulder wound when a Zero had attacked his plane after its pullout. Unsure of his ability to land an unfamiliar plane while wounded, McClusky insisted on waiting until his other planes had trapped on deck before making his final approach. For all the mistakes he made during the morning mission, this selfless act more than made up for it, and I forever applauded McClusky afterward. When we examined his bullet-riddled plane, we discovered that he had less than five gallons of fuel remaining.

My own plane, Sail-Seven, had even less. Only three gallons remained of the original 310, a consequence of my plane being a few planes back from the lead. I was lucky to have returned at all. Few of the planes from the rear divisions had made it back. Perhaps I would have been lost on the ocean, too, if it hadn't been for Admiral Halsey taking a shine to me and recommending me for section leader. Altogether, only fourteen of our thirty-two SBDs returned to *Enterprise*—eight from Scouting Six, five from Bombing Six, and our air group skipper, McClusky.[*]

Even before John and I dismounted Sail-Seven, three *Enterprise* ordnancemen dashed under our plane and held up the three arming wires to show that our bombs had been armed to detonate, proof that the ordnancemen had contributed to the victory in their own small way. The excited sailors took the wires, cut them into sections, and bent them into the shape of an aircraft, twisting the ends so they could be attached to a uniform like a medal. They gave an improvised award to each person who had serviced Sail-Seven prior to the morning attack. They also gave a piece of the arming wires to both John and me.

---

[*] The returning planes included CEAG, Sail-One, Sail-Two, Sail-Seven, Sail-Eight, Sail-Eleven, Sail-Sixteen, Sail-Seventeen, Sail-Eighteen, Baker-One, Baker-Two, Baker-Three, Baker-Twelve, and Baker-Sixteen. Of the thirty-two SBDs that set out with McClusky that morning, one had crashed during its dive (possibly shot down), killing the pilot and gunner (Sail-Three); another had crashed from fuel exhaustion before the attack (Baker-Eight); two others landed safely on *Yorktown* with both crews surviving (Baker-Five and Baker-Fifteen); and fourteen others had crashed from fuel exhaustion during or after the attack on the Japanese carriers. Of the fifteen planes that crashed from empty fuel tanks, all but one belonged to the second and third divisions of Scouting Six and Bombing Six. I repeat: it paid to be flying at the front of the pack. These fourteen planes were Sail-Four, Sail-Five, Sail-Six, Sail-Ten, Sail-Twelve, Sail-Fourteen, Sail-Fifteen, Baker-Six, Baker-Seven, Baker-Nine, Baker-Eleven, Baker-Thirteen, Baker-Fourteen, and Baker-Eighteen. Some controversy exists surrounding the ditching of one Bombing Six plane, Baker-Nine, piloted by ENS Eugene Greene. Some histories claim that Greene's SBD-2 ditched shortly after the *Enterprise* dive bombers sighted *Arashi*. However, one of the surviving Bombing Six pilots, ENS Lew Hopkins, claimed that Greene's plane survived the morning attack on *Kaga*, and in fact, it formed on his wing during the recovery phase. However, after a time, Greene's plane ran out of fuel shortly after he and Hopkins lost sight of the Japanese fleet. In any event, Greene ditched his plane in the empty ocean, and he and his gunner, RM 3/c Samuel Muntean, were never seen again.

What a morning! Despite the losses, we were drunk with triumph. For the past six months, our situation had looked grim. With the codebreakers' spectacular success, all eyes turned to us, the aviators. We had to deliver a victory. We had to prove that our training, our equipment, and our resolve had not been a waste of time. Here, now, Thursday, June 4, we had our proof. We had done it. We had demonstrated to all doubters that U.S. naval dive bombing really worked. Now it seemed we might just have a shot at winning this thing.

But it would be a great mistake to say that we rested on our laurels. It was still only noon of what would be a very long day. The battle was far from over.

|||||||||||||||||||||||||||||||||||||||||||||||||||||||||||||||||||||||||||||||||||||||||||||||||||||||||||||

CHAPTER 14

THE BATTLE OF MIDWAY, PART 2
The Afternoon Attack, June 4, 1942

A powerful Japanese fleet was still out there, and the surviving carrier, *Hiryu*, was like a wounded animal, thirsting for revenge. We had to deliver the coup de grâce or suffer the same fate ourselves. As I walked across the flight deck, I learned some terrible news. Members of *Enterprise*'s deck crew told me the Japanese had counterattacked. At 11:55, dive bombers from *Hiryu*—the very same pack that I saw during my return flight—attacked one of our three carriers, USS *Yorktown*. During the ensuing engagement, the Japanese lost five of their six fighter planes and thirteen of their eighteen dive bombers, but they damaged *Yorktown* with three bomb strikes.

Diving through layers of flak, they put two holes in the deck and another near the smokestack. Although this did not sink *Yorktown*, it did put the big ship out of action. Because *Yorktown*'s deck was a shambles, the carrier's returning dive bombers—twenty-three of them—had to land on *Enterprise*. At first I worried things might get a little crowded, but as I entered the hangar deck, I realized a terrible truth—the arrival of *Yorktown*'s fliers filled out our own losses. Most of our Devastator squadron, Torpedo Six, had been destroyed during the morning mission.

I instantly thought of my friend Tom Eversole. I rushed into Torpedo Six's ready room. I found a few surviving Torpedo Six crewmen resting in the chairs, all of them stunned, heads hung low, eyes glassy and remote. The sight of all the vacant seats filled me with a creeping dread. Clearly, Torpedo Six had been through some kind of hell.

I asked them point-blank, "What happened to you guys?" They told me their sad story. After my squadron departed Task Force 16, Torpedo Six launched fourteen planes. The squadron roughly followed the path taken by my squadron, that is, until around 9:30, when Torpedo Six's commander, LCDR Lindsey, saw smoke on the horizon.[*] Lindsey turned his squadron hard to starboard, and his squadron reached the Japanese carriers at about 9:40, about forty-five minutes before my squadron attacked.[†] Without fighter cover and wielding their defective torpedoes, Torpedo Six barreled into the enemy fleet and took heavy casualties. In a few minutes, the Zeros splashed nine planes. Five crews managed to escape the carnage, but one of these, Tare-Eight, ditched on its return trip, leav-

---

[*] This smoke was caused by Torpedo Eight's attack against the carrier *Soryu*, which had occurred just minutes before. Torpedo Eight belonged to USS *Hornet*. That squadron had broken off from its air group and encountered the enemy fleet on its own. It was the first squadron from either task force to encounter the Japanese carrier fleet. In a few minutes, the Japanese fighters and antiaircraft gunners shot down all fifteen planes. Twenty-nine of thirty crewmen died. The next day, a PBY scout plane recovered the one survivor, ENS George Gay, who was found floating on the ocean.

[†] Torpedo Six's after-action report indicated that the squadron made contact at 10:00 A.M., but most histories contend that the engagement started earlier, at 9:40.

ing only four forlorn crews to return to *Enterprise*.* The survivors believed they had scored two torpedo hits, but later studies proved that none of their torpedoes had exploded.

Down in *Enterprise*'s hangar deck were the shredded remains of Torpedo Six—just four TBD-1 Devastators, two them badly shot up. How the survivors got home and landed at all was a miracle. They were shot full of holes and about half of their fuselage skin was missing. One of those planes had only four aluminum pipes connecting the tail section to the rest of the plane. It looked like a gutted fish with only the head and tail intact. It was so badly filleted as to be useless even for parts. The crew shoved it overboard.

Tom Eversole's plane was not among the surviving quartet. I couldn't stop thinking about my best friend on the ship. I asked the survivors what happened to him. They told me that Tom's torpedo bomber had been shot down. The news hit me like a thunderclap.

I admit that I held on to a distant hope that Tom might have survived the crash, and that maybe he was floating in his life raft, exactly as had happened to him on February 18. Deep down, however, I knew he was gone. This realization hurt me profoundly, perhaps even more than when I saw Bill West drown two weeks earlier. Tom and I had gone through so much together and had shared in so many dangers. I always believed that if I was ever so foolish as to fall overboard, Tom would jump in the ocean to save me without pausing to consider the danger. He was that kind of person. Now he was gone and there was nothing I could do about it. Curses to whoever ordered those fourteen brave torpedo bomber crews to fly into battle that morning! Even today, I can't think about

---

* On June 21, after seventeen days at sea, a PBY rescued the crew from Tare-Eight, Machinist Albert Waldo Winchell and RM 3/c Douglas Marvin Cossitt.

Tom's death without a bit of anger, as he should never have been there in the first place.

When I first learned of Tom's death, I tried not to dwell on it. The battle was not yet won and our air group was hurting from losses in men and planes. Can you believe it? *Enterprise's* air group had lost 43 percent of its personnel during that morning mission.

The Scouting Six ready room offered a sorry sight, too. Seventeen of our pilots had filled that room only six hours earlier, but now only nine remained.* The situation in Bombing Six was even worse. Fifteen planes had launched in the morning, but only five had returned.† Some of these missing pilots might still be alive, I thought, floating on the ocean, waiting to be picked up. But others might be dead. Even with the orphans from *Yorktown*, I wondered, could our meager air group carry on operations with losses like these? My squadron would have to fight the remainder of the battle with only 50 percent of our pilots available.‡

---

* ENS John Q. Roberts had died during the attack, his plane shot down by *Kaga's* antiaircraft batteries. Seven other pilots—Dickinson, McCarthy, Lough, Peiffer, Ware, O'Flaherty, and Shelton—had failed to return, all of them having run out of gas flying the inbound leg. Two of these pilots—Dickinson and McCarthy—were later found. The nine pilots who returned were me, Gallaher, Rodenburg (who returned to the carrier shortly after takeoff), Dexter, Stone, Micheel, West, Pittman, and Jaccard. Scouting Six also possessed two additional pilots, Patriarca and Vammen, who remained on *Enterprise* with the spares. I did not count these two men with the seventeen pilots who launched on the morning attack.

† The five planes that returned belonged to LT Richard Best, LTJG Edward Kroeger, ENS Frederick Weber, LTJG Edward Anderson, and ENS Lewis Hopkins. Although we did not know it yet, two other planes—those belonging to ENS George Goldsmith and LTJG Wilbur Roberts—had landed on *Yorktown*. Those crews survived, but their planes were destroyed when USS *Yorktown* sank. Every other plane had crashed from fuel exhaustion. Of the eight missing crews, only two were later found.

‡ My carrier accommodated fifteen dive bombers from Bombing Three and eight from Scouting Five. That squadron had taken off from *Yorktown* shortly before

I reported to Scouting Six's office and gave Gallaher my report on the morning's action. I proudly told him how I had returned Sail-Seven without a scratch. Once the crew had rearmed and re-fueled it, I could fly in the afternoon. I told Gallaher about the ditched Bombing Six crew, and I confirmed that my bombs had struck one of the Japanese carriers. I felt certain I had hit *Kaga*, but really, all Gallaher and I could agree on was that we had left three enemy flattops burning and useless. At the time, that was enough for the two of us.

I scarfed down a quick lunch of sandwiches and coffee, eat-ing them out on Vulture's Row. Even as I ate my meal, *Hiryu* launched a second air strike, this one consisting of six fighters and ten torpedo bombers. By 2:30, this second wave of Japanese planes reached *Yorktown*, the same carrier that *Hiryu*'s fliers had damaged hours earlier. Sandwich in hand, I watched this engagement un-fold. I saw six of *Enterprise*'s fighter planes swarm into the Japanese planes, helping *Yorktown*'s fighters shoot down five torpedo bomb-ers and three fighters. *Yorktown*'s task force was far from our own, so the aerial battle looked like a bunch of angry dots swirling on the horizon. In the end, the enemy got the upper hand. *Yorktown* endured two torpedo hits. If the bomb damage had not rendered it dead in the water, the torpedoes certainly did. *Yorktown* developed a list—a tilt—preventing it from launching or landing any more planes. Admiral Fletcher, the senior commander, transferred to a cruiser and gave Spruance free rein to command all further air operations.

By this point everyone in our ready room was chomping at the bit to get airborne again. Even though we had brushed elbows with

the attack by *Hiryu*'s planes, and when it returned, the pilots needed a place to land.

death just hours before, we were all eager to go back out there. In fact, I can't remember another time when my squadron was as unified with battle fever.

All we needed was a target.

Our answer came at 2:45. An SBD pilot who belonged to Scouting Five, *Yorktown*'s scout bombing squadron, radioed the position of *Hiryu* and its escorts. That pilot, LT Samuel Adams, brilliantly located the missing Japanese carrier and accurately identified its location some 110 miles from our position.* Immediately we prepared for a second strike. With McClusky confined to sick bay, having returned from the morning attack with a shoulder wound, LT Gallaher took command.† Gallaher was the most senior of the remaining pilots. I was overjoyed to hear our superb skipper would be leading us. He was a true genius when it came to naval dive bombing. Gallaher's leadership shined immediately. He drew up a plan that differed greatly from the morning attack. Instead of wasting time trying to unite the air groups, Gallaher wanted *Enterprise* to launch its dive bombers and not wait for *Hornet*'s air group to unite with us. This way my squadron could conserve its fuel, we could take our time when making our attacks, and we didn't have to worry about coordinating with other groups.

Gallaher organized the three dive bomber squadrons—Scouting Six, Bombing Six, and Bombing Three—into appropriate groups.

***

* Providentially, at 11:30, *Yorktown* had launched ten SBD-3s belonging to Scouting Five, fanning them out in two-plane sections. One of those planes, Sail-Seven, flown by LT Sam Adams, called in the sighting. This was one of the most important moments of the battle. Minutes after the staff officers on *Enterprise* received Adams's data, they accurately relayed it to our ready rooms.

† The next ranking officer would have been LCDR Maxwell Leslie, commander of Bombing Three; however, Leslie had no plane, and in fact he was not even on *Enterprise*. During his return from the morning attack, Leslie's plane, Baker One, ditched near USS *Astoria* (CA-34) when it ran out of fuel.

Gallaher told me that since my aircraft, Sail-Seven, could still fly, I should expect to join the mission. I was eager for it. With Tom's death looming over me, I felt the need to do something to make his sacrifice meaningful.

Initially, we counted thirty operational dive bombers; however, five of these never launched and a sixth plane, Norman West's, experienced engine trouble and had to return to the carrier. In the end, *Enterprise* deployed twenty-four SBDs: six from Scouting Six, four from Bombing Six, and fourteen from Bombing Three. The second launch began at 3:30. When the speaker blared, "Pilots, man your planes!" I bolted onto the flight deck and found John Snowden smiling and ready to go. We had our propeller spinning smartly and I gave a firm thumbs-up during my equipment check. Gallaher's plane took off first, followed by his two wingmen, Stone and Jaccard. Then the takeoff officer spotted me. I revved my engine, and for a second time, John Snowden and I lofted heavenward. I had my old wingman, ENS James Dexter, following me, and also a new one, ENS Vernon Micheel. Both men were excellent, trustworthy pilots. Those of us in Scouting Six carried our usual complement of three bombs, one 500-pounder and two incendiaries. Once we got airborne, the other squadrons, Bombing Six and Bombing Three, joined us, each plane carrying a 1,000-pound bomb. The launch was complete by 3:45. With that, cruising at 13,000 feet, our air group proceeded on its next date with destiny.

The second air strike proceeded nearly flawlessly. By comparison, the morning mission had lasted five hours, with more than three hours devoted to locating the Japanese fleet. In contrast, our afternoon mission took only ninety minutes to find *Hiryu*. We spotted our target at 4:55, seeing it easily to our north through a layer of scattered clouds.

The Japanese carrier was circled by six surface ships, including a battleship. We could see thick columns of smoke off to the south,

the scene of the previous attack. We assumed the other enemy surface ships were there, rescuing their survivors and scuttling the
wrecks. As we closed on our new target, I noticed about a dozen
Zeros circling *Hiryu*. John and I anticipated a rougher battle. In the
morning, the Japanese fighters were nowhere to be seen. Clearly
they had been chasing the torpedo squadrons and had no idea that
we dive bombers were approaching from above. Now, in the afternoon, the enemy fighters were out on patrol, wiser for what we had
done to them that morning and eager to test their luck against us.

Gallaher gave a signal to the group. He instructed us to climb
to 19,000 feet and use that as our attack altitude. Further, rather
than send us into our attack directly, as McClusky had done, Gallaher told us to circle clockwise around the enemy fleet. As we approached *Hiryu* from the south, Gallaher wanted us to swing to the
west. That way we would emerge from the clouds on the sunny side
of the carrier. Ideally we'd be invisible to the Zeros and to *Hiryu*'s
antiaircraft gunners, who wouldn't be able to see us with the glare
of the sun in their faces.

When we reached a point directly west of *Hiryu,* with the carrier steaming directly at us into the blazing afternoon sun, Gallaher broke radio silence. He ordered Bombing Three to continue
arcing northeast and attack the battleship *Haruna*. Meanwhile,
Gallaher ordered Scouting Six and Bombing Six to follow him
against *Hiryu*. Although we were understrength, Gallaher believed
that nine SBDs could finish the job. Like any good leader, he had
incredible faith in us.

The battle above *Hiryu* began at 5:05. A cluster of five Zeros
swooped in at us, causing our gunners to blaze away. At least two
of them lunged at Gallaher's plane, but his intrepid gunner, ACRM
Thomas Merritt, kept them at bay. We opened our throttles, reaching the pushover point at high speed. Gallaher went first, dropping
downward and pushing into a nearly vertical angle. He aimed his

bomb perfectly, but suddenly *Hiryu* made a radical turn to port. The helmsman on that carrier saw our approach and tried to spin the carrier 180 degrees. When *Hiryu* commenced its turn, Gallaher had just gripped the bomb-release lever and he jerked his plane to correct for the error. The skipper's bombs jolted loose and the force of it caused his plane to shudder like a T-boned automobile. The trauma wrenched his back. I watched as he pulled out of his awkward dive, his bombs splashing harmlessly astern of his target.

I had just pushed over and I could see the string of three planes in line ahead of me. Had *Hiryu* remained on a steady course, Gallaher would have hit it, but the ship's sudden turn prevented that. The next pilot, Reid Stone, also missed. He was following Gallaher closely in his dive and likewise did not have time to correct. Thankfully, the third pilot, Richard Jaccard—a junior pilot who missed *Kaga* during the morning attack—delivered the first hit. The rookie's 500-pound bomb plunged through *Hiryu*'s forward elevator, flinging the big steel slab up against the bridge.

As I plunged toward the sea, fourth in line, I remember thinking this was my toughest dive yet. In the morning, I had to hit a moving target. Now I had to hit not only a moving target, but one that was also in the middle of a sharp turn. In a few seconds, I sized up the enemy carrier and determined its speed and turning radius. *Hiryu*, smaller than *Kaga* and *Akagi*, turned remarkably fast. Its bow would be off its own port quarter in twenty seconds, meaning it could complete a 120-degree turn in that short a period of time. Yikes! Once again I aimed for the unblemished Rising Sun on the flight deck. I didn't aim directly to hit the ship, but aimed for where the ship was going to be as it continued that turn.

I took my plane down to a low altitude—about 1,500 feet—and released my payload. My bombs plunged into *Hiryu*'s smoking flight deck.

When I pulled up, I stood the plane on its tail. This time I really wanted to see the damage unfold. Looking over my shoulder, I could see that my 500-pounder had landed about sixty feet in front of where Jaccard's bomb had hit. My bombs smashed into the flight deck and, like a giant hand rolling a taco, just folded it over. I must say, the sight of *Hiryu*'s destruction seared itself into my memory. Even now I can close my eyes and see the image of the mutilated flight deck clear as day. It's probably my most vivid recollection of the battle. With the deck peeled away, I saw *Hiryu*'s innards, rows of planes kept belowdecks. Flying debris and flames pulverized them and produced such a huge fire that little else could be seen on *Hiryu*'s bow. Still, the fire was nothing in comparison to the fires I had seen in the morning attack.

I leveled out and tried to gain altitude, but I kept looking back to watch the other SBDs coming down. I saw several other good hits smack *Hiryu*. Contrary to orders, LT DeWitt Shumway led his squadron, Bombing Three, against the carrier. Gallaher had told Shumway to attack the battleship, but when Shumway saw Gallaher's and Stone's bombs miss the flattop, he directed his squadron to dive on it, unintentionally cutting in front of Bombing Six in the process. Bombing Three scored at least one hit, and Dick Best of Bombing Six claimed a hit as well. This last bomb smacked the forward flight deck, about ninety feet from the bow. As it turned out, Dick Best and I were the only two American dive bomber pilots to score two hits on June 4. Best hit *Akagi* in the morning and I hit *Kaga*. Both of us hit *Hiryu* in the afternoon. All the while, as we attacked, Zeros hounded us during our dives. One fighter zoomed at Gallaher immediately after he pushed over.* When I leveled out

---

* Zeros shot down two SBD-3s belonging to Bombing Three, Baker-Twelve and Baker-Sixteen, killing both pilots and their gunners. Finally, a Zero splashed

following the attack, a Nakajima E8N2 reconnaissance seaplane—one of four attached to the Japanese carrier force—swooped in. John Snowden unleashed a burst of machine gun fire, setting its engine smoking, and it veered off.

Even after the attack was over, *Hiryu*'s fighters harassed us as we flew back to *Enterprise*. What else was there for the enemy pilots to do? They were as good as dead men, with nowhere left to land. I joined up with Gallaher and two Bombing Six planes. A single Zero tailed us most of the way, taking leisurely shots, but our resolute gunners kept the Zero at a distance. At 6:15, all of our surviving aircraft reached *Enterprise*. Each plane landed safely, including three battle-damaged SBDs. I landed with no trouble. Amazingly, I returned to base for a second time without my plane suffering so much as a scratch. LT Gallaher was lucky to land cleanly with his severely wrenched back.

Initially he refused to land. His injury prevented him from reaching the lever that lowered his plane's tailhook. Without a tailhook down, you can't catch a wire, and if you can't catch a wire, you're going to bounce down that long flight deck, hitting everything in your path, potentially going over the bow and into the drink. For a few minutes it appeared as if he might have to ditch. From the flight deck I watched in horror, worried that he'd go into the water and be carried down by his sinking plane. It would be the fate of Bill West all over again! I don't know how he did it, but Gallaher managed to ignore the blinding pain long enough to pull the lever. At 6:34 his plane landed perfectly, although the carrier's

---

Bombing Six's Baker-Three. This occurred when Bombing Three cut in front of Bombing Six; Dick Best held back his planes for a few crucial seconds and one enterprising Zero pilot used this opportunity to get behind the last plane in the group, shooting it down, killing ENS Frederick Weber and his gunner, AOM 3/c Ernest Hilbert.

corpsmen had to lift Gallaher out of the cockpit. His injury left him too stricken to move.

That legendary day was almost at its close. I reported my actions to LT Frank Patriarca, now Scouting Six's commander. Once again I was proud to say I had struck an enemy carrier. I tried to tell him how *Hiryu* looked like a big smoking taco, but I'm not sure he appreciated my metaphor. Patriarca gave me a nod and told me that due to all the casualties, I was de facto second-in-command of Scouting Six.

Thoroughly fatigued from the day's exertions, I wandered back to my room and recorded the day's events in my logbook. Meticulously, I wrote down every detail I could remember. Strange as it is to say, I knew I had just been part of a battle that would be forever remembered. I wanted to get every detail right. Devoted as I was to preserving these facts, it was hard to put it all together. I wanted to narrate what I had done, commit every anecdote to paper. But my mind drifted to Tom Eversole and the torpedo bomber pilots.

Saddened beyond measure, I wrote this in my journal: "Breathe a prayer for our suicide TBD squadrons." As the last hours of daylight faded, I jotted my prayer: "Now, oh Lord, won't you please take care of those Wonderful Ones who loved us so much. They were willing to die for us without hesitation." At that moment, another Scouting Six pilot brought in a slug of whiskey. I gulped it down and fell fast asleep.

|||||||||||||||||||||||||||||||||||||||||||||||||||||||||||||||||||||||||||||||||||||||||||||||||||||||||||||||||

CHAPTER 15

THE BATTLE OF MIDWAY, PART 3
June 5 and 6, 1942

After a deep, dreamless sleep, I awoke early the next day, June 5, ready to head back into action. Unlike the previous day, my squadron's morning got off to a slow start. We knew we had crippled or sunk four Japanese carriers, but we did not yet know what the Japanese surface ships intended. Would they continue their course toward Midway or would they retreat? All morning the admirals vacillated, or so it seemed to me, wondering what move to make. Hours passed.

Finally, at 2:00 P.M., Admiral Spruance elected to send out a search mission. At the request of his chief of staff, CAPT Miles Browning, Spruance ordered the SBDs on a 270-mile scouting mission carrying 1,000-pound bombs. This announcement resulted in a near revolt among us aviators. We did not want to travel so far and with such a heavy load. Our disagreement was understandable. The previous day, eighteen planes had failed to return from Scouting Six and Bombing Six. Nearly all had been lost because fuel exhaustion had caused them to fall out of the sky. Heavy bomb loads at extreme range gambled with the pilots' lives, and no one relished the idea of dying slowly of sunstroke and thirst out on the lonesome Pacific. When news of Browning's plan reached us in the ready room, the walls practically rumbled with our displeasure.

Pushed to the limits by our superiors, we complained vociferously. I didn't see what happened, but I heard about it afterward. An argument erupted on the bridge as some of the dive bomber pilots decided to tell Browning and Spruance what they thought of the plan. The contingent included two pilots from *Yorktown*, LT DeWitt Shumway and LT Wally Short, and it also included Wade McClusky and Earl Gallaher, who both hobbled out of sick bay to be there. McClusky and Gallaher suggested that Spruance order a later takeoff so the task force could close the distance and shorten the inbound leg. Second, they wanted the planes fitted out to carry only a 500-pound bomb load. This would allow the crews to fill our tanks to maximum capacity. After a protracted argument in which the four pilots all had their say, Spruance altered Browning's plan, allowing the aviators—not his staff—to formulate the mission.

I should repeat, I did not witness this heated argument on *Enterprise*'s bridge, so I do not have firsthand knowledge of what actually transpired, but I have often thought about what it suggested about American leadership at Midway. The senior officers on *Enterprise* had taken a big risk when they sent us on the morning mission on June 4. That risk had paid off, but at high cost. We destroyed four Japanese carriers, but at the price of 70 percent of *Enterprise*'s torpedo bomber squadron and half of our two dive bomber squadrons. We pilots had endured these risks without complaint, but now, a day later, Browning's decision to execute a high-risk air operation seemed unnecessary and reckless. A day makes all the difference. I'm glad that Gallaher and McClusky voiced their concerns. They probably saved many pilots' lives on June 5.

Even so, we pilots planned this mission poorly. At first, I expected Dick Best would operate as the new air group commander, but that morning he reported to sick bay. Overnight he had come down with a respiratory illness induced by breathing caustic soda from his SBD's malfunctioning oxygen system. For a second time in a matter of hours, another valuable squadron commander had been grounded. Without Gallaher or Best available, our new air group commander was LT Shumway, who until recently had been a division commander on *Yorktown*. Shumway had to take charge of thirty-two planes: ten from Bombing Three, six from Bombing Six, seven from Scouting Five, and nine from Scouting Six.

Our mission was simple. We had to find the Japanese carrier force and make certain *Hiryu* had gone down. If it was still afloat, we had to finish the job. If it was already sunk, then we had to do all we could to damage the surface ships.

We had a pretty good idea where to find the Japanese ships, since reports from the PBYs had been streaming in all morning. Our objective was reported only a short distance from the previous day, and included roughly the same assortment of ships: two battleships, three cruisers, and four destroyers. Importantly, the PBYs reported a damaged enemy carrier still afloat. We supposed it had to be *Hiryu.**

At 3:12 we launched our mixed contingent of thirty-two SBDs. After forming up near our carrier, LT Shumway led us toward the Japanese for 265 miles. The scouting squadrons, our own and Scouting Five, flew at low altitude. We formed into a "scouting line," that is, with the planes arranged in something like a half chevron, spread out so we could see as much of the horizon as possible, but close enough that we could signal each other without radios if any of us spotted something important. Meanwhile, Bombing

---

* The previous day's targets—based on LT Adams's report—was 31-40°N Latitude, 172-10°W Longitude. The June 5 objective was 30-00°N Latitude, 176-32°W Longitude.

Three and Bombing Six cruised above us at 13,000 feet, taking in a bird's-eye view of the ocean. Poor weather hampered the search. All the way, fog and mist enshrouded the horizon. From where I was, I could see very little. Eventually, after hours in the air with no enemy contact, Shumway signaled to the scouting squadrons to pull out of our scouting line. We joined Bombing Three and Bombing Six at their attack altitude.

At 6:00 P.M. we reached the intercept point, finding nothing but empty ocean, a frustrating repeat of the day before. Shumway led us to the southwest and we kept searching. At 6:20 we picked up a message over the radio. The other carrier in our task force, USS *Hornet,* had launched thirty-three SBDs about the same time as *Enterprise.* Those planes had made contact, and their air group commander, LCDR Stanhope Ring, called out, telling us that his planes were engaging a light cruiser. Shumway gave us a signal and we changed direction yet again. In ten minutes we arrived on the scene. We did not see a cruiser, but a lone destroyer, the *Tanikaze.* Apparently the Japanese had left behind this ship to scuttle *Hiryu,* which had slipped beneath the waves long before we got there.

When we reached the scene, *Hornet's* dive bombers had already made their attacks and were forming up to head home. All thirty-three of their planes had dived on *Tanikaze* and none of them had hit their target. As soon as our air group arrived, the destroyer started peppering us with antiaircraft fire. Shumway signaled to us, waggling his wings: "Attack!" The dive bombers from Bombing Three went first, followed by six Bombing Six planes commanded by LT Lloyd Smith. All of them missed. Then it was our turn.

LT Patriarca waggled his wings and our nine planes from Scouting Six tried our luck. One by one, we went into our dives, but due to the inclement conditions, the choppy seas, and the diminutive size of our target, we hit nothing. The destroyer made tight

S-turns, slicing back and forth. The overcast and growing darkness made the target difficult to see. I could only make it out by sighting the muzzle flashes of the antiaircraft guns and by looking for the white flare rising up behind the ship, which indicated the direction of the vessel. In the end, I missed with the rest of my squadron. I came in low and dropped my bomb, but it splashed harmlessly to the side. Later that evening, this was how I described the attack in the June 5 entry of my war journal: "The little devil fired everything he had at us, put on full speed (about 40 kts.), zigzagging nicely, and was most difficult to hit. I saw several close misses, but no hits."

After I pulled out of my dive, I watched as the seven planes from Scouting Five tried to sink the slippery destroyer. Once again, they all missed. Even worse, one plane crashed into the water. This SBD belonged to LT Sam Adams, the same *Yorktown* pilot who had spotted *Hiryu* the day before and radioed its position perfectly. One of the most important figures of the battle had died a watery death in a mission that accomplished nothing. We had all just whiffed a game against a lonely little tin can. God has funny ways of humbling men.

Beyond the loss of Adams and his gunner, RM 2/c Joseph J. Karrol, our group got away unscathed—a few minor dings to the aircraft, but no further casualties. Our group orchestrated a running rendezvous, with the lead planes cruising slowly so the rear planes could catch up. Using our YE-ZB, we homed in on *Enterprise* and made it back at 7:45. It was completely dark, which posed something of a danger because six pilots from Scouting Six had never made a night landing before. I had already made several of them myself, but even with my experience, the process was not easy. I have since heard Navy pilots compare night landings to jumping onto a moving skateboard with your eyes closed. I think that about sums it up. *Enterprise* had its sidelights and search lights on, which made the carrier easy to see, but being able to tell the status of one's approach was virtually impossible in the dark. During daylight landings, I could always get visual cues from the landing signal officer or from the photographic contingent up on Vultures Row—if they ever raised their cameras toward you, look out! Unable to see them in the darkness, I had to determine my speed, altitude, and rate of descent all on my own. This night landing was confusing, particularly with so many planes returning at once, but I trapped on board with no trouble. Our big problem during the June 5 recovery was that our pilots couldn't identify which carriers were which. USS *Hornet* and USS *Enterprise* looked virtually indistinguishable in the dark. Five *Hornet* pilots accidentally landed on *Enterprise,* believing it to be their own carrier, and one Scouting Six pilot, ENS Clarence Vammen, landed on *Hornet.* In any event, I was not at all pleased with the results of the June 5 mission. In my war journal, I summed it up succinctly: "This flight was not worth the gas, bombs, and loss of a plane."

The next day, Saturday, June 6, offered one final opportunity for action. I arose early yet again, had a decent breakfast and a short mission briefing, and at 7:00, answered the familiar call, "Pilots, man your planes!" This morning I joined a "scouting hop," a mission intended to scour a sector of ocean northwest of our carrier. Eighteen SBDs were assigned to this mission, six belonging to my squadron. We launched at 7:10, and once again, John Snowden and I were airborne. We cruised for two hundred miles but reported no contact in our sector. We returned to *Enterprise* without incident. None of the other planes reported contacts, either.

The real action occurred in the afternoon. One of our scout planes reported another group of enemy surface ships 170 miles from our task force. This group of ships consisted of two cruisers, *Mogami* and *Mikuma,* and two destroyers, *Asashio* and *Arashio.* During the night, the two cruisers had collided. Now they steamed slowly in the water, leaking oil. Due to a transmission error, the scouting report identified a Japanese carrier with the group. (The radioman meant to send the letters "CA," the code for "heavy cruiser," but instead sent the letters "CV," the code for "aircraft carrier.") In fact, in our ready room, LT Patriarca told us that a battleship had also been spotted by the scouts, a discovery that proved erroneous once our squadron arrived on the scene. Our leaders worried that another flattop and its escorts had arrived. After quick consultation, Admiral Spruance ordered one last air strike. He wanted us dive bombers to intercept this group and send the unknown carrier to the bottom.

USS *Hornet* launched first, sending twenty-five SBDs and eight F4Fs into the air. They gave the Japanese cruisers a decent whacking, or so they claimed. They hit *Mikuma* five times and *Mogami* once. Two of their planes were shot down, one of their own pilots and also ENS Vammen of our squadron. Since he had landed aboard *Hornet* the previous evening, Vammen had orders to return to *Enterprise* after this mission. Sadly, his plane took a direct hit from antiaircraft fire and he and his gunner, AMM 1/c Milton Clark (who had flown with me when I earned my nickname), were killed. Two more wonderful friends were added to Scouting Six's growing death roster.

Despite the accuracy of their attack, *Hornet*'s pilots failed to sink either of the two cruisers, so Spruance ordered us *Enterprise* pilots into the fray. At 11:00 A.M. we launched thirty Dauntlesses, all under the command of LT Wally Short.* John Snowden and I

---

* Once again, our mission consisted of *Enterprise* and orphaned *Yorktown* aircraft. LT Short led seven Scouting Five aircraft, LT Patriarca led six Scouting Six aircraft, LT Smith led five Bombing Six aircraft, and LT Shumway led ten Bombing Three aircraft. Also, two SBD-3s from USS *Hornet* accompanied VB-6 for this mission.

made up part of Scouting Six's six-plane contingent. As usual, I led one of the three-plane sections, supervising wingmen Micheel and Dexter. In addition, we also had twelve F4Fs accompanying us, providing fighter protection. Spruance even allowed three TBDs from Torpedo Six to take off and accompany us, although he gave specific instructions to the three pilots to abort the mission should it appear too dangerous for them. None of the three planes reached the target, wisely turning back. This was the last combat operation performed by TBD-1 Devastators.

About one hour after takeoff, we discovered *Mogami* and *Mikuma,* an easy enough task given that we merely had to follow the trail of leaking oil. We were a little disappointed in what we saw. The word sent to us from *Hornet* was that they had sunk one of the destroyers and that both of the cruisers were dead in the water. Our mission was supposed to "mop up" what they had started.

The reality was quite different. In the heat of battle, the *Hornet* pilots had exaggerated the results of their attack. Although *Mikuma* was noticeably damaged, all four ships were afloat and operational. Antiaircraft fire whizzed in as soon as we got there. The Japanese still had plenty of fight left in them, and this would be nothing like the "mop-up" we were led to expect. Further, we wasted precious time searching for the supposed battleship, circling around the cruisers hoping to see it. We found no battleship because none existed. The report had been in error. When LT Short became convinced that the only ships in the area were the two cruisers and the two destroyers, he ordered us to attack.

Our attack on the cruisers began at 12:35. We were up at 19,000 feet. Scouting Five went in first, dropping its bombs on *Mikuma,* scoring as many as five hits. My squadron went next. Mine was the fourth of our six planes to dive. Compared to the earlier dives against the enemy carriers, this one was just as exciting, perhaps even more because we came into the middle of a running engagement. The diving attack by *Hornet*'s planes had already put the Japanese on alert, so their antiaircraft fire was ferocious and determined. The destroyers buffeted our squadrons with puffs of smoke, a desperate salvo to save their stricken cruisers. Meanwhile, it seemed that everyone was chattering on the radio, breathlessly shouting out their feelings, saying such obvious things as "Look at it burn!" or "You nailed that SOB!" I didn't indulge in any histrionics, but I'll admit I felt the peculiar rush of adrenaline at knowing I'd get another kill. As my plane plummeted downward, *Mikuma* reminded me of a wounded animal bleeding inky black blood. Somehow it felt right to put it out of its misery. The cruiser was a smaller target and harder to hit, but as I approached my release altitude, *Mikuma*'s smoking deck wandered lazily into my bomb scope. I must have grinned with pride. I had made another perfect dive. I was dead-on with no chance of side slippage. For the third time in as many days, I knew I was going to hit something big.

Scouting Six delivered three perfect hits, all amidships, with my bomb exploding just aft of *Mikuma*'s smokestack, adjacent to its No. 4 turret. When I pulled out of my dive—my fourth combat dive of the battle—I looked backward to observe the battered cruiser. It was an absolute wreck with no chance of survival. As I wrote in my journal, "[We left] our target a complete mass of wreckage dead in the water and burning from stem to stern. . . . No one will probably ever know who hit what today, but two bits says the battle cruiser we hit is now resting on the bottom."

Mikuma did sink, although it took several hours to slip beneath the waves.* Confirmation came later in the day when my friend Cleo Dobson volunteered to fly an SBD on a photographic mission.

---

* Bombing Six and Bombing Three added to the carnage, and later on the cruiser endured another dive bombing attack delivered by pilots from *Hornet*.

At 3:00 P.M. he found *Mikuma* smoking and abandoned. Dobson's rear-seat gunner, chief photographer J. A. Mihalovic, snapped several shots of the stricken vessel, which became some of the best-known images of the Pacific War. (Rare is the day when I can pick up a book on the Pacific War and fail to see Mihalovic's photograph.)

As he flew overhead, Dobson soon noticed about twenty survivors clustered around the stern, some of them making their way into the water. Someone on *Enterprise* had given Dobson orders to strafe any Japanese sailors he found, but when he saw the panicked men splashing in the water he refused to add to the bloodbath. When he returned to *Enterprise,* he confided to me, "They were waving at me and I just couldn't do that!"

In the end, *Mikuma* took 650 officers and men to a watery grave. My other targets, *Hiryu* and *Kaga,* sank as well. *Kaga* went first, slipping beneath the surface at 7:00 P.M., June 4, taking with it the bodies of 811 sailors. Finally, *Hiryu* took with it 389 victims.

Sometimes these statistics are hard to think about. After all, I had something to do with the loss of life. God's commandment says, "Thou shall not kill." My job in the Navy involved dropping bombs on people, killing them. Only rarely has anyone ever asked me how I felt about that. Perhaps, at one brief moment, the thought of killing concerned me. However, I feel no shame in admitting that it did not worry me at the time and it does not worry me now. I did my duty to my country, plain and simple. I performed the tasks the Navy taught me. I dropped out of the sky like a meteor and released my bombs, pulling up within spitting distance of the ocean, just so I could reload, refuel, and rearm to perform the same dangerous task again later. This was no job; this was my duty— sacred, inviolable, and uncompromising. In the end, I can only hope I lived up to my obligation and the only individuals who shall be judged for the act of killing were those who were in power, those who brought on the cruel and bloody war in the Pacific.

When I returned to USS *Enterprise* at around 1:40 P.M. on June 6, I appreciated one fact above all else. *I was alive!* More than anything, I was thankful to have survived without a scratch. Six months earlier, I worried I would be killed by this war and miss out on the greatest opportunity of my life, being with lovely Jean forever. As I exited the cockpit of my trusty SBD, sun on my face, I realized how lucky I was. I would be going home—I was sure of it—and I had my chance to make amends for all I had done wrong.

I had barely changed out of my flight gear when I started penning a letter to Jean to let her know I was safe and sound:

[After]Noon
6 June 1942

Jean, darling,

Just have a second to let you know I'm OK but am tired as the dickens. Have been wearing your nice soft sweater and it keeps me warm way up thar' and keeps me safe way down below. If anything should get me now I just want you to know and Dad to know that recently I've had more than my share of luck and that Tojo is most unhappy about it all. Will write again soon as I can find a whole minute all at one time.

I love you darling. Don't worry or let anyone else worry about me, and bye for now.

Love you lots,
Jack

"I've had more than my share of luck." That's what I wrote on June 6 and it is still just as true today as it was back then. I realized my squadron had helped cripple the Japanese fleet and I was lucky enough to have played an important role, hitting three Japanese ships with bombs. But as the empty bunks attested, this victory came at a high cost. I survived while others died. It could just as easily have been the reverse.

The next four days passed anxiously. I wondered whether the admirals would pursue the Japanese surface ships westward across the Pacific. At first it seemed as if Admiral Spruance intended to take Task Force 16 to the Aleutians, the scene of the attack of June 3. This realization vexed us pilots. Although we were battle-weary, we wanted nothing more than to stay at Midway and finish off our foe. My frustration was evident when I wrote this in my war journal: "Wish we had Wild Bill Halsey along instead of Spruance. Believe he was a little too cautious." I was hot-headed and opinionated back then. At the time, I believed our fleet should have stayed longer. But history has proven Spruance right. We did not need to linger in the area, but in the aftermath of the battle, I could not fathom why he decided to leave the island unprotected. I continued, "Someone knows more of the answers than I do."

Slowly but surely, good news filtered in. As Task Force 16 steamed north, I learned that several of *Enterprise*'s missing pilots had been rescued. After the battle, destroyers recovered two Scouting Six pilots and their gunners: Clarence Dickinson, Mac McCarthy, Joseph DeLuca, and Earl E. Howell. Additionally, destroyers and PBYs rescued three Bombing Six crews. Finally, on June 21, a float plane discovered a lone Torpedo Six crew, pilot Machinist Albert Waldo Winchell and his gunner, RM 3/c Douglas Cossitt, the last two American aviators recovered after the battle.* In the final tally, ten crews from *Enterprise*—five Scouting Six crews and

---

* A few squadrons possessed one or two enlisted pilots. Albert W. Winchell was one of them.

five Bombing Six crews—remained unaccounted for. All ten planes had ditched after the June 4 morning attack and their crews were never to be seen again.

The fate of one of our aircrews in particular has never stopped bothering me. We learned years later that on the afternoon of June 4, the Japanese destroyer *Makigumo* fished out of the sea ENS Franklin Woodrow O'Flaherty and his gunner, AMM 1/c Bruno Peter Gaido, of Scouting Six. With little delay, *Makigumo*'s officers interrogated the two men, later claiming they had coerced from them vital information about Midway's defenses. Then, sometime after the battle, Commander Isamu Fujita determined that O'Flaherty and Gaido had outlived their usefulness. Fujita ordered his sailors to tie weights around their ankles and toss them back into the sea. On June 15, three petty officers carried out the murder. According to Japanese accounts, both aviators faced death stoically, without a word of complaint. Of course, I did not learn of this barbarous act until May 1947, when the Office of Naval Intelligence (ONI) published a translated copy of Admiral Nagumo's after-action report, which described the interrogation and execution of O'Flaherty and Gaido.

I could never fathom why the Japanese had to kill these friends of mine. Certainly I doubted that my two faithful comrades would have told their captors anything of value before they died. As it stood, the ONI report carried the insinuation that O'Flaherty and Gaido had given up crucial information that endangered our fleet. This story and its controversial legacy forms the subject of a later chapter, but on June 15, 1942, this untold story of the Battle of Midway set into motion a sequence of events that later captured my attention. It was this event that forced me to confront the history of the battle during a period of my life when I was trying to leave it behind.

Of course, as of June 11, all of this lay in the unforeseeable future. That day, word reached us aviators that Nimitz had recalled *Enterprise* to Pearl Harbor. We didn't know it at the time, but the Joint Chiefs of Staff had already ordered the First Marine Division to head to New Zealand in preparation for what would become the invasion of Guadalcanal. Having savaged the Japanese carrier fleet, Nimitz now had to keep our carriers safe until the operation in the Solomon Islands began. Accordingly, the Big E planned to enter port on Saturday, June 13. I wrote this in my journal: "The gang went wild. Seems as though a big Saturday night is in the offing." We bristled with anticipation. We believed we had fought hard and therefore deserved plenty of rest and relaxation. That day, I slumped contentedly into my bunk, lazily imagining my life with Jean. At the time, I realized that I had had a hand in one of the most important naval battles the world would ever witness, but I had no idea its memory would never leave me alone.

|||||||||||||||||||||||||||||||||||||||||||||||||||||||||||||||||||||||||||||||||||||||||||||||||||||||||||||

CHAPTER 16

RETURN TO THE STATES

June–October 1942

U SS *Enterprise* returned to Pearl Harbor on June 13. As the crew sauntered down the gangways to the pier, my squadron mates and I experienced a kaleidoscope of emotion. We felt the overwhelming physical and mental effects of prolonged fatigue. There was no doubt about it, we were tired. On one hand, we had survived one of the most epic battles in naval history. In defiance of the odds, we had returned alive. Against even longer odds, our out-numbered task force had destroyed an experienced Japanese fleet, which had enjoyed six months of continuous victory. The release of our pent-up nerves encouraged daredevilry among our merry group of survivors.

One of us—a Scouting Six ensign—displayed his cavalier blus-ter during the first day back at the naval air station in Kaneohe, Hawaii. During gunnery practice, he flipped his SBD on its back while firing on a tow sleeve. He scored perfect hits on this upside-down run, but he killed his engine. It starting smoking, and he landed it on a nearby beach, just ten feet from the waves. For his bravado, Gallaher made him guard the plane all night while the rest of us enjoyed happy hour in Honolulu. I felt no need to show off. I only wanted to be careful so I could return to my lady love the same as when I last saw her.

On the other hand, we had suffered the loss of a carrier. Although it survived the damage it suffered on June 4, USS *Yorktown* did not make it back to Pearl Harbor. While the wounded carrier was being towed at a near walking speed of only five knots, a Japanese submarine, *I-168*, slipped through *Yorktown*'s ring of escorts and torpedoed it, sending it to the bottom of the Pacific along with an escorting destroyer, USS *Hammann* (DD-412). Once again the Pacific Fleet was in a tight spot. Now only two carriers—*Enterprise* and *Hornet*—remained operational.

Even though USS *Enterprise* had suffered no physical damage, it had lost heavily in terms of its air crew. The Battle of Midway cost our air group forty-four men: fourteen from Scouting Six, eighteen from Torpedo Six, and twelve from Bombing Six. Overall, our two task forces had lost 277 sailors and airmen.

I found it difficult to weigh the importance of the victory against the terrible loss of life. I understood that battles were often exercises in cruel arithmetic, and yet it wasn't about numbers. The loss of Tom Eversole weighed especially heavily on me. He was no statistic to me, but a good friend. It felt as if a piece of me had been torn out, that I wasn't truly whole. At the time, when I weighed the loss of life against the consequences, I tried to stay positive.

On the first night back in Hawaii, we received a free stay at the Royal Hawaiian Hotel. As we drank a sentimental toast to the fallen, we overheard a group of B-17 pilots boasting about the great victory won by Army fliers based on Midway Atoll. They had been working the press for a full week before our arrival. An Army press release dated June 11 stated, "The Army fliers . . . kept up an incessant attack on the Japanese fleet until the invading force was completely shattered, and fleeing back toward its own bases. The Chief of bombing operations in the Hawaiian sector, Brigadier General Hale, said that the total destruction inflicted on the Japanese by Army flyers may even exceed present estimates." Believe it or not, a few papers in Hawaii bought and published some of this bilge.

Of course, those of us who had actually turned four enemy aircraft carriers into burning hulks knew the truth. Not one bomb from a B-17 Flying Fortress had struck an enemy ship. When he heard these boasts resonating above the gabble, an ex–Torpedo Six pilot who joined us at our table could not contain himself. He stood up and shouted that it was a "damned lie," starting a twenty-minute brawl that Shore Patrol could not subdue.

I scribbled angrily in my logbook, "Guess the Navy should go home. I saw some spots before my eyes—red ones on CV [carrier] decks. But the above t'ain't the way I saw it. May be the Army team burns 'em down with some new invisible flame." Oh boy! I was bristling with rage!

Of course, I possessed all these feelings when the long-term ramifications of the battle were not immediately evident to us. Although we had lost heavily in terms of aviators and planes, we had taken out four of Japan's six heavy carriers, the pride of their fleet. (During the war, Japan produced only two additional heavy carriers; thus we erased 50 percent of their wartime heavy carrier force in just one day.) To put it succinctly, Midway took away Japan's initiative. With no carrier force to threaten us in the Central Pacific, our Marine and Army forces could commence their counteroffensives, rolling back Japan's vast island empire. It took another three years to subdue our foe, but Japan never counterattacked us in a strategic sense. From July 1942 to August 1945, our armed forces executed a series of important amphibious invasions at such faraway places as Guadalcanal, Betio Island, Kwajalein, Saipan, Peleliu, Iwo Jima, and Okinawa, among many others. In essence, our victory at Midway shifted the momentum of the war. The story of our nation's long, bloody victory in the Pacific began with our unexpected success at Midway Atoll in June 1942.

By the third week of June 1942, the Navy reassigned me. On June 16, I received a promotion to full lieutenant, which meant, first and foremost, more money. I wrote to Jean, "Gosh, but won't we have fun spending it."

Then the Navy disbanded Scouting Squadron Six, reassigning the remaining pilots to other duties.* On June 21, orders arrived from the headquarters of the commander in chief, Pacific Fleet (CINCPAC), Admiral Nimitz, sending all of the senior pilots back to the States. A transport was scheduled to leave in three days. Nimitz believed that six months of combat duty represented valuable expertise best reserved for training the next generation of dive bombers. The junior pilots—the ensigns who joined after Pearl Harbor—all received reassignments to Bombing Six. Finally, the eight surviving rear-seat gunners received orders to report to Kaneohe Bay Naval Air Station and await reassignment. I hurried to make the necessary arrangements to leave Hawaii for good. I sold my car, collected all my personal items stored under *Enterprise*'s elevator No. 1, and bid farewell to my shipmates.

It was hard to leave Scouting Six. For thirteen months I had trained and fought with this capable group. To say goodbye to them, especially when the war in the Pacific remained unfinished, proved difficult. It was hardest of all to leave behind my dutiful gunner,

* Later on, in November 1942, the Navy reactivated Scouting Six as part of Air Group Three, the group assigned to USS *Saratoga*. It served at Henderson Field on Guadalcanal, participating in bombing raids over New Georgia and Kolombangara. In March 1943, Scouting Six was redesignated as Bombing Squadron Thirteen. It served for seven additional months until finally decommissioned in September.

John Snowden. We bade each other a final, tearful goodbye on
June 24, just as I made my way to the transport. John survived the
next few months without me, although not easily. As it happened,
the Navy transferred him to another SBD squadron, and later that
autumn, he served in the Guadalcanal campaign, eventually con-
tracting malaria after the bombings of Munda and Kolombangara.
In 1943, the Navy sent him back to the States, where he took up
flight training. Early in 1944, Snowden wrote to me. It's one of the
nicest letters anyone has ever written to me and to this day I still
keep a copy with me, a reminder of the rapport John and I had. Our
fellowship ended up saving both of our lives on more than one occasion. Allow me to quote from it:

> After you left, I thought I'd never fly with anyone else. But
> Dusty, I felt immensely experienced and someone had to help
> train those new gunners. I was about the only one left and the
> navy has sort of grown on me so that my duty is to think first
> of the navy. I never quite got over breaking us up. I didn't care
> so much about where we went so long as we went together. I'd
> gone to hell and back with you in that front seat. It's quite a
> thing to have that much confidence in someone when you're sit-
> ting backwards diving down [against] A.A. guns and feel you're
> never coming out and can't see what's below. Felt like I should
> turn around and grab those controls lots of times but I got over
> that. They never quite could get us could they? Lots of times I
> wouldn't have given a plugged nickel for our chances though.
> I've often wondered how you felt on those attacks. Probably as
> scared as I was.

Enterprise was the best ship on which I ever served and it was
sad to leave it and my friends behind, but my new orders instructed
me to report to the commander of the Advanced Carrier Training

Group, Pacific Fleet, stationed at Naval Air Station San Diego. At long last, I thought to myself, I would be near Jean.

At 4:00 P.M., June 24, I boarded a transport ship bound for San Francisco. I just relaxed. I think I slept for hours, the kind of deep, blissful sleep that only comes when all of life's worries have been pushed half a world away. My first glimpse of San Francisco was a patriotic crowd eager to buy me drinks—the typical reward for any sailor returning from service in the Pacific. They believed every sailor who came back from the Pacific had fought at Midway and they wanted to reward him accordingly. It just so happened that I actually had fought in it. However, I had no time for drinks. I called up Jean, telling her to meet me at the train platform in Los Angeles.

The next day we had a reunion of hugs and kisses at the station. Oh my! I cannot describe the feeling of that reunion. How can someone capture the pure efflorescence of love? Well, after fighting in an aerial duel to the death in the Pacific, I understood it clearly. I asked Jean to marry me, to hell with what my family thought about our religions. With a smile that sent fireworks shooting through my heart, she said, "Yes." Quick as we could, we drove off to Las Vegas.

On July 3, we got married at a chapel that advertised "speedy weddings" on its marquee. Immediately I submitted paperwork to the Navy requesting a thirty-day leave of absence, citing my honeymoon as sufficient cause. In my life, I've had to make many life-changing decisions. I've regretted a few and been unsure about others. The decision to marry Jean did not fall into those categories. I made the best decision of my life that day, one that led to everlasting happiness. I loved and cherished her every day thereafter. For how I had treated her during our courtship, she had every right to say no or act with indifference, but as God or fate would have it, we were going to be together forever, a loving couple united amid the worst war the world has ever known.

I took my new bride on a drive to Kansas to introduce her to her new father-in-law. News of my imminent arrival set Coffeyville into a bit of a stir. No one yet knew of my exploits at Midway but the papers had already picked up on the story that Admiral Nimitz had awarded me the Distinguished Flying Cross. The *Kansas City Star* published the now-famous photograph of Dorie Miller and the *Enterprise* aviators. Noticing my presence in that image, the *Coffeyville Journal* ran its own article a few days later. Naturally, my friends and family went out of their way to express their pride and gratitude. One of my pals, Mary C. Rosebush, later wrote to me, "That [news article] shows you, Jack, how proud we are of you. I don't like to think about you being in so much danger but we have to expect that in time of war. . . . My greatest hope is that the war will be over before long (tho' I don't really expect it) and that you boys will all come back safe and sound. Wouldn't that be a happy reunion?" When I returned home, the sheer number of well-wishers embarrassed me. I've always been shy of praise, so I made no mention of the fact that I had participated in the Battle of Midway, not even to my father.

Our reunion was not easy. Dad wasn't exactly pleased I had married a Catholic girl, and furthermore, he disliked being outflanked by our speedy Las Vegas wedding. Jean's demeanor softened him, though. She was always loquacious and charming, capable of handling awkward situations with poise, whereas I barreled into tense familial disputes with characteristic bluntness.

Anyway, after dealing with my father, Jean and I made preparations to head to San Diego. Originally, none of the available billets allowed for Jean to accompany me. Thankfully, the officer in charge, CDR Howard Young—my former air group commander—found a way to keep us together. He wrote me a fourteen-day order to "see" his friend who issued orders to Navy pilots. Thanks to Young's intervention, on July 4, the Bureau of Personnel modified my orders, reassigning me to the Advanced Carrier Training Group, Atlantic Fleet.

I spent a total of three days at San Diego before leaving for the east coast on August 10. Jean and I packed our belongings and made a fourteen-day cross-country trip. Initially we relaxed on a train to Washington, D.C., but upon arrival, we learned about the newly imposed restrictions on gasoline. The Office of Price Administration doled out rationing cards labeled A, B, C, T, and X, which represented different levels of gasoline priority. (For instance, the lowest-priority vehicles, Class A, received three gallons of gasoline per week. By contrast, Class X entitled the holder to unlimited gasoline.) We were told we would receive our card when we reached Norfolk. We thought we rated a card higher than Class A, but having left our best cars in California, we had to purchase an old Model-T Ford in Washington for the price of a few dollars, driving the outdated hulk the rest of the way to our destination, NAS Norfolk, Virginia, where we arrived on August 24.

Within five days of our arrival, I was flying again as an instructor for the Atlantic Fleet's Advance Carrier Training Group, or ACTG. The training group was the last stop for any new navy pilot before heading into combat, either to the Atlantic or the Pacific. Each trainee spent about one month learning the systems of his aircraft, practicing his dive bombing and learning to work with his assigned radioman-gunner. The original syllabus called for seventy-five flying hours in various areas, including tactics, navigation, gunnery, bombing, night flying, and instrument identification. However, during the war, the Bureau of Aeronautics reduced trainees' required number of flying hours to speed up the pipeline to war. Prior to the war, pilots had to log more than 600 hours' flying time before they could go into battle. Under the ACTGs, trainees needed only 300 hours.

Further complicating the situation, Norfolk's ACTG—one of the two original ACTGs created on July 28, 1941—suffered for lack of modern aircraft. Rather than supply the group with modern SBD-3s, the Navy issued Vought XSBU-1 biplanes and SB2U-2 Vindicators. Neither aircraft proved capable of surviving a modern diving attack. The thoroughly obsolete biplanes were too delicate to handle steep dives, and the SB2U-2s could not handle a 9-g pullout by a seventy- to eighty-degree dive without risk of ripping off their wings.

Pressed for time, I went to work teaching my students, making sure they did not incur more than 5 or 6 g on their pullout. Each day I tested the accuracy of Norfolk's rookie pilots. I placed a target in a remote area and watched from an observation platform as they dropped their smoke bombs. Of course, I always made certain I had a quick path to escape, in case any of the smoke bombs overshot their target. Few of the youngsters ever hit the bull's-eye. Even my best squadron had an average twenty-five-foot error from the center of the target.

I watched these pilots closely, trying to discover their deficiencies and correcting them before they hurt themselves or any innocent bystanders. About 80 percent of the pilots listened to me, but there were always some who did not. One particular pilot always struggled during his takeoff. Normally dive bomber pilots carrying a full load of bombs rolled their flaps down to pick up additional speed before they ascended. This particular pilot rolled his flaps and tried to ascend simultaneously. Without sufficient airspeed, he threatened to nose his plane back into the ground. He never heeded my several warnings and one day the worst came to pass. His creaky old Vindicator skimmed the treetops, and must have caught a branch too heavy for the whipping propeller. The SB2U-2's nose went straight down. When we pulled him out of the wreckage, he was just pieces.

After this tragic death, a personnel officer consoled me, telling me the accident was not my fault. A few weeks before I arrived—so the officer revealed to me—this same trainee had nearly crashed into a moving car. Furious, I asked why I had not been allowed to see the pilot's flying record beforehand. I never received a solid answer. Eventually the Bureau of Aeronautics decided to transfer my group to another location, one less likely to cause civilian deaths if a trainee crashed. By mid-autumn, the bureau selected Jacksonville Naval Air Station in Florida as that location. Beginning in mid-October, I began transferring some of Norfolk's ACTG planes to Jacksonville. That is, the Navy paid me to fly each aircraft there, and then take civilian transportation back to Norfolk. On October 25, 1942, after several successful deliveries, I received a transfer order, and I left for Jacksonville permanently.

The Navy wanted me to continue to teach the lessons I had learned during the first six months of the Pacific War to the new pilots. I wondered whether the trainees in Florida would listen to me. From my brief experience in Norfolk, I had my doubts.

|||||||||||||||||||||||||||||||||||||||||||||||||||||||||||||||||||||||||||||||||||||||||||||||||||||||||||

CHAPTER 17

FLIGHT INSTRUCTOR

1942–1945

Jacksonville Naval Air Station was a mammoth facility located a few miles south of the city. The Navy had commissioned it in October 1940. By the midpoint of the war, it stood as one of the nation's largest air stations. In addition to the main facility on the St. John's River, Jacksonville NAS consisted of forty-one auxiliary fields, one of which served as my primary base. I joined the scout-bombing ACTG squadron at Cecil Field, sixteen miles west of the city, deep in the Florida swamps.

Although far removed from the battlefront, sad news from the war managed to reach me at my new base. My old ship, USS *Vincennes*, had been sunk at the Battle of Savo Island. Back in August 1942, in a confusing night battle off Guadalcanal, eight Japanese surface ships hammered an American and Australian task force, sinking four cruisers. *Vincennes* went down, losing 332 crewmen. I wondered if any of the sailors in turret No. 2 (still painted with the big "E" we had won in 1939) had died. Then, in November, I learned more terrible news. My friend from the surface fleet, CDR Tom Fraser, had also been killed. On the night of November 14–15, 1942, Admiral Halsey's South Pacific Task Force 64 engaged Japanese ships north of Guadalcanal, losing three destroyers, including USS *Walke* (DD-416). When *Walke* sank, it took with it eighty-two crewmen, including Fraser. This was hard news to bear, but I told myself that if Tom Fraser had to die, this is the way he would want to go: leading a pack of destroyers in an important battle. Their victory that night finished the Japanese for good in the South Pacific.

Some cheerful news arrived a little later. The Department of the Navy wanted to award me another medal; in fact, it wished to award me the highest decoration for valor it could bestow. On November 12, 1942, the Associated Press announced that Secretary of the Navy Frank Knox planned to award sixteen aviators with the Navy Cross, all for heroism at the Battle of Midway. Ten of those sixteen belonged to Scouting Six.* Lo and behold, I was one of them. My citation read as follows:

> *The President of the United States of America takes pleasure in presenting the Navy Cross to Lieutenant, Junior Grade Norman Jack Kleiss, United States Navy, for extraordinary heroism in operations against the enemy while serving as Pilot of a carrier-based Navy Scouting Plane of Scouting Squadron SIX (VS-6), attached to the U.S.S. ENTERPRISE (CV-6), during the "Air Battle of Midway," against enemy Japanese forces on 4–6 June 1942. Participating in a devastating assault against a Japanese invasion fleet, Lieutenant, Junior Grade, Kleiss, with fortitude and resolute devotion to duty, pressed home his attacks in the face of a formidable barrage of anti-aircraft fire and fierce fighter opposition. His gallant perseverance and utter disregard*

---

* All of the survivors of the June 4 morning attack—Earl Gallaher, Reid Stone, Clarence Dickinson, Bill Pittman, Alonzo Jaccard, Norm West, James Dexter, Vernon Micheel, John McCarthy, and me—received the Navy Cross for service at Midway.

for his own personal safety were important contributing factors
to the success achieved by our forces and were in keeping with the
highest traditions of the United States Naval Service.

News of the Navy Cross turned me into a minor celebrity among the aviators at Cecil Field. The *Jax Air News,* the air station's newspaper, often ran articles that recounted the history of its veteran instructors. I avoided an interview for nearly a year until an editor finally caught me in September 1943. The article was titled "Lt. Kleiss Has Had Enough Close Calls for Lifetime." This was the first time anyone tried to make me a hero. The first line in the article gushed with unnecessary praise: "Holder of the Navy Cross for bravery during the Battle of Midway, and the DFC for a courageous display during the raid on the Marshall and Gilbert Islands, Lieut. Kleiss has been in the thick of it since the Japs fired the opening gun at Pearl Harbor on the morning of December 7, 1941." Talking to that editor was the first time I was forced to recall these brutal events. It would be the first of many times I would have to relive the Battle of Midway.

At the time, the act of recalling incidents from the battles was not too difficult. The images were still fresh and raw. Actually, I spent most of my time with the author recounting the Battle of the Marshall Islands. More than Midway, the Marshall Islands, with all its complexity, justified a more thorough retelling than the events of June 4. When I tried to explain what happened on the morning of June 4, I don't think I did a very good job. I was worried that if I narrated my experience truthfully—mentioning all the mistakes I'd observed—I'd be court-martialed for insubordination. This was supposed to be a "puff piece," an effort to keep folks on the home front happy with good news. My first "war story" from the Battle of Midway was only an impressionistic image, not a play-by-play account of the action. I described the sensation of seeing the Japanese carriers untouched, right before Scouting Six attacked, and what they looked like after they had been set aflame.

All this puffery aside, I did not stand out from the other instructors. The Jacksonville staff was filled with luminaries. My story paled in comparison to that of Cecil Field's XO, CDR William Oscar Burch Jr. Already Burch had compiled an impressive war record. A Naval Academy graduate of 1927, he had earlier distinguished himself as the commanding officer of *Yorktown*'s Scouting Squadron 5, even receiving a Navy Cross for his actions at the Battle of the Coral Sea. He had also fought at Tulagi, Lae, and Salamaua. As Jacksonville Naval Air Station's newspaper explained, accurately, "Comdr. Burch has seen widespread combat duty. He wrote a brilliant page in the history of naval aviation during the Pacific War."

Burch was great under pressure as the executive officer. I remember an incident in March 1943 when a terrible windstorm swept across the area, damaging eighty-seven aircraft and twenty-eight buildings. As the storm moved in, both Burch and I expected that our commander, CDR Thomas D. Southworth, would order an immediate evacuation of the aircraft at Cecil Field. Without sheltered hangars, the high winds could fling the planes about like loose shingles. We hurried the crew, getting the planes ready so they might be moved to a safer airfield. For hours we waited for Southworth to render a decision. At one point a brutal wind gust flung some debris through our office window, throwing glass everywhere. Suddenly the phone rang. Dodging debris, Burch crawled under his desk and answered it. Southworth was on the other line. I couldn't hear the conversation terribly well, but Burch gave me permission to evacuate the planes. He screamed: "Permission allowed for you to take off!" I grabbed my gear and went to inform the squadron. As I left, I heard Burch screaming at Southworth. Many of his words are unrepeatable.

When Burch became CO, he made noticeable changes to discipline and decorum. Under Southworth, we instructors used Cecil Field's Guest Lodge lobby to relax. There we completed our students' log books, added reports to our files, and drank free coffee. We wore our flight suits in the lobby and used the telephone to call our wives. Under Burch, all of this changed. We could not wear flight suits in the lobby, only dress whites; we could not have free coffee; and if we used the telephone, Burch docked our monthly pay. I did my best to avoid getting my pay docked. Despite my improved salary, Jean and I did everything to conserve our money and our scarce resources. We lived about thirteen miles from Cecil Field. It was a short trip, but naturally I relied on conserving precious gasoline ration coupons (civilian grade) to get to and from work. Lacking anything more affordable, I kept driving the old Model-T just to get around.

I relied on the Model-T whenever something went wrong. I had to be at the beck and call of the tower operator at Cecil Field if an emergency arose. Burch told me to purchase a telephone line for my home so that I could respond to those situations. Getting a telephone line installed proved easier said than done, and for weeks the telephone company refused to connect our residence with a serviceable line. Finally, I paid a visit in person.

An agent asked me, "Why do you want a phone?"

It annoyed me that the telephone company viewed all requests as a matter of "want," not "need." I replied, "My boss, Commander Burch, at Cecil Field, wants me to get a telephone."

Nonplused, the telephone employee asked, "Well, why does your boss want you to get a telephone?"

I saturated my response with sarcasm: "Well, it's like this: after I do my duties at the field, if anyone at Jacksonville finds a submarine or any Axis ships out there, they call me up to go get a squadron to go dive bomb them."

The telephone agent blinked. I continued: "To be honest, I really don't want a telephone. I'd rather sleep!"

The agent said flatly, "Well, I guess we'll give you a telephone."

These problems took on minor importance when I learned that Jean was pregnant with our first child. Using every available hour, I worked to find a top-notch hospital facility for her. I made inquiries, and soon officers at Jacksonville gave me the telephone number of a Navy captain, an experienced medical officer who specialized in births. I called him, but an intern answered, telling me that the doctor was unavailable and that I should call back later. I called day and night, always getting the same intern, finally telling him that Jean would deliver a baby in a couple of days. The intern, who sympathized with my plight, told me how the Navy doctor was unavailable and no Navy hospital bed was available, and that I should call an ambulance to deliver Jean to a Catholic hospital, and that he—meaning the intern—would meet her there.

Under that arrangement, on June 9, 1943, Jean gave birth to our first child, Nancy Jean Kleiss. I used my last gasoline coupon to visit them at St. Vincent's Hospital, a medical facility on the waterfront overcrowded with enlisted personnel. When I reached the ward, I was shocked. Jean was in agony. The intern had never delivered a baby before, nor did he have the proper medical instruments. Somehow Jean worked through the pain and both mother and child, our daughter Nancy, survived. The overworked intern dismissed Jean without a follow-up appointment. As a result she suffered a life-threatening impetigo infection on her breast that soon spread to the baby's mouth. St. Vincent's staff administered an antibiotic, but the infection continued to grow in size. I received no help at all from the Navy. That blasted doctor never returned any phone calls. I feared I was going to lose Jean and Nancy, so I decided it best to put them on a train to Long Beach. Nancy was only two months old. I didn't want to send them away when she was that young, but I had no choice. The Navy had failed me. I hoped Jean's family physician would take care of her and the baby, giving them the attention they needed.

In the end, Jean and Nancy—or "Jeannie," as I called her—survived their brush with death. Overlooking all the heartache from the episode, I adored my "little sweetheart." When Jean took the baby to California in late July, I wrote to them every other day. "Puleeeze come back," I wrote on August 13. "Papa needs Mama, and little Jeannie too." Two days later, I wrote, "My darling Jean & precious Jeannie how I love you—how I love the pretty names. Please hurry home." My little sweetheart opened a kindness in me I didn't know I had.

However, in some ways Nancy's birth strained my relationship with naval aviation. I wanted to remain a pilot, but with a family, I worried what might happen if an accident or mishap intervened. I explained it to Jean this way in one of my letters: "Sometimes I wonder just how you feel about aviation—honest & truly. It takes a lot of confidence to make a good aviator and you've got my heart and it isn't mine anymore. But that's something we'll have to talk over one of these minutes—I mean days." Further, the ever-present threat of "sea duty" always loomed. When Jacksonville changed commandants in the summer of 1943, the new staff began listing more and more instructors as available to go back to sea. A possibility always existed that I might go back to war.

If managing the realities of life on a far-flung auxiliary airfield proved difficult, training these green pilots offered an even greater challenge. Every month a new batch of dive bomber trainees arrived, eager to test their mettle. Many of them were mere boys, youngsters who had been in high school when the war started. Now, eager to join the fray and avenge Pearl Harbor, they rushed into naval aviation, looking for their own Navy Cross. None had ever flown a dive bomber. I like to believe my lessons saved some lives. I recalled the teaching methods of my former instructor, LT Lanier, and put them to work on my students. Particularly, I taught them how to survive a crash landing. I told my boys that if their engine ever lost power, they had to pick two strong trees, like goalposts, and skid between them. The trees would shear off the wings, and small brush on the ground would slow down the wingless fuselage. This would destroy the plane, of course, but it could allow a pilot to walk away. Sure enough, on two occasions my pilots used this technique and came away from crashes uninjured.

We instructors knew precious little about the incoming pilots. Stunningly, the Navy kept no records pertaining to incoming ACTG aviators' flight experience. Nothing indicated whether a pilot had ever crashed an aircraft, or had trouble with his eyesight or hearing, or suffered from dizziness while in the air. Simply put, to assess the capabilities of incoming trainees, we could only review their flight logs and calculate the amount of hours each ACTG pilot had spent in the air. This posed a tremendous problem, since during the instructional period we had to recommend some ACTG pilots to serve as section or division leaders. Barring better information, as a general rule, CDR Burch insisted that the pilots with more flight time serve as the section and division leaders. At various times, this was a recipe for disaster.

For instance, one pilot always lost his bearings at night. (I'd rather not give his name, so allow me to refer to him as "Student M.") One evening, the training squadron came back after dark. Upon landing, the junior pilots vented openly, complaining to me and instructor Herm Krol. The squadron leader, Student M, could not locate the airfield, and after circling for hours, he reluctantly let another pilot take command. This other pilot finally led the squadron back to the ground. Krol and I agreed. Student M was a threat not only to himself, but to others. We had tried to flunk trainees on previous occasions, but each time, Southworth and Burch had disallowed us. But Student M was so bad he just had to be an exception. We hammered out a convincing case, taking it to Burch, who dutifully sent the request up the chain of command. Orders soon returned that all student pilots meeting a certain number of flying hours had to be retained as assistant instructors. Not only could we not flunk Student M, but we had to work with him as a fellow instructor.

Naturally, more chaos ensued. A short time later, Student M fouled up a bombing drill. On one beautiful day, I sent my ACTG squadron to attack a tow target out on the ocean. As usual, a Navy tug with a camera pulled the target, recording the bomb strikes. Not long into the exercise, a division of SB2U-3s returned to Cecil Field. Visibly shaken, the pilots exited their planes, swearing loudly. Soon I noticed that some of their aircraft had sustained battle damage. One plane had a couple of holes. I asked the trainees what happened. The pilots explained that the tug pulling the target had fired on them. Unwilling to dive near a firing ship, the pilots came home, scrubbing the exercise. I wondered, Who was in the previous attack? A quick communication to the tug revealed the problem. The first division to practice dive bombing had attacked the *tug*, not the *target*. Unwilling to risk another such attack, the tug crewmen fired on the next wave of bombers, scaring them off. Sure enough, the squadron leader who had mistakenly attacked the tug was Student M. He stupidly attacked the ship—endangering the lives of the poor sailors on it—and the rest of the planes simply followed their leader. Luckily, Student M also possessed exceptionally poor aim, so when he and his division attacked the tug, they missed. Somehow we still won the war.

Other incidents proved even more ridiculous. One evening the telephone rang (the telephone company having finally installed my line). I answered it. I recognized the crisp, clear voice of one of the on-duty WAVES, the female naval auxiliary corps. Calling from

Cecil Field's air control tower, she explained quickly that one of the crew chiefs wished to see me about an unusual landing that had just taken place. I made haste for the field. There the crew chief pointed to a recently landed SB2U-3.

"What's wrong?" I asked.

"What's wrong?!" exclaimed the chief. "What's wrong is that no rear-seat gunner came back with this plane. It took off with a pilot and gunner, and it landed with only a pilot."

I must have looked befuddled. "Are you sure?"

"Positive."

I asked, "Is there anything wrong with the plane?"

The chief replied, "Well, yes. There are some strange markings on the tail."

I examined the stabilizer. Sure enough, a massive heel print marked up the rudder. It seemed the gunner had either fallen out of the plane while it was in flight, or had purposefully jumped out of it.

"What's the name of the missing gunner?" I asked.

"Radioman Bale, sir."

I questioned the pilot, who looked terribly embarrassed. When the pilot had landed his plane, he had dismounted it happily, chart board in hand, not even bothering to check the rear seat. Ashamed he had lost his rear-seat gunner and not even noticed, he stammered as he tried to answer my questions.

I asked, "Did you notice anything wrong with Bale?"

The pilot swallowed, "No sir, I called to him through the interphone every so often, just to see if he was all right."

"Did he answer?"

"Yes, he did!" The pilot paused. "Well, maybe he didn't answer the last time."

For a while, there seemed to be no solution to the mystery of the missing gunner, but then a farmer contacted Cecil Field by telephone.

The farmer explained, "I've got an airman who landed in my field. He's a little shaken up, but he's all right. Do you want to talk to him?"

I replied, "No, wait. First off, what's his name?"

"He says his name is Bale."

I sighed in relief. The gunner had parachuted safely. I asked, "What did he tell you? How did he come to parachute into your field?"

The farmer replied, "He said he thought the plane was going to crash and his pilot told him to jump. Do you want me to put him on the phone?"

I replied, "No, no. Just keep him there, and we'll talk to him at your place."

With that, I drove to the farmer's house, finding the shaken gunner waiting patiently, still wearing his flight gear. I asked him what had happened.

He explained, "My pilot shouted over the interphone, and I realized we were going to have a collision with another plane. He told me to jump."

I was perplexed. The pilot had not mentioned a possible midair collision. I asked him to confirm his last statement: "Wait, your pilot told you to bail out?"

"Yes, sir. He practically shouted it into the interphone."

"What did he say, exactly?"

"He shouted, 'Bail!' sir."

I blinked. "Isn't that your name?"

"Uhm?"*

---

* As a matter of disclosure, I must admit, I'm unsure of the exact name of the gunner who bailed out of the SB2U-3. I've told this story many times, because it is incredibly funny. However, in retelling the incident, I've often garbled the gunner's name. I admit it might not be the right name, but I've put it in here as it

In July 1943, the Navy finally sent us a supply of SBD-5s, the latest combat model of Ed Heinemann's Dauntless dive bomber. The SBD-5 had a stronger engine and a larger ammunition supply than the SBD-3. Despite these improvements, mechanical failures still occurred, and if these happened, the trainees lacked the experience to rectify problems in flight.

One day the tower operators called, warning me of an emergency. A new pilot—one who was flying his new SBD-5 for the second time ever—could not land his plane because the throttle had broken. I instructed the tower controllers to radio the pilot and tell him to keep circling. I mounted my own SBD-5 and took off, joining the frightened pilot. Picking up the radio, I asked, "What is your airspeed?" The pilot answered me, but I already knew it; I wanted to hear the pilot answer so I could judge his state of mind. Speaking over the radio, I instructed him to use his flaps to slow down the SBD-5 and then, once above the strip, cut the engine, gliding the plane onto the tarmac. Our two planes flew side by side, with me landing first, and then taking off again in preparation for the real attempt. Once the pilot saw how I did it, he followed me in a second attempt and landed the plane safely.

Sabotage—real or imagined—also concerned me. On June 17, 1942, a German submarine landed four saboteurs at Ponte Vedra Beach, four miles south of Jacksonville. The FBI caught them, and after a speedy trial, all four went to the electric chair on August 8. After that incident, we received instructions about keeping our eyes peeled for spies at Cecil Field. I don't know if we ever caught any, but we sure believed we did. One day in 1943, I witnessed an SBD-5 taxiing down the runway. Suddenly its engine began froth-

---

seems to be the most likely candidate. I hope that readers will forgive this faultiness of my memory.

ing like a dog with rabies. The plane sputtered to a halt and the pilot and gunner dismounted, confused as to what had happened. I was equally confused. What could cause a plane's engine to spew frothy bubbles? Fearing that some new lubricant had caused the accident, I ordered no one to clean the plane until it had been stripped and examined. When the mechanics tore open the engine, they discovered the problem. Someone had taken lumps of .50-caliber ammunition powder and dumped it into the engine. Then, to cover his tracks, the saboteur—whoever he was—had poured oil over top of it. Apparently the saboteur expected the heat from the engine to ignite the powder, thus exploding it like a bomb. Instead the chemical mix of the powder, oil, and heat produced white foam. I don't know how this was resolved, but rumor followed that military police found the culprit and arrested him, and that was the last I ever heard of the incident. Was it a German spy? It's hard to say. That was the world we lived in.

Indeed, a few weeks later, I experienced a troublesome takeoff. As I pulled back on the stick in my SBD-5, it refused to give. My plane taxied down the runway but it could not get airborne. I drove it back to the hangar and turned it over to the chief. Upon taking apart the controls, the crew chief discovered pieces of a lead pencil jammed into the stick apparatus. Perhaps some fool had dropped it there, but at the time I remember thinking that I was the victim of sabotage.

By the autumn of 1943, I made a move to leave Cecil Field. After serving as an instructor for a year, I came to realize that I wasn't a good disciplinarian. Don't get me wrong, I loved training new pilots and I held fast to my solemn obligation to help win the war by imparting my knowledge. I know that some of my students went on to fight in important battles in 1944 and 1945: Philippine Sea, Leyte Gulf, and Okinawa. Undoubtedly, my duty as an instructor influenced the course of the war in its own small way. I was proud of the new generation I sent to war, but when I reflected on my life as an instructor, I couldn't stop thinking about the pilots who died (or nearly died) by accident. Granted, some of them were untrainable dolts, but for the most part I worried that *I* had failed *them*. I feared that if I continued on as an instructor, the Navy would make me a squadron commander. Even worse than going to sea again, I hated the thought of being skipper. I'd have to make important disciplinary decisions. I doubted I had what it took to stand tall under the microscope.

I believed my talents were in engineering. And what an exciting field that was. All that new technology! I was drawn to solving problems of inefficiency. So many planes just drove like trucks. I had skills that could help us develop better weapons of war. If I wasn't going to use my experience to fly in combat against the enemy, I decided I could best make a contribution by working to improve the quality of the aircraft flown by the U.S. Navy. I knew how big a difference engineering could make in the combat effectiveness of our aviators—and in preserving their lives. I sought an assignment as an Aircraft Engineering Duty Officer, part of the Bureau of Aeronautics. I sent a flurry of letters, asking my former superiors to recommend me. I sent letters to Admirals Halsey and Nimitz, and to CAPT Stevens, my former CO on USS *Vincennes*.

On October 26, 1943, after months of seeking endorsements, my transfer orders arrived. Jean and Jeannie returned from Long Beach in good health. In the winter of 1944, as my final days at Cecil Field wrapped up, my family packed our belongings. When laden with two adults and a baby, our tiny car could not carry a single suitcase, so we had to send all our personal baggage by freight. In addition, I saved all my civilian gasoline coupons, having just enough to make it to our destination, the U.S. Naval Academy's Postgraduate School. We arrived in Annapolis, Maryland, on March 6, 1944.

I wasn't the best student, but I made decent marks, and the instructors took notice. During my second year at Annapolis, my new commanding officer—the head of the postgraduate school, Randall Jacobs—assigned me to "Project Paperclip," a program that brought German scientists and technicians to the United States to exploit their military knowledge. The Joint Intelligence Objective Agency (JIOA) ran the project. I provided escort for ten scientists, engineers, or managers of aircraft factories to their new occupations. It was simple. All I had to do was go with them on a train, taking them to their destination. For two months I traveled the country, dropping off the Project Paperclip scientists in Pennsylvania, New Jersey, New York, Ohio, and Virginia. I liked the German expatriates, as they all possessed incredible knowledge and none of them expressed any Nazi sympathies.

By the spring of 1945, I had one more year of postgraduate education, which I intended to complete at the California Institute of Technology. As I stuck gamely to the task of completing my tedious classes, exciting news arrived. On July 23, 1945, Jean gave birth to our second child, Norman Jack Kleiss Jr. In contrast to the previous birth, Jean received excellent care at the Navy Hospital. After sitting in the waiting room for several hours, a nurse arrived, holding Jack Jr. She said, "Here's your slugger!" He was much larger than any of the other births at the Navy Hospital in Annapolis.

Even bigger news arrived three weeks later. On August 14, 1945, the nation exploded with joy. We learned that Japan's emperor had accepted the Allies' call to surrender. In an outpouring of bliss, midshipmen began snake-dancing through the streets of Annapolis. In less than a month, the Pacific War would be over.

Japan's surrender gave me so much joy that words cannot express how I felt. At long last, the killing had finally ceased. Though I sat out the war's last three years, I liked to think I made a difference training young dive bomber pilots to carry on the task we started in 1942. I don't know if I was a good instructor. I tried my best to keep them safe and weed out those who lacked the right stuff. I just hope and pray that some of my students went out there and made a real difference in the war.

Victory certainly gave a new sense of meaning to all of the tragic deaths we had suffered. I have never stopped thinking about the gallant lost aircrew of Scouting Six, Tom Eversole, the crew of *Vincennes*, Tom Fraser. Their priceless sacrifices had not been in vain.

CHAPTER 18

|||||||||||||||||||||||||||||||||||||||||||||||||||||||||||||||||||||||||||||||||||||||||||||||||||||||||||||||||||

MY LIFE AFTER THE
SECOND WORLD WAR
1946–1976

On February 15, 1946, an envelope reached my desk. Bearing the signature of Secretary of the Navy James Forrestal, here was my eagerly anticipated assignment to aeronautical engineering duty. In June 1946, after finishing my current duty assignment, my family packed our belongings again and moved to Washington, D.C. Once there, I reported to the Bureau of Aeronautics, Structures Branch. At BuAer, I served as assistant head of the Air Frame Division, which tested the durability of new aircraft designs. I worked for RADM Alfred Melville Pride, one of the oldest naval aviators in the country. Pride had served on board the Navy's very first aircraft carrier, USS *Langley* (CV-1), and in 1931 he had made the first helicopter landing on an aircraft carrier.

We did important work at the Air Frame Division. I worked on the report that led to the deactivation of the Navy's newest dive bomber, the Curtiss SB2C-5 Helldiver. During the war, I had never piloted an SB2C, but even without firsthand experience I deemed it an unworthy successor to our beloved Douglas SBD Dauntless. Particularly, I believed the SB2C's tail was too weak to handle the rigors of dive bombing. During the war, several Helldivers had lost stabilizers when they were pulled off by the tailhook as the planes caught on to their carrier's arrestor cables. My recommendation produced some blowback from Curtiss-Wright, which had already started a 970-plane production run. In May 1947, when RADM Pride received a promotion to assume command of BuAer, I became head of Structures Branch. In May 1949 my change-of-duty orders arrived. I began a series of transfers, moving from base to base, staying three years at a time, always working with new aircraft. I went to Burbank, California; to Norfolk, Virginia; to Philadelphia, Pennsylvania; and then to Washington, D.C. At the last location I became the director of Catapults and Arresting Gear, Ship Installation Division.

I remember my time at Catapults and Arresting Gear with pride. Our most important task was to prepare takeoff and recovery systems for a nuclear-powered aircraft carrier then under construction. Workers at Newport News Shipbuilding and Dry Dock Company had just laid the keel for CVN-65, which soon bore the name USS *Enterprise*. My former carrier, CV-6, had been stricken from the Navy's register in October 1956. Despite protestations from veterans who wanted to convert it into a floating museum, the Navy sold CV-6 for scrap in 1958. Still, the Navy was eager to carry on the name, and it awarded the unfinished hull of CVN-65 that illustrious title. Several issues held CVN-65's success in doubt. Notably, BuAer needed to install an updated catapult system before the carrier's 1961 commissioning. We expected *Enterprise* to carry powerful jet-powered aircraft, some of them six times as heavy as the long-defunct SBD dive bomber.

When I arrived, we had to hustle to meet the ambitious deadline. We supervised the installation of the new landing mirror system and a replacement for the outdated hydraulic catapult. The first of these tasks came easiest. British engineers had already designed a landing mirror system. During the Pacific War, we landed aircraft by following the directions of the landing signal officer, a sharp-eyed sailor who stood on the fantail and gave advice by waving a set of colored paddles. After the Second World War, the Royal Navy developed a system of gyro-controlled mirrors and angled lights that showed an approaching pilot whether or not he was on the correct glide path. In the Royal Navy, landing signal officers still existed, but now they guided each pilot during his approach by talking to him over the radio. I liked the landing mirror system designed by the British and I wanted CVN-65 to get a version of it. We simply needed to copy it.

My division's second challenge—the new catapult—presented a deeper conundrum. I held a low opinion of carrier-mounted catapults, yet the advances in aviation technology required the U.S. Navy to adopt them. My old CV-6 had three Type-H, Mark-2 hydraulic catapults, one on the flight deck and two on the hangar deck. These were capable of hurling a 7,000-pound aircraft into the air in just fifty-five feet; however, in operation, this rarely happened. Whenever Air Group Six used the hydraulic catapults, the shaking of the hydraulic engine, the imperfections of the cable, and the pitching of the deck all conspired against the pilot. Planes barely got airborne, and some nervous pilots even slammed on the brakes to prevent takeoff. In short, we hated to use them. Sometimes it felt like you were being thrown skyward by a drunken giant.

The postwar era, though, changed the Navy's needs. The Navy began employing heavier types of aircraft and powerful jets, both of which required a new system of launching. They could not get airborne across a short distance unless supplemented by an external source of thrust. In the end we turned to the Royal Navy for a solution. Back in 1950, a British officer, Commander Colin C. Mitchell, had designed a slotted steam-powered catapult. The Royal Navy graciously shared its design with us, and in 1954 aviators tested it on USS *Hancock* (CV-19). I admired Mitchell's design and considered it smooth and safe. I recommended we call in Mitchell and employ him as an advisor. Mitchell and I became friends as we adapted the steam-powered catapult to a nuclear-powered carrier. I had a team of wizards working for me, and between us, we found a way to implement Mitchell's design. Four steam catapults went underneath the flight deck of USS *Enterprise* (CVN-65). It's been something of a habit of mine to write its commander every few years and make sure our catapults are still working. Though *Enterprise* was deactivated in 2012, it pleases me that the catapults were in operation for fifty-one years. I like to believe they saved many pilots' lives. Those catapults were my last useful contribution to the Navy.

In June 1961, after another three years had gone by, I received my fifth reappointment since the war. I became an administrative officer for the Office of Naval Materiel, responsible for investigating complaints about defective equipment. Of all my postwar assignments, I liked this one the least. It was draining to be immersed in an endless stream of problems, rather than contributing solutions. I considered it best to retire from the Navy now. I had put plenty of stress on my family, moving them from place to place every three years. It was time to give them a sense of stability.

By January 1962, I found a new job in the private sector. April 1, 1962, was my last day wearing Navy blue. When I retired as a captain after twenty-eight years of service, I surrendered my nickname as well as my commission. I was no longer "Dusty." I reverted back to Jack Kleiss.

My new job came from Hercules Powder Company, a chemical and munitions manufacturing company. In 1945, Hercules began operating a subsidiary company of the U.S. Navy's Allegany Ballistics Laboratory, located in Rocket Center, West Virginia. Allegany wanted experienced aviators familiar with rocketry to join the staff, and offered a generous salary.

I reported to my new job two days after my retirement from the U.S. Navy. Allegany Ballistics Laboratory was a sprawling facility nestled deep in the woods of West Virginia's mountainous panhandle. I held the position of Senior Staff Engineer, Explosives Division, the unit assigned to fulfill all contracts for the U.S. Navy's expanding missile program. I remember a few of the dangers at the laboratory. One night, I received an assignment to transport nitroglycerine using one of the company's trucks. Partway into the trek, the truck struck a bump and the headlights went out. I pulled over to the side of the road and tried to fix the problem, but the headlights were unfixable. Uncertain of my ability to navigate the night-shrouded West Virginia wilderness with my explosive payload, I remained with the truck until daylight came. The next day I delivered the nitroglycerine safely, but the danger inherent in handling these materials was real—as we would soon discover. On April 27, 1963, a blast shot a pillar of flame about four hundred feet into the air, eviscerating a building and several trucks, and killing three workers and injuring ten others.

After three years, I decided I had enough. I went seeking another, safer, career, operating as a surveyor, builder, and developer. I also took up teaching at West Virginia's Berkeley Springs High School, joining the faculty in August 1966. I taught mathematics, science, chemistry, and physics. More than anything, I loved taking my students on field trips. I don't know if I was popular with the students, but I felt vindicated when I rediscovered how much I thoroughly enjoyed teaching. At the risk of oversimplifying, I found it easier to teach high school students than to teach trainee pilots preparing for war. That is, I didn't have to worry about students dying in tragic aircraft accidents. Without that fear holding me down, I thrived in the classroom. In June 1976, after ten years at the high school, I decided to retire. I had several land investments that now paid off ample dividends.

Jean and I raised five children. My oldest son, Jack Jr., was born at the end of the Second World War. My middle son, Roderick Edward Kleiss, was born November 1, 1947. Albert Louis Kleiss was born November 19, 1950. Like his father, he possessed a fondness for engineering, and at a young age he began designing small motors. He even built a brushless DC electrical motor, which caused him to win West Virginia's state science fair. Albert was set to present at the prestigious International Science Fair in Baltimore, but then tragedy struck. On Mother's Day, 1970, he was flying a model plane, showing it off to family and friends. The wind shifted suddenly, blowing the plane into a nearby high tension wire. The collision shot a bolt of electricity into Albert, killing him. I was there to see it. I desperately tried to revive him with CPR, but it was to no avail. It was one of the darkest days of my life.

Jack Jr. married and settled in Cloverdale, Indiana, where he found work as an engineer. Rod married in 1972 and moved to Grantsburg, Wisconsin, where he established Kleiss Gears, a manufacturer of small, polymer gears used in automobiles, medical instruments, pencil sharpeners, toys, and robotics. I also have two daughters, Nancy and Jill. Nancy (my oldest) attended Trinity College (now Trinity Washington University). She moved to San Francisco. My youngest child, Theresa Jill Kleiss (born August 5, 1954), married in November 1992 and became a senior sales representative for Johnson & Johnson.

Although many changes happened to my family over the years, the legacy of the Battle of Midway always remained. Every June 4, I said a prayer for my fallen comrades, and each year, it became increasingly difficult to forget the battle. This was contrary to what I wanted. Initially I had no desire to recollect the events of that fateful day. Honestly, the battle's action had occurred so rapidly, I found it hard to recall all of its details in any event. Further, the loss of my good friends rendered those memories unpleasant.

Public interest exploded in 1967 when Walter Lord published *Incredible Victory*, a narrative that incorporated first-person accounts from pilots. Funded by a New York–based grant called the Midway Project, Lord, a well-known Baltimore-born author who had written definitive accounts of the Pearl Harbor attack (*Day of Infamy*) and the sinking of the Titanic (*And the Band Played On*), set about collecting accounts from living participants in order to fill the pages of a serial to be published by *Look* magazine. During his research, Lord contacted Cleo Dobson of Scouting Six, who graciously shared his personal letters, flight log, and journal. In turn, Dobson put Lord in contact with other veterans, and by the time he finished, Lord received questionnaires from eight Scouting Six pilots and gunners, myself included.*

This was the first time I had to recall the events of June 4, 1942, for posterity's sake. On January 25, 1966, Lord sent me a letter and a three-page questionnaire. Lord wrote me, "This is to help me describe what the Battle of Midway was really like—what happened to people like yourself and how it felt to be there. I need every point of view—high rank and low; Navy, Marine, and Air Force; duty on shore, at sea, or in the air." Lord anticipated a lengthy, informative response. In fact, he took time to add a small comment in the margin, encouraging me to write to my heart's content. "As a member of VS-6, you really must have a fascinating story to tell."

Lord's questionnaire consisted of seven sets of questions, most of them suggestive, an undisguised attempt to get me to offer up

---

* These were: Earl Gallaher, John Snowden, Vernon Micheel, Cleo Dobson, John McCarthy, Frank Patriarca, Eldor Rodenburg, and me.

human interest stories.* It took me about four months to draft my reply. When I finally submitted my answers, I admitted I had trouble recalling events. I wrote, "June 4th 1942 was a long time ago and I hesitated to give you the facts without reviewing the 'log' which I kept during the action." Ultimately I sent nine pages of material, but I had trouble describing what the battle "felt like." It had been twenty-four years. Memory of my emotions did not resurface vividly—or, rather, subconsciously, I did not want them to. No one had ever asked me how the battle made me feel. It was a strange question.

Despite my reticence, a few emotional memories emerged. Like a movie playing inside my head, I could see *Kaga, Akagi,* and *Soryu* burning brightly after being struck by bombs. For a moment, a mental image spread across the page. I wrote, "I can still see the three carriers burning like haystacks drenched with gasoline. First,

---

* The sets of questions were: 1) "What was your duty? Your rank at the time?" 2) "When did you first realize that something big was up? Some of our top command knew the Japanese were on the way long before they came . . . what was your first clue?" 3) "Did you have any actual contact with Japanese planes or ships yourself? If so, what did you see first? Any close calls?" 4) "Do you remember seeing or hearing anything that seems funny now, even though it did not, of course, seem so funny at the time? For instance, a radioman who warned that the Japanese were cutting in on our own transmissions. 'What did you say?' asked a slightly Oriental voice. 'I said you Jap SOBs were using our radio' cracked back the operator. Anything funny happen to you?" 5) "Do you recall any incident, sad or brave, or just plain memorable, that struck you more than anything else? Every man who saw it, for instance, vividly recalls the Japanese pilot who stunt-flew up the Eastern Island runway after delivering his bomb. What do you remember?" 6) In times of great stress, some people show unusual ingenuity or self-reliance; others do incredibly stupid things. Do you remember any outstanding examples of either? There was, for instance, a rear-seat man who somehow cradled a heavy machine gun in his arms when the mount broke . . . and the pilot who splashed and rowed six miles back to his carrier in his rubber raft . . . and the Yorktown men who neatly arranged their shoes side-by-side before abandoning ship. Can you recall anything too?" 7) "Do you have the present address of someone else who was at Midway and might have something worthwhile to contribute?"

I saw a spreading field of flames looking downward during my dive. Then as I pulled out of my dive near the water I saw flames spurting as high as three hundred feet. And finally several minutes later as I reached 1,500 feet I saw giant flaming chunks of debris from the Akagi [sic]* thrown several thousand feet high. I had to look up to follow them." Lord thanked me for my time. He wanted to get the story right. He wrote, "So many people like yourself have gone to such trouble to help me, I only hope the finished product does justice to all your time and effort."

The next year, when *Incredible Victory* appeared in print, it expanded America's interest in the battle. In describing the two battling fleets, Lord painted the picture of David versus Goliath: a diminutive, undersized, unprepared U.S. fleet defeated a vast, battle-hardened Imperial Japanese Navy. In winning, the hardscrabble Americans had lofted the name of "Midway" up alongside "Marathon, the Armada, [and] the Marne." The Battle of Midway proved "that every once in a while, 'what must be' need not be at all." I liked the book a lot, but I did not completely agree with Lord's conclusion. Put simply, Lord linked victory with "Lady Luck." He believed uncontrollable quirks of fate handed us our victory: "They had no right to win. Yet they did, and in doing so they changed the course of the war." Commenting further, Lord explained, "the margin [of victory] was thin—so narrow that almost any man there could say with pride that he personally helped turn the tide at Midway. It was indeed, as General Marshall said in Washington, 'the closest squeak and the greatest victory.'"

I hated that idea. In my opinion, more than luck had won the battle. We had trained long and hard to be the best pilots in the air. That must have had something to do with it.

---

* For whatever reason, I repeatedly stated that I bombed *Akagi,* not *Kaga.*

||||||||||||||||||||||||||||||||||||||||||||||||||||||||||||||||||||||||||||||||||||||||||||||||||||||||||

CHAPTER 19

REMEMBERING MIDWAY
1976–2016

For a long time, I stayed away from public commemorations of the Battle of Midway, until I realized they served as excellent opportunities to reconnect with other survivors. One of my first commemorations occurred in 1979 at the Wyoming State Museum, which opened an exhibit in honor of the thirty-seventh anniversary of the battle, called, "Midway: The Turning of the Tide." Pat Hall, the curator, invited several veterans to come speak, including Earl Gallaher, Dick Best (of Bombing Six), Paul Holmberg (of Bombing Three), and Benjamin G. Preston (of Scouting Five). The museum displayed several artifacts from the battle, including Gallaher's flight log and my Navy Cross. It was wonderful for me to see some of my old aviator friends.

With interest in the Battle of Midway ever increasing, it didn't take long for local writers to find me. Every so often, West Virginia newspaper writers profiled me, and each year I received letters from relatives of aviators who had been killed in the battle. Quite often they attempted to coax out personal details about their deceased relative. I struggled to answer these letters. I found it hard to write, especially if their relatives had died in horrifying ways, drowned at sea or burned alive when their planes were shot down. I tried to be as positive as I could. I hope I did right by them, but I often worry I may have failed to eulogize them in the best way possible.

I often thought about Tom Eversole, my friend from Torpedo Six, who had gone into battle carrying a faulty torpedo. In the back of my mind, I considered journeying to Pocatello, Idaho, to tell Tom's family what really happened to their son. But I always thought to myself, What good would that accomplish? In the end, I never went. He was gone and there was nothing I could do. What could I say? It wouldn't have helped them to hear from me how horrible the torpedoes were.

In 1979 I quit my last public occupation, resigning my post as president of the Morgan County, West Virginia, Planning Commission. Fully retired and with our children off on their own, Jean and I went on a mission to give back to society. We volunteered at St. Jude's Ranch, an institution devoted to the care of abandoned, abused, or neglected children. Eventually we moved to the Tohono O'odham reservation, a 4,400-square-mile reservation spread across three counties in southern Arizona. I volunteered there, cleaning out water pipes. Meanwhile, Jean played the organ at the local Catholic church. Making the day better for St. Jude's children and the Tohono O'odham offered us a sense of spiritual redemption.

After years of making war, I found solace in the selfless trades of peace. The Tohono O'odham adhered to strict scruples against violence. They are one of the most peaceful groups of people you could ever imagine. At some point in time, they came to the idea that fighting won't get you into heaven. I really enjoyed that philosophy. In 1997, Jean and I moved to the Air Force Village, a retirement community for military families on the southwestern outskirts of Lackland Air Force Base in San Antonio, Texas. That's where I've been since. It's a swell place. Every week, the residents get together for a sing-along. Jean played the piano and I trotted out for a solo of "Show Me the Way to Go Home," acting the part of a drunken sailor. I don't know how they deal with me.

It's been the greatest challenge of my life to make peace with the memory of the Battle of Midway. For years it was always there, lurking in the back of my mind like a shadow. I kept quiet about it, rarely sharing my thoughts. I spoke to the *Jax Air News*, I wrote for Walter Lord, and I spoke to local newspapers, but I didn't become truly interested in revisiting the battle until 1997.

That year, something triggered me.

In 1997, V. Dennis Wrynn wrote "Missing at Midway," the first comprehensive account of the Japanese war crimes committed after the battle. Wrynn's six-page article appeared in the June issue of the *Barnes Review*. In it he described how the Japanese murdered three American prisoners: ENS Wesley Osmus of Torpedo Three, ENS Frank W. O'Flaherty of Scouting Six, and AMM 1/c Bruno Peter Gaido, O'Flaherty's gunner. It had been public knowledge for some time. The first account appeared in 1947, when the Office of Naval Intelligence (ONI) published a translation of VADM Chuichi Nagumo's official report of the Battle of Midway. In it Nagumo revealed that the crews of two destroyers, *Arashi* and *Makigumo*, had pulled these three men from the ocean, interrogated them, and then killed them. At the end of the war, the Supreme Allied Command Headquarters in occupied Japan attempted to prosecute the responsible Japanese officers but discovered that none had survived the war. In 1943, during the Battle of Vella Gulf, American destroyers sank *Arashi*, and that same year, *Makigumo* struck a mine and sank. In both cases, the sinking ships took nearly all hands to a watery grave. With no one left to prosecute, high command set the matter aside.

For years the murders remained an unknown part of the Battle of Midway, acknowledged only by friends and family of the deceased men. When Wrynn wrote "Missing at Midway," it proved to be the first real attempt by an author to deal with this controversial subject. Though I considered it an otherwise good article, I took issue with Wrynn's description of what O'Flaherty and Gaido had told their captors. Wrynn had stated, "Even though neither American had ever been to Midway Atoll, they supplied the Japanese with valuable intelligence about the Marine, naval, and air dispositions on the strategic island." Specifically, he alleged that they offered eight pieces of intelligence. Wrynn guessed: "They may have thought that revealing apparently useless information (considering the destruction of the Japanese carriers that they had helped to inflict) would save their lives." The article plainly intended to censure the Japanese for war crimes. But to me it seemed the finger was pointed at these three brave aviators, portraying them as too weak of mind or too weak of flesh to hold their tongues.

I could not allow this to stand. In January 1998, I wrote a letter to the editor of the *Barnes Review,* defending O'Flaherty and Gaido. I wrote, "As stated in the article, neither man had ever been to Midway. They could not have received information on the Midway build-up because they were at sea with me in Scouting Six. And most certainly they were never briefed on the strengths of our military installations." I argued that Wrynn had no idea what O'Flaherty and Gaido might have said when the Japanese captured them. His essay hinged on an assumption that could not possibly be true. Perhaps O'Flaherty and Gaido had fed the Japanese misinformation. If they had had "loose lips," perhaps they had even saved Midway from invasion. I concluded, "Traitors or Heroes? The Navy evaluated and made its decision: For O'Flaherty, a Navy Cross and a ship named in his honor. For Gaido, a Distinguished Flying Cross and selection as the first inductee into the Enlisted Combat Aircrew Roll of Honor."

My letter to the editor was an important moment for me in how

I remembered Midway. For the first time, I decided to embrace my memory of the battle. In the past, whenever I spoke about it, I had relied on my impressionistic images or on my logbook. I hated talking about the battle, so I spoke quickly and perfunctorily. No longer. My decision to criticize the "Missing at Midway" article gave me confidence. I had been there. I was an actor in these events, and an eyewitness. I decided to unlock memories hidden in my subconscious for fifty-six years and share them with others. I realized that people wanted to hear my stories. It was selfish to keep them to myself.

I have an old photograph of Scouting Six. It was taken on May 12, 1942. There were twenty-one pilots in that photograph, including me. I looked to see who was still alive. Ten of them were killed during the war. Since the war, another eight had died. As of 2001, only three pilots from my squadron who fought at Midway were still alive: me, Eldor Rodenburg, and Vernon L. Micheel. I'm a very religious person. I believe God will not summon us to heaven until we've accomplished all the various missions he's given us. I've always wondered why God spared me but took the lives of my friends. As I entered my eighties, I arrived at the conclusion that God would not find me worthy until I accomplished one last mission for him. My squadron was filled with heroes, the pilots and gunners who died during the war. I had to share their stories before they were forgotten. I had to finish making my peace with the Battle of Midway.

I started out as a quiet veteran who tried to suppress his chaotic memories of the Battle of Midway. In the years since, the sequence of events has become permanently transcribed upon the tablets of my memory. From our apartment in San Antonio, Jean and I compiled original documents, photographs, and my logbook into a short self-published book we titled *VS-6 Log of the War*, printed by Debbie Ehrstin, a family friend. *Log of the War* recounted my participation in the Pacific War with Scouting Six from Pearl Harbor to Midway. In my dedication, I made it clear the Navy owed its victory to those pilots who had perished at Midway. I explained:

> *Earl Gallaher and I . . . were the lucky ones. At the front of the formation we had targets free from smoke and fire but, more importantly, we used a little less fuel than planes in the rear. Of the first division, most landed back to the carrier, but with less than a dozen gallons of gas. Some landed short, into the sea. The second division was never found. Many of them surely knew, before they dropped their bombs, that they could not reach the carrier. They, not the survivors, were the heroes. The real super heroes, however, were the unflinching torpedo bomber crews, pressing their attack until almost none survived. They permitted our dive bombers to make an unopposed, perfect attack.*

Log of the War has had limited circulation. I give away copies at various talks. However, it has attracted historians as a valuable collection of primary-source documents. I'm also the subject of a piece of aviation art. David Gray painted a limited edition print titled *Dauntless Courage,* which portrayed me inside my dive bomber swooping down from the sky, just seconds after dropping my bomb on *Kaga.* Finally, the History Channel interviewed me for a television show, *Battle 360,* a ten-part documentary that narrated the combat career of USS *Enterprise.* The miniseries ran from February 29 to May 2, 2008, featuring interviews with *Enterprise* veterans spliced together with computer-generated simulations of Pacific War battles. I appeared in Episodes 1, 2, and 10, and in them I got a chance to narrate my experiences at Pearl Harbor, the Marshall Islands, and Midway.

Unfortunately, Jean never got to see my "fifteen minutes of fame" on the History Channel. In early 2006 she was diagnosed with pancreatic cancer. We tried chemotherapy, but nothing seemed to stop it. My amazing wife of sixty-four years bore her struggle with a smile. If she was hurting, she never let anybody know. She kept playing piano every week right up until the end. She died on October 25, 2006. We buried her in the national cemetery at Fort Sam Houston in San Antonio. (One day, my remains shall lie next to hers.) Needless to say, nothing could fill the emptiness her death created. We had known each other for sixty-seven years. I survived the war only from my unfaltering desire to see her again. Her love saved me from death. I miss her so much.

After Jean died, the memory of the battle flowed out of me like a broken dam. I wrote notes for myself—I still write notes for myself—everywhere. They contained trigger words intended to transition me to the next phase of the battle. Some folks might find it funny, but I use the word *taco* to remind myself of what it looked like to bomb *Hiryu*. The instant I see the word, I can envision *Hiryu*'s flight deck rolling over, as I described earlier. I know I'm not the best public speaker. Old age has creeped up and made it harder for me to speak for a long time and in a consistent manner, but I truly love to share my war stories while I still have time left. In the past two decades, I've been a frequent visitor to the National Museum of the Pacific War in Fredericksburg, Texas, seventy miles north of my home in San Antonio. The kind folks there have offered me several opportunities to speak at their symposia on the Battle of Midway.

Generally, I like to assume a contrarian posture, challenging the current literature for its deficiencies. Allow me to list a few of my themes.

1. I disagree with the "luck theory," as I noted at the end of the last chapter. Ever since Walter Lord's *Incredible Victory*, the public has come to believe the U.S. fleet won the Battle of

Midway through sheer luck. To say that luck served as the only key to victory cheapens what our aviators accomplished. Our squadrons were capable. Prior to the war, we trained tirelessly. I prefer to believe we won the battle because we knew our stuff just a little bit better than our foes knew theirs. If luck played any role at all, it came in the fact that a few of us pilots lived to fly another day, while many others died. Luck determined who survived, not which side won the battle.

2. I tend to believe the historians give too much credit to the admirals and not enough to the pilots. Our task force commanders—Spruance and Fletcher—concocted an overly elaborate plan, one that contained several flaws. They tried to unite all of our squadrons from all three carriers into a giant swarm, what they called a "combined, joint attack." This was too hard to accomplish. My squadron's experience is a case in point. After we got airborne on the morning of June 4, we had to circle for about fifty minutes to await the other squadrons, which never joined us. If we had proceeded immediately we would have saved many pilots' lives because we would have had enough fuel to stage an orderly attack and then return. Further, the admirals sent us in the wrong direction. We flew southwest when we should have been flying almost due west to intercept the Japanese fleet. Only because our superb squadron and air group commanders changed the plan in the air were we able to find the enemy fleet. In short, I think we found the enemy fleet in spite of Spruance's and Fletcher's plan, not because of it.

3. The pilots of those martyred torpedo bomber squadrons were on a suicide mission and knew it. For months everyone knew the Mark-13 aerial torpedo suffered from glaring defects. It exploded only 10 percent of the time, and then only when conditions were ideal. If deployed in a combat situa-

tion, the torpedoes were certain to detonate zero percent of the time. High command should have ordered those lousy fish condemned before the Battle of Midway, but no one had the guts. A complicating factor arose in that, on May 7 and May 8, 1942, at the Battle of the Coral Sea, two of our torpedo squadrons claimed a slew of hits on the carriers *Shoho* and *Shokaku*. These were likely exaggerations caused by the fact that near bomb misses looked similar to torpedo strikes. (During that battle, the dive bombers and torpedo bombers attacked simultaneously.) The Coral Sea reports gave the erroneous impression that our torpedoes worked splendidly. On *Enterprise*, we knew they were dysfunctional. We ought to have spoken up. Someone ought to have said something. Perhaps the brave torpedo crewmen might not have died on June 4.

4. Credit should go to the SBD-3 dive bomber, not just the pilots, but to the designers and builders of that remarkable aircraft. Our planes were the newest, most accurate of naval weapons. They were the only weapons we had available in 1942 to sink a fast-moving, swirling ship. Just as ironclads replaced wooden ships during the Civil War, so did our new carrier-based planes replace torpedoes and surface weapons during the campaign in the Central Pacific. Our nation owes a great debt to the designer of the SBD, Ed Heinemann, and his brilliant team at the Douglas Aircraft plant in El Segundo, California. Not only that, but our nation owes thanks to our excellent squadron commanders who knew how to operate the SBD, to push it to its limits, and to instruct us new pilots. I saw two of the best in action—Earl Gallaher and Dick Best. Dear reader, if you are ever in Arlington National Cemetery, please place flowers at the foot of their graves on my behalf. More than anyone, those two men whipped Scouting Six and

Bombing Six into shape. They transformed us into the best pilots we could be.

The real heroes of the battle were the crews who died, the torpedo bomber crewmen lost in their attack and the dive bomber crewmen and fighter pilots who ran out of gas and suffered a lonely death out on the vast ocean. I am haunted by the memory of my final farewell to Tom Eversole. I owe it to Tom to tell the story right. I've always thought about how he must have felt the night before the big battle. He knew we were not going to provide any smoke tanks to give our TBDs any cover. He grasped that death likely awaited him the next day. I prefer to believe his sacrifice meant something. His squadron attacked the Japanese about fifty minutes before mine did. Perhaps his selfless act—and those of the other crewmen in his squadron—did enough to distract the Japanese fighter pilots to draw them down to low altitude, making it easier for my squadron to arrive later on and deliver the coup de grâce from on high. I repeat what I wrote on the evening of June 4: breathe a prayer for our suicide TBD squadrons.

I've always enjoyed telling listeners about the bravery of my friends in Scouting Six. Yet, as I said, public speaking has always been a challenge for me, because I hate to talk about myself. I abhor arrogance and I scrupulously try to avoid appearing that way. Naturally, this memoir has been something of a challenge to write. I prefer to speak about my squadron in flattering terms, but not glorify my own actions. This is hard because whenever I tell my war stories, fond wishes and accolades flood in unbidden. One of the most challenging honors came on May 26, 2011, when the United Services Automobile Association invited me to be the guest of honor at its Memorial Day commemoration in San Antonio. Five hundred people attended the ceremony and historian Hugh Ambrose delivered the keynote address. I did my best to avoid going. I didn't want people to make such a big fuss over me. I might have declined the invitation, but some friends told me I should accept because it showed good manners. The USAA had assembled an excellent program. Ambrose introduced a twelve-minute clip, a short video in which I narrated the events of the Battle of Midway. In it I described the death of Bill West, my friend who died in a tragic takeoff accident a few weeks prior to the battle. When asked to reflect upon the deaths of all those who died, I replied in my usual way: "Each one of them, I know that they did their best. Some of them won medals, some of them were not even really known at all. But each one of them did it for their country. Hopefully, now, people will finally think about this on Memorial Day and give full thoughts for all these people who gave everything. They lost their lives, their fortune—their everything—but they gave us a great country."

At that point, the lights came on and Ambrose asked me to stand up and be recognized. Reluctantly I arose from my seat in the corner, and the spotlight came on me. Without prompting, the audience surged from their seats and gave me a standing ovation. Gosh! I think it lasted for two minutes. All the while, I clutched my USS *Enterprise* ball cap nervously. I didn't know what to tell them. When the clapping subsided, I spoke from my heart: "I don't deserve it, but I sure thank you." It was an honor, and I'm glad I went.

Hero is a strange word, is it not? We use it to mean "protector" or "defender," or, quite often, we use it to refer to someone who is an example to others, admired for their courage. People have used that word when referring to me and I find it foreign and terrifying. It's a word that carries too much baggage for my taste. Heroes cannot be among the living, only the dead. A living hero would succumb to pride, I think. Never call me a hero, but just a lucky fool. Remember as heroes men like Bill West, Bruno Gaido, Tom Eversole, and those other brave aces who fought and died during the early days of the Pacific War, when all was dark and victory appeared as distant as a dimly lit star.

I'm ninety-nine years old. Like the last leaf at the end of autumn, I am the last dive bomber pilot from Midway still living. There has to be a reason I've lived this long. I hope this act of telling my tale fulfills part of it.

AFTERWORD

Laura and I did not intend to write this book. In a way, the subject found us. In 2010, we had just moved to Norfolk. Laura commenced work at the Hampton Roads Naval Museum, assuming the role of that institution's special events coordinator. Looking ahead to the year 2012, she expected to be in the midst of an important commemoration, the seventieth anniversary of the Battle of Midway. Our new community, Hampton Roads, played an important role in that battle. All three U.S. carriers had been built just across the water from us at Newport News and several of the squadrons had trained at Norfolk's naval air station. Was it possible, we wondered, to get a veteran aviator to come to Hampton Roads and reflect upon his experiences at Midway?

Through the help of Ron Russell, then manager of the Battle of Midway Roundtable, we began our search. Within a few days of our inquiry, Dusty Kleiss gave Laura a telephone call. He originally planned to come to Norfolk, but a bout of pneumonia canceled his plans. Still, Laura and Dusty spoke regularly, becoming fast friends. As his life story came together through these telephone interviews, we realized he had a remarkable tale to tell. As we chatted about Dusty's experiences during our afternoon walks, Laura and I worried that an opportunity to preserve a vital piece of naval history was about to pass us by. If we failed to record his tale, would we end up regretting it? We took a momentous step. We asked him if he'd like to write an autobiography with our help.

Initially Dusty expressed mixed feelings about all this. On one hand, he was eager and excited to tell us the thrilling tale of his naval career. On the other hand, he was uncomfortable with a book that made him the central figure. He frequently scoffed, "Who would want to read a book about *me*, anyway?" As we came to learn, a strong sense of modesty shaped his personality; he did not want us to produce anything that might portray him as a hero. To assuage his concerns, we told him that he could organize the memoir the way he wanted, within reason. In fact, we said, his memoir could stress the idea that he was *not* a hero, but an ordinary pilot doing ordinary work.

This is the result. *Never Call Me a Hero* is a retelling of Dusty Kleiss's naval career and the battle that seared his soul forever, the Battle of Midway. Dusty made the process of writing especially easy. To our surprise, he had assembled a massive pile of luggage that contained all of his official documents. His apartment was a veritable archive, chock-full of information. He kept his wartime logbooks, particularly his flight log and his self-published war diary, *Log of the War*, which, among other things, contained the official after-action reports of his squadron, Scouting Six. Dusty also preserved his personnel files, which provided an essential road map for his twenty-eight-year military career. He also kept his love letters to his girlfriend (later his wife), Jean Mochon, and the letters that she wrote back to him. Finally, we completed thirty-three hours of oral history interviews. Dusty shared his intimate stories, opinions, and confessions. He approached these interviews hoping to be as honest as he could be. "I have no secrets!" he stated flatly.

Of course, no person is an open book, no matter how forthcom-

Never Call Me a Hero involved four years of collaboration. Here, Laura, Dusty, and I enjoy a moment of relaxation at the Air Force Village's restaurant.

ing they intend to be, so we cannot say he shared absolutely everything with us. However, we went over and over various incidents with him, pressing him on certain issues and double-checking others. With his help, the book went through several revisions, some stories added, some removed, until we had something that satisfied him.

Almost. Even to his death he was still working on this book. When his family invited us to his funeral, they had waiting for us piles of notes he had intended to mail to us. In short, some of the final revisions came from Dusty himself, from beyond the grave.

On March 7, 2016, Dusty celebrated his one hundredth birthday surrounded by family and friends. He received birthday cards from dozens of well-wishers, including Senator John McCain and

President Barack Obama. Former president George H. W. Bush—who was himself a naval aviator in the Pacific War a long time ago—called on the telephone to wish Dusty a happy one hundred years. So did Secretary of Defense Ash Carter, who wrote soon after the conversation, "I called Dusty today and told him that one of my jobs is to fight today's wars but also to make sure that our force is as fine as the one that won World War Two. Dusty, your country remains proud of you and we are grateful for your service. It was an honor to speak with you. Happy Birthday!" During the final weeks of his life, Dusty gratefully absorbed all the fond wishes that came his way. He repeated a question that he offered over and over during the years we knew him: "Why am I so lucky, anyway?"

Perhaps he wasn't far from getting an answer to that question. Dusty died in his bed on April 22, 2016. Seven days later, Laura and I joined the Kleiss family at Fort Sam Houston National Cemetery to say our final farewell. As per tradition, we listened to "Taps" and a twenty-one-gun salute. An officer handed to Jack Jr., Dusty's eldest son, the flag that draped his father's coffin, thanking him "on behalf of a grateful nation." I like to believe that we, as human beings, make our own luck. Our choices in life determine who we are. Dusty made many good choices in his. Bravery, love, and duty earned him every crisp note, every solemn discharge, every star, every stripe, every bit of gratitude. For the first time in a long while, the historian in me was silent. Normally, I might have pointed out how one of our nation's last living connections to the Battle of Midway was gone. I couldn't think of anything like that. I was in grief. I just wanted my friend back. Dusty always wondered aloud why he didn't die at Midway. Laura and I always said to him, we're just thankful that you lived, or else you never would have become our cherished friend.

For that reason, I found it hard to write this book. Most days, I'm immersed in the Civil War. It's always been easy for me to write dispassionately about the war of 1861 because I've never expected Ulysses S. Grant to invite me to dinner or Robert E. Lee to tell me a silly joke. Dusty was more than just a historical subject to me; he was friend in whom I developed a rapport. Further, I didn't merely create a bond with Jack Kleiss, the ninety-five-year-old retiree; I also became friends with Dusty, the twenty-six-year-old pilot. Occasionally, when the moment was just right and the storytelling had taken over his soul, Dusty's face changed. His voice got more determined. He gripped an imaginary stick, putting his dinner table into what I could only imagine was a death-defying vertical dive. His fingers flicked imaginary switches and he lifted his invisible goggles. He spoke to me like a brash pilot, like someone who didn't care that he cheated death every day. This was a thrill for me. It was nothing like studying the Civil War. I miss the brash pilot as much as I do the one-hundred-year-old veteran.

Still, the historian in me would like the last word. I hope readers will appreciate *Never Call Me a Hero* for what it is: the story of a U.S. naval aviator at war. Military history would be drab indeed if we could not read colorful accounts of outspoken observers who noticed their place in history. The American Revolution would be nothing without Joseph Plumb Martin. The Civil War would be a shade less interesting without the scrawling of E. Porter Alexander. The Pacific War never forgets Eugene Sledge, nor does the Vietnam War overlook Philip Caputo. Those exciting personalities have given historians irreplaceable observations of war as seen from the ground. Thank you, Dusty Kleiss, for giving us an unmatched view from the cockpit.

—*Timothy J. Orr*

ACKNOWLEDGMENTS

Writing is not a solitary art. We learned this truth long ago. No book is written without the assistance of friends and colleagues. We are lucky to have many. Thanks to all those who read through chapters, offering their unrivaled wisdom. Rousing cheers go to Brett Bebber, Erin Jordan, Anna Mirkova, Jelmer Vos, John Weber, Elizabeth Zanoni, Gordon Calhoun, Matthew Eng, Jonathan W. White, Elijah Palmer, and Jack Beal. All of you helped make this a better book. Also, applause must go to John Heiser, our cartographer, for drawing us a map of the Pacific and to David Colamaria of NHHC for helping us track down several historic photographs. We are indebted to you for the time you spent helping us to tell Dusty's story.

A hearty huzzah goes to our agent, Jim Hornfischer—an excellent author in his own right—for taking on this project, offering suggestions, and seeing it to completion. Jim was indefatigable, insightful, and reassuring. This book prospered because of him.

A standing ovation goes to Peter Hubbard of HarperCollins, who believed in this project enough to steer it through the publishing process on a very short deadline.

Special thanks go to our other dive bomber friend, George Walsh of Bombing Squadron Eighty. With George we've spent many fond hours having conversations about the history of dive bombing and the Battle of Midway. George was Dusty's friend. He cared deeply about him and about getting his story in print. George's support was essential for this project and a strong handshake goes to him for all his assistance and for his devoted service during the Pacific War. Thank you, George!

Most especially, we'd like to offer our eternal thanks to the Kleiss family, particularly to Jack Jr., Rod, and Jill. Ever since we started this project, years ago, the Kleiss family has shown us nothing but the utmost kindness and gratitude. They've always treated us like family. Without their generosity and support, this book would never have happened. We only hope we've done right by your wonderful father. We're proud to have known him and to be a part of your extended family.

||||||||||||||||||||||||||||||||||||||||||||||||||||||||||||||||||||||||||||||||||||||||||||||||||||||||||||||||||||||||||

APPENDIX: ROSTER, SCOUTING SQUADRON SIX, MAY 1941 TO JUNE 1942

OFFICERS

1. LCDR Ralph Dempsey Smith (Commanding Officer, Killed in Accident, May 21, 1941)
2. LCDR Halstead Lubeck Hopping (Commanding Officer, Killed in Action, February 1, 1942)
3. LT Wilmer Earl Gallaher (Commanding Officer)
4. LT Clarence Earle Dickinson Jr.
5. LT Frank Anthony Patriarca
6. LT Reginald Rutherford
7. LT Charles Rollins Ware (Missing in Action, June 4, 1942)
8. LTJG Edward Thorpe Deacon
9. LTJG Carleton Thayer Fogg (Killed in Action, February 1, 1942)
10. LTJG Hart Dale Hilton (Captured in Action, March 4, 1942)
11. LTJG Norman Jack Kleiss
12. LTJG Perry Lee Teaff (Wounded in Accident, February 24, 1942)
13. LTJG Benjamin Henry Troemel
14. LTJG John Norman West
15. ENS Robert Keith Campbell
16. ENS James Campbell Dexter (Missing in Action with Bombing Six, July 19, 1942)
17. ENS Cleo John Dobson
18. ENS Earl Roe Donnell Jr. (Killed in Action, February 1, 1942)

19. ENS Thomas F. Durkin Jr.
20. ENS Percy Wendell Forman (Captured in Action, February 24, 1942; Drowned in Captivity, March 13, 1942)
21. ENS William Edward Hall
22. ENS Alden Wilbur Hanson
23. ENS Richard Alonzo Jaccard (Killed in Action with Bombing Six, September 15, 1942)
24. ENS John Cady Lough (Missing in Action, June 4, 1942)
25. ENS John Reginald McCarthy (Wounded in Action, December 7, 1942)
26. ENS Milford Austin Merrill
27. ENS Vernon Larsen Micheel
28. ENS Franklin Woodrow O'Flaherty (Captured in Action, June 4, 1942; Executed in Captivity, June 15, 1942)
29. ENS Carl David Peiffer (Missing in Action, June 4, 1942)
30. ENS John Quincy Roberts (Killed in Action, June 4, 1942)
31. ENS William Robinson Pittman
32. ENS Horace Irvin Proulx
33. ENS Eldor Ernst Rodenburg
34. ENS Daniel Seid (Killed in Action, February 1, 1942)
35. ENS James Arnold Shelton (Missing in Action, June 4, 1942)
36. ENS Reid Wentworth Stone
37. ENS Clarence Earl Vammen Jr. (Killed in Action, June 6, 1942)
38. ENS John Henry Leon Vogt (Killed in Action, December 7, 1941)
39. ENS William Price West (Wounded in Action, February 1, 1942; Killed in Accident, May 20, 1942)
40. ENS Walter Michael Willis (Killed in Action, December 7, 1941)

ENLISTED SAILORS

1. Thomas Edward Merritt, ACRM
2. Floyd Delbert Adkins, AMM 2/c
3. Erwin G. Bailey, AMM 3/c
4. William Hart Bergin, RM 1/c
5. Thomas James Bruce, Sea 2/c
6. Milton Wayne Clark, AMM 2/c (Killed in Action, June 6, 1942)
7. Mitchell Cohn, RM 3/c (Killed in Action, December 7, 1941)
8. Audrey Gerard Coslett, RM 3/c (Wounded in Action, December 7, 1941)
9. David Bruce Craig, RM 3/c (Missing in Action, June 4, 1942)
10. Ferdinand Joseph Cupples, RM 1/c
11. John Dewey Dance, RM 3/c

12. Joseph Ferdinand DeLuca, RM 1/c
13. Otis Lee Dennis, RM 3/c (Killed in Action, February 1, 1942)
14. Fred John Ducolon, COX (Killed in Action, December 7, 1941)
15. Bruno Peter Gaido, AMM 1/c (Captured in Action, June 4, 1942; Executed in Captivity, June 15, 1942)
16. David Franklin Grogg, AMM 3/c (Killed in Action, February 1, 1942)
17. Louis Dale Hanson, RM 3/c (Missing in Action, June 4, 1942)
18. Donald Hoff, RM 3/c
19. Earl Edward Howell, RM 2/c
20. Roy L. Hoss, RM 3/c
21. Frederick Charles Jeck, RM 3/c (Missing in Action, June 4, 1942)
22. Edgar Phelan Jinks, RM 3/c (Killed in Accident, February 24, 1942)
23. Jack Leaming, RM 2/c (Captured in Action, March 4, 1942)
24. William Cicero Miller, RM 1/c (Killed in Action, December 7, 1941)
25. Sidney Pierce, RM 3/c (Killed in Action, December 7, 1941)
26. Porter William Pixley, RM 3/c
27. John Warren Snowden, RM 3/c
28. William Henry Stambaugh, RM 1/c (Missing in Action, June 4, 1942)
29. Alfred R. Stitzelberger, RM 2/c
30. Thurman Randolph Swindell, AOM 1/c (Killed in Action, June 4, 1942)
31. Harold Thomas, RM 1/c (Killed in Action, February 1, 1942)
32. Alton John Travis, AMM 2/c (Killed in Action, February 1, 1942)
33. John Edwin Winchester, AMM 2/c (Captured in Action, February 24, 1942; Drowned in Captivity, March 13, 1942)

GLOSSARY OF
MILITARY ACRONYMS

RANKS AND RATINGS

1/c, 2/c, or 3/c—First class, second class, or third class
ACRM—Aviation Chief Radioman
AMM—Aviation Machinist's Mate
AOM—Aviation Ordnanceman
CAPT—Captain
COX—Coxswain
CDR—Commander
ENS—Ensign
LCDR—Lieutenant Commander
LT—Lieutenant
LTJG—Lieutenant (Junior Grade)
RADM—Rear Admiral
RM—Radioman
VADM—Vice Admiral

SHIPS

BB—Battleship
CA—Cruiser, heavy
CL—Cruiser, Light
CV—Aircraft carrier, heavy
CVL—Aircraft carrier, light
CVN—Aircraft carrier, nuclear
DD—Destroyer
SS—Submarine

U.S. AIRCRAFT

B-17—"Flying Fortress," Boeing, Type 17 (a four-engine, ten-person, long-range bomber)

F2F-1—Grumman Fighter, Type Two, Mark 1 (a single-seat fighter biplane)

F3F-1—Grumman Fighter, Type Three, Mark 1 (a single-seat fighter biplane)

F4B-4—Boeing Fighter, Type Four, Mark 4 (a single-seat fighter-bomber biplane)

F4F-3—"Wildcat," Grumman Fighter, Type Four, Mark 3 (a single-seat fighter)

F4F-4—"Wildcat," Grumman Fighter, Type Four, Mark 4 (a single-seat fighter)

N3N-1—Naval Aircraft Factory, Type Three, Mark 1 (a tandem-seat trainer biplane)

NJ-1—"Texan," North American T-6 Variant (a two-seat advanced trainer)

O2U—"Corsair," Vought Observation Plane, Type 2 (a two-seat scout biplane)

O3U-1—"Corsair," Vought Observation Plane, Type 3, Mark 1 (a two-seat scout biplane)

PBY—"Catalina," Consolidated Patrol Bomber (a ten-person flying boat)

SB2C-5—"Helldiver," Curtiss Scout Bomber, Type Two, Mark 5 (a two-seat scout bomber)

SB2U-2—"Vindicator," Vought Scout Bomber, Type Two, Mark 2 (a two-seat scout bomber)

SB2U-3—"Vindicator," Vought Scout Bomber, Type Two, Mark 3 (a two-seat scout bomber)

SBC-4—"Helldiver," Curtis Scout Bomber, Mark 4 (a two-seat scout bomber biplane)

SBD-1—"Dauntless," Douglas Scout Bomber, Mark 1 (a two-seat scout-bomber)

SBD-2—"Dauntless," Douglas Scout Bomber, Mark 2 (a two-seat scout-bomber)

SBD-3—"Dauntless," Douglas Scout Bomber, Mark 3 (a two-seat scout-bomber)

SBD-5—"Dauntless," Douglas Scout Bomber, Mark 5 (a two-seat scout-bomber)

SNJ-1—"Texan," North American T-6 Variant (a two-seat advanced trainer)

SOC—"Seagull," Curtiss Scout Observation plane (a two-seat amphibious scout plane)

SU-2—"Corsair," Vought Scout, Mark 2 (a two-seat scout biplane)
SU-3—"Corsair," Vought Scout, Mark 3 (a two-seat scout biplane)
TBD-1—"Devastator," Douglas Torpedo Bomber, Mark 1 (a three-seat torpedo bomber)
XSBU-1—"Corsair," Vought Scout Bomber Variant, Mark-1 (a two-seat scout bomber biplane)

JAPANESE AIRCRAFT

A5M-1—"Claude," Mitsubishi Type 96 fighter, Mark 1 (a single-seat fighter)
A6M-2—"Zero," Mitsubishi Type 0, fighter, Mark 2 (a single-seat fighter)
BN5-2—"Kate," Nakajima Type 97 torpedo bomber, Mark 2 (a three-seat torpedo bomber)
D3A-1—"Val," Aichi Type 99 dive bomber, Mark 1 (a two-seat dive bomber)
GM3—"Nell," Mitsubishi Type 96 medium bomber (a seven-person medium-range bomber)

INDEX